D1230684

That We Might Become God

That We Might Become God

The Queerness of Creedal Christianity

Andy Buechel

Foreword by
Mark D. Jordan

CASCADE *Books* · Eugene, Oregon

THAT WE MIGHT BECOME GOD
The Queerness of Creedal Christianity

Cascade Books
An Imprint of Wipf and Stock Publishers
199 W. 8th Ave., Suite 3
Eugene, OR 97401

www.wipfandstock.com

ISBN 13: 978-1-4982-0022-6

Cataloguing-in-Publication Data

Buechel, Andy

That we might become God : the queerness of creedal Christianity / Andy Buechel, with a foreword by Mark D. Jordan

xiv + 174 p. ; 23 cm. Includes bibliographical references.

ISBN 13: 978-1-4982-0022-6

1. Queer theology. 2. Queer theory—Religious aspects. 3. Jesus Christ—Person and offices. 4. Sacraments. 5. Deification (Christianity). 6. Homosexuality—Religious aspects—Christianity. I. Jordan, Mark D. II. Title.

BT83.65 B822 2015

Manufactured in the U.S.A.

Dedicated to Mom and Dad:
With Eternal Thanks for Their Unfailing Love and Support,
Personally and Academically

Contents

Foreword

THE WORD "QUEER," WE are sometimes told, once meant odd or strange. Now it is a neutral name for certain expressions of sexual desire. So too with the phrase "queer theology." If it referred to anything, it must have been theology that was off-kilter or outlandish. (Imagine a book-reviewer shaking his grey beard over some piece of "queer theology" by a troublesome woman. Or the local squire muttering after a difficult sermon by the new curate.) Today "queer theology" only announces a theology devoted to the rights of increasingly recognized sexual minorities.

This little story about the word is much too simple. "Queer" has long been used—and not only by squires—to mark desires that were also accounted sins or perversions or affronts to decency. "Queer" was hissed to pass judgment or shouted to excuse an assault. So when you read in older books that someone else espoused a queer theology, you must wonder how much is left unsaid. With these implications, the English word registers tacitly an old Christian prejudice: heretics have always been portrayed as prone to one sexual sin or another—likely to all of them—while unrepentant sexual sinners were inevitably heretics.

Today the word "queer" still retains some of this history of shame. (That is one reason for liking it.) Applied to persons, it implies not just a statistically unusual sexuality, but an uncontainable excess of desire or a blurring of the body's boundaries. If seminary jargon now often speaks of "queer theology" to specify a sub-set of theological topics, the phrase may still mean—especially in its most accomplished writers—the artful perversion of academic certainties, the subversion of standard theological methods.

Andy Buechel's book teaches its readers to hear these meanings together. On his account, Christian theology has always been queer—strange but also erotic, endlessly excessive and subversive. He urges that Christian thinking never try to elude the suspicion of queerness. He shows that it cannot honestly disavow its preoccupation with strange bodies: bodies made fertile out of season, healed, transfigured, resurrected, lit up by the flickering of grace through sin.

If this book is right, there can never be a tidy beginning to the story of queer theology in Christianity. Should its story be told from the late 1980s, with the appearance of queer theory and ACT UP's protests against the churchly denials of AIDS? Or from the 1970s with the extension of liberation theology to gender and sex? Does the story start in the 1960s, when what were then called "homophile" groups began to collaborate with progressive churches? Or a few years earlier, with the first churchly publications advocating the decriminalization of sodomy? In fact, as Buechel reminds us, the story of queer theology goes back to two ancient gardens. In Eden, a woman and a man seek knowledge only to find their nakedness and shame (Gen 3). In the second garden, near Jerusalem, another woman searches for the body of her teacher. She watched him die and has come to finish preparing his body for burial. He stands before her, but she cannot recognize him until he calls her name. He cautions her not to cling to him—not yet. His body, still carrying its mortal wounds, has not yet ascended to be with God (John 20).

Looking back over the centuries of Christian speech, we can rightly wonder how much queer theology was lost to the violence of one orthodoxy or another. (A certain Agostino, a Florentine accused of sodomy, was bold enough to defend himself before his persecutors. The official scribe pointedly refused to record the "detestable and unpleasant things" he said to them. More effective than burning words is not allowing them to be written.)[1] Still Buechel reminds us that the greater fund of queer theology is to be found in the libraries of the orthodox themselves—in the generations of queer meditation on the irrepressible scandal of God made flesh.

These libraries can help contemporary Christian efforts to write adequately about embodiment. Too much of contemporary theology of sex or gender, especially in progressive churches, has been content to import fundamental categories from current medicine or psychotherapy or social engineering. The result has often been identity theology in the service of

---

1. The incident is recorded in Rocke, *Forbidden Friendships*, 26.

identity politics. Identity politics cannot be the (queer) gospel. It is only a sort of outraged Cartesianism, an aggressive method for stamping labels onto human lives in order to manage them more efficiently. As Buechel shows, following Elizabeth Stuart, there can be no Christian algebra of identities. Queer theology must reject this world's certainty about human identity precisely because of its faith in the mystery of what humans will one day become.

Andy Buechel's book exerts itself to avoid false certainties, easy algebras, in order to acknowledge the full queerness of Christianity. That effort is one of the queerest things about the book. Some readers may pick it up expecting that anyone who criticizes church teachings on sexuality will *of course* reject every article of the creed. They will be surprised to read here that a radical reconsideration of sexed bodies can also affirm very traditional preoccupations and pieties. Indeed, they will learn that radical reconsideration arises from *within* the deepest parts of tradition.

Michel Foucault once remarked that what some people find disturbing about male homosexuality is not the (imagined) sex, but two men in love beyond social forms.[2] In the same way, I would suggest that what makes queer theology disturbing to some is not that it is anti-Christian, but that it is so unashamedly Christian. In this book, Andy Buechel is less interested in justifying (once again) the permissibility of certain sexual acts than in understanding the relations of sexed life to divine incarnation, Christian sacrament, and the divine consummation of history. What does revelation teach us, he asks, about our embodied lives as we actually live them? What do our lives reveal about the divine? He writes, "Montage allows us to see that which we cannot see." Buechel has in mind certain film sequences, but he refers as well to the startling montage in the phrase "queer theology."

This book speaks to the effects of sin not only in lives, but in the institutions that call themselves churches. On some pages, Buechel describes poignantly the wounds that he received while coming of age as a Roman Catholic. Rome has no monopoly on institutional violence, of course. Living in any Christian church means living with organized sin. Buechel is also clear eyed about his own complicity in his earlier suffering. Much more important to him and to his reader is the hope that moves through the failures of "Christian" communities ever fully to be churches. He expresses the hope in a language of erotic desire for the divine remaking of the whole world, including its churches. This original desire for God's transfiguring

2. Foucault, "De l'amitié comme mode de vie," 38–39.

presence is not greed. It is the "dispossessive" desire that seeks to have only to share. (Buechel takes the term from Gerard Loughlin.) A theology animated by this desire hopes to encourage unexpected perceptions of the divine by directing attention through new languages and the forms of practice they evoke.

What is it that we want a book of queer theology—of any theology—to do? Maybe we want it to replace so-called theologies that have wounded us. Maybe we count on its helping us to correct or combat oppressive errors of biblical interpretation and moral regulation. Maybe it will guide our campaigns to reform states and churches. Maybe—tender wish—maybe it can actually show us more of what life with God is like. I have heard each of these desires brought to queer theology. I have carried them at different times myself. More important than trying to compile them or rank them is to see what they imply. Queer theology is not so much the study of certain desires as their urgent expression. It enacts desires for union with the divine that surely deserve to be called queer. Indeed, the particular vocation of queer theology in our time is not to extend theology over unmapped desires, but to return desire in all its queerness to the writing of theology.

Mark D. Jordan

Andrew W. Mellon Professor of Christian Thought
Harvard Divinity School

Acknowledgments

This book project has been long in the making, and many people are owed profound thanks for its final fruition. First among these are Drs. Mark D. Jordan and Wendy Farley, who read the manuscript at various stages in its composition and were unflagging in both excellent feedback and support. Others who have read the text in its entirety, with insightful comments that have made it better than it was and with many needed words of encouragement, are Francis Beaumier, Debbie Buechel, Father Justin, Dr. Steffen Lösel, Stephen Rieger, Dr. Don Saliers, Axel Takács, and Bonnie Wessendorf. For reading and commenting on particular chapters, I thank Ed Buechel, Gregory Clines, Father James Heft, Reba Hennessey, and Michelle Rudowicz-Lux. Andrew Knapp was kind enough to answer some questions on Hebrew for me, and Meghan Henning gave me good guidance on Greek. Robin Parry, my editor at Wipf and Stock, gave numerous suggestions that strengthened the text, both in clarity and content. Special thanks to all my friends in South Bend, Atlanta, and Cambridge for the numerous conversations where so much of the contents here first germinated.

INTRODUCTION

Folly and Stumbling Blocks

. . . our Lord Jesus Christ, who did, through his transcendent love, become what we are, that He might bring us to be even what He is Himself.

—ST. IRENAEUS OF LYONS[1]

. . . yes, I say, the Word of God speaks, having become man [*sic*], in order that such as you may learn from man how it is even possible for man to become a god.

—ST. CLEMENT OF ALEXANDRIA[2]

For he was made man [*sic*] that we might be made God . . .

—ST. ATHANASIUS OF ALEXANDRIA[3]

"For He has given them power to become the sons [*sic*] of God" [John 1:12]. If we have been made sons of God, we have also been made gods . . . .

—ST. AUGUSTINE[4]

1. Irenaeus, *Against Heresies*, 554.
2. Clement, *Exhortation to the Greeks*, 23.
3. Athanasius, *On the Incarnation*, 107.
4. Augustine, *Exposition on the Book of Psalms*, 178.

1

EXAMPLES OF THIS LINE of thinking, which views Christian salvation as entering into the very life of God, that is, becoming God could easily be multiplied. For these early generations of Christian thinkers, the incarnation of God in Jesus Christ was so that we might become "incarnated" in the eternal life of the Trinity. Christ came down to bring us back to where he was. These same thinkers were also those whose thought and work helped shape the "rule of faith" (*regula fidei*) and the major creeds that emerged in the first Christian centuries. The thought could not be more orthodox or traditional.

It is also very queer.

Queerness and creedal Christianity are usually presumed to be opposed to one another, and partisans on both sides of the divide are quite happy to maintain this division. I contend, however, that some iterations of contemporary queer theory allow us to appreciate more deeply the fundamental insights and aims of these ancient creeds, to realize their vitality in the modern world, and to help us to move past some of the dead-ends modernity has created for us, most specifically reified and essentialized categories of gender and sexuality. Thinking of theology queerly means seeing the tradition that has been handed down to us with fresh eyes, allowing us to better understand and live certain dangerous realities of faith, such as the ancient belief that when we encounter each other, we encounter those who are becoming God. It helps us to live authentically an ancient faith as modern people. As theologian Jay Emerson Johnson notes, "rather queerly, the past is not settled and fixed. History, including theological history, remains fluid and restless, waiting to be refashioned in the hands of contemporary communities."[5] This refashioning is not arbitrary or boundless, for the creeds exist in order to ensure the preservation of essential mystery. Nonetheless, queer theory can help us discover new ways to be traditional.

In talking to friends and family about the topic of this book, the first question that I have usually been asked is what I mean by "queer theology." This is sometimes because, for many, "queer" is still a word that has primarily pejorative connotations, though I find that this objection tends to come from those of generations older than my own. Another question is whether or not this is a project about gay and lesbian people, and if so, what its relevance is to larger topics of Catholic-Christian belief and practice. Finally, from some more theoretically-minded friends, I am asked if my use of the term "queer" isn't overly broad and possibly anachronistic. Permit

5. Johnson, *Peculiar Faith*, 46.

me, briefly, to respond to all of these questions; to say a bit more about what I mean by "queer."

What is Queer?

What do I mean by the word "queer" itself, outside of theological contexts? This is a far more complicated question than it first appears, for queer is a term that has been intentionally left open, with parameters, but nothing like a simple definition. For instance, David Halperin has famously defined queer as "an identity without an essence," meaning that people use it as a mark to describe themselves and others, but that it does not have any set, pre-formed content.[6] For him, it is a position that places the speaker in opposition to the normal, whatever the normal is in a given instance. Further, this open-endedness leads those who utilize the term to avoid any attempt at rigid definition or normative understanding of its use. There may be as many meanings of queer as there are those who deploy it. Some of these, which I will discuss, I find quite useful in thinking through creedal Christian faith; others—such as the "anti-social" queer theories found in Lee Edelman's influential, but deeply wrong-headed, book, *No Future: Queer Theory and the Death Drive*—are fundamentally antithetical to Christian faith (which Edelman no doubt would rejoice in). Thus, I will not even attempt to give "The Definition" of queer, for no such monolith exists, but will rather describe my own use of it.

This procedure allows me to clarify my own meaning, as well as summarize how it will be used in the coming pages. For my purposes, there are four inter-related and overlapping, yet distinct, senses that I have in mind: queer as instability of identity, strategy of subversion, boundary transgression, and, finally, as "simple" strangeness. The first three of these all involve a theoretical discussion about the play of borders and how those borders are rendered visible, whereas the fourth highlights the way that all of this is done in opposition to a hegemonic ideology of the "normal." This last one is a bit more basic and encompassing, showing that the particular theoretical valences are also present, to an extent, in "ordinary" speech. All, however, highlight how the queer allows new ways of seeing and living to rise out of the (perceived) solid hegemonies within which we live.

---

6. Halperin, *Saint Foucault*, 62. For a more thorough discussion of the various ways "queer" is deployed, especially in relation to theology, see Cornwall, "What is Queer?" in her *Controversies in Queer Theology*, 9–42.

Queer as Instability of Identity

The first sense is the one most often considered when scholars discuss the queer. It is also, to my mind, the most important, for it is to this meaning that the others to be discussed relate. It has to do primarily with gender, sex, and sexuality categories that are facets of personal and communal identity.[7] Many understand "queer" to be simply a synonym for gay and lesbian, or more broadly, the LGBTQI alphabet soup that is currently used to discuss this "community." This understanding, though not wholly inaccurate, is nonetheless inadequate, since it maintains the dichotomy of "gay/straight" rather than challenging it.

Like most queer thinkers, I accept that human desire is created and sustained through discourse and culture. In other words, there is no such thing as a purely "natural" sexual desire, one that is simply "there." Even the bases of sexual desire, which may have their roots in instinctual drives, are never simply experienced as such, but are always influenced by the cultures within which we are embedded. For example, I may have a certain "libidinous" urge towards men, but the particular "kind" of man that I find attractive is always already formed by the world I live in, perhaps by a preference for lighter rather than darker-skinned bodies, young rather than old, muscular rather than slight of build. Class considerations often play decisive factors in sexual attraction, and these are simply the constructions that are most evident in the modern West. In other societies, clan affiliation, perceptions about purity (ritual or otherwise), and other markers of masculinity and femininity play other roles. The pathologies as well as virtues of the societies in which we live are written into our very experiences of desire.

If desire is not then simply a biological given, how much less so the identities that are predicated on those desires? The insight that desire is socially constructed allows us to realize that these desires, and the identities connected with them, have histories. They are not simply givens that have always "been there." There has been same-sex and opposite-sex activity throughout every culture and civilization in history, but the idea that those activities and desires constitute *who I am* at my deepest, most primal and

---

7. I tend to use queer in relation to these identifying markers, but it can also be expanded to include other—and all—identities. For example, M. Shawn Copeland uses "queer" as discussed by Robert Goss within a larger matrix, not only of homosexual desire, but also of race and human bodies in general: see Copeland, *Enfleshing Freedom*, esp. 78–81. For more on race as itself a queer category within dominant US culture, see Somerville, *Queering the Color Line*.

important level, is a much more recent innovation: as Foucault famously says of this nineteenth-century invention, "Homosexuality appeared as one of the forms of sexuality when it was transposed from the practice of sodomy onto a kind of interior androgyny, a hermaphrodism of the soul. The sodomite had been a temporary aberration; the homosexual was now a species."[8] This creation of sexual *identity* as opposed to *practice* applies not only to the modern category of "homosexual," but to the even more recent category of "heterosexual" as well.[9] Since these identities are not immutable, the question necessarily arises as to whether they are really the best way for us to understand ourselves, especially when this means that we must stand in opposition to others (either heterosexual or homosexual) in order to somehow "be what we are."[10]

Beyond this, though, there is "slippage" between the neat binaries that we have established between homosexual and heterosexual. The categories are unstable and artificial, and thus cannot account for the lived nuances, complexities, and paradoxes of human sexuality. This is true for any facet of human life, but when these facets are about who we take ourselves to be essentially, the problems resulting from these instabilities are multiplied. Sometimes this leads to comic consequences. For instance, in the episode "Cougars" of *30 Rock*, Frank (Judah Friedlander) falls for Jamie (Val Emmich), a much younger man. Part of Frank's character through the series, though, is that he is a very slobby, very heterosexual, and very perverted man (in a different episode he is the envious Salieri to Tracy Jordan's [Tracy Morgan] Mozart of porn). Yet, for whatever reason, he finds himself sexually drawn to Jamie; not to men at large, but just this particular man. Frank ends up going through a crisis of identity, trying to understand what this means for him and how he can score with Jamie. He starts shopping for what he takes to be trendier clothes and fashions, becomes artier, and attempts to dress better. These, of course, are common things we are taught gay men do, and thus it is "natural" for Frank to enact these scripts as he undergoes his crisis of sexual identity. "Who he is" as a character is thrown

8. Foucault, *History of Sexuality I*, 43.

9. "Heterosexual" is an even newer identity which, like homosexual, originally denoted a pathology—immoderate desire for one of the opposite sex—and dates from the very end of the nineteenth century: see Katz, *Invention of Heterosexuality*.

10. The identity of the Masturbator is a fascinating analogue to the construction (and demolition?) of other sexual identities. The history of how this activity has been understood culturally, was turned into a pathologized and essentialized identity, and then returned once more to a rather unexceptional activity is told in Laqueur, *Solitary Sex*.

into question because of one sexual desire toward another human being, even though the episode ends with a cheerful resolution and Frank returns to the same characteristics that define him throughout the series. Liz (Tina Fey) suggests at one point that this crisis cannot be real, at least for men: "You can't be gay for one person. Unless you're a lady. And you meet Ellen." The line exposes not only that social tolerance for boundary instability is itself gendered, but also serves to increase the tension over fleeting attractions that can be, for some, all too real and disturbing.

Though *30 Rock* uses this fluidity for comic purposes, it can nonetheless be quite troubling for some. After all, it threatens not only self-identity, but also one's position in society as belonging to the "normal" majority and the corollary power and privilege that this position brings. Norbert Reck writes:

> This [division of humanity into homosexual and heterosexual] is injurious not only to those who are discriminated against by that division, but to all others. For even if the unconscious aim of categorization was to ascribe disconcerting sexual feeling to a precisely defined group of "others," in order to conceive of oneself as "normal," that does not mean that those feelings are banished in any way. Every human being experiences forms of desire for other people—wholly irrespective of their gender. The occasional appearance of same-sex desires [among heterosexuals] means insecurity and anxiety for many of those who have constructed an unequivocally heterosexual identity in which to enclose themselves. Am I possibly not truly heterosexual? Could I possibly be one of the others, those deviants? If that is so, what will happen to my marriage, or to my position in society?[11]

Part of what any discussion about queerness seeks to do, then, is bring these issues of fluidity and instability to the fore. By doing so, it is my hope that we can decrease the angst created around these matters—both social and psychological—which, when left within a rigidly binary matrix, have the potential to lead to violence and abuse. If one needs to shore up one's own sexual identity, the easiest way to do it is by attacking those who are their "others," be it physically by gay bashing or, perhaps even more insidiously, verbally, as with the often glaring misogyny among many gay men, to name but two possible manifestations.

11. Reck, "Dangerous Desires," 25.

These breaches in the supposedly solid walls of sexual identity are also present in our experiences of gender and sex. Throughout this book, I employ the basic distinctions from so-called "Second Wave" feminism when using these terms. When not referring to erotic activity, "sex" then means the biological configuration of bodies that one is born with. Thus, one is male or female based on genitals and/or chromosomal markers. Sex in this sense is natural and given. "Gender," on the other hand, refers to the cultural meanings that overwrite the physical body. For example, one common assumption is that the feminine is passive, emotional, and nurturing, while the masculine is active, rational, and distant. Whereas sex is still construed as given and immutable in this feminist account, gender roles are viewed as constructed and changeable. The important consequence of this distinction is that gendered stereotypes can be separated from particular bodies, though this is more complicated than it first appears, as I'll discuss below. Finally, "sexuality" is a much broader and vaguer term that can encompass not only sexual orientation, but also erotic tastes or other styles of relating to others—even on a non-genital level.

These distinctions are helpful, but only provisionally. This is because human reality simply does not reduce easily to these binaries, any more than it does to those of sexual orientation. Queer theorist Judith Butler has greatly influenced my thinking on this matter.[12] For instance, in *Bodies That Matter*, she points out that there is never a point of "pure nature" at which the body exists separate from or prior to cultural constructions.[13] As soon as the sex of an infant is discovered, that child is already being gendered: bedrooms are being painted pink or blue, dolls are bought rather than trucks, and so on. Indeed, in our present culture, this is necessary if the child is to be even recognized as a human being. If, for example, the child is born intersex with ambiguous or otherwise unusual genital configurations, there is a very real way in which the humanity of that child is difficult to recognize. "It" is spoken about, rather than "he" or "she," and surgeries are quickly performed to "assign" a more legible sex to the infant. One cannot even enter into human discourse without having a clear sex that is always already gendered. Our gender/sex binaries make it difficult—if not impossible—for

12. When discussing queer authors, the reader must remember that I am not attempting to give anything like a comprehensive—or even non-comprehensive—survey of the literature in queer theory or theology. The diversity and equivocal usage of major terms makes such a project much too complicated for the space I have here—assuming it is possible at all.

13. See, for a highly condensed version of this, Butler, *Bodies That Matter*, 1–10.

some actual genital configurations, or ambiguously gendered sexes, to be even recognized as human.[14] But, as Thomas W. Laqueur has convincingly argued, our "common sense" binary of sex as male and female is itself not the only way sexed bodies have been interpreted historically. Indeed, for much of Western history many thought that there was only one sex (male) and two genders, where women were "incomplete" men.[15] Like sexual orientation, even something so apparently evident as humans coming in two and only two sexes has a history and has developed over time.[16]

Since our understandings of both sex and gender *have* changed over time, there is no reason to think that those changes are not still occurring. In other words, gender and sex identities are as restless as those surrounding sexual orientation, with the borders between those markers constantly crossed, re-crossed, and changed in the crossing. The fact that they have a history and have only hardened into rigid binaries in the modern era indicates that there is no reason why these binaries cannot be loosened and the reality of their flexibility made more evident in the future. This would allow us to give a more honest and accurate assessment of the complexities of these phenomena—of the complexity of ourselves. Queer theory has helped expose this historical implication and make it somehow speakable.

For some, the claim that these identities are all constructed somehow implies that they are unreal, fictitious. If we align the "real" only with the purely "natural," then this is not incorrect, but it is misleading. Simply because a reality is socially constructed does not mean that it is not animated by strong physiological, psychological, emotional, cultural, and familial forces. Social construction of identities does not mean that one can simply wake up tomorrow morning and decide to be a man after having long been a woman. Gender transitions *can* happen, of course, but they require a very long process of learning and unlearning. That is why these identities are so often spoken of as being created by discourses: they are like languages. There is no doubt that the fact that I speak English is socially constructed—if I were born elsewhere, I may have spoken something else. English has certain words and concepts that are readily expressible, and these are not always the same as those readily expressible in other languages, and

14. The numbers of those born intersexed is not negligible either, with estimations of around 1 in 2,500 children born with ambiguous genital configurations. See Cornwell, "Intersex and Ontology," 2.

15. Laqueur, *Making Sex*.

16. For the scientific complexities that challenge gender and sex binaries, even on a biological level, see Ainsworth, "Sex Redefined."

vice versa. In turn, we are more likely to notice those aspects of reality that we have definable concepts for, and these may be different from those of other cultures and languages. Truly learning a language is not simply about memorizing the parallel term for an object in a different tongue, but is closer to forming a different way of seeing the world. I *can* learn other languages, perhaps even become as fluent as a native speaker, but I cannot simply get up tomorrow and decide that I'm no longer an English speaker, but a French speaker, with all the worldviews, biases, and insights that that implies. The same is true for sex and gender identities as well. They are real, but they are unstable and can be lived and enacted in different ways from what we are trained to do.

In addition to pointing out how sex is constructed, Judith Butler has helped form my thinking by showing how gender and sexual identities are best understood, famously, as repeated performances.[17] The term is perhaps unfortunate, since it gives the implication of a conscious "acting," of choosing to do one thing rather than another. Rather, what she means is that we learn what it is to be male and female, gay and straight, and act these out accordingly, if usually subconsciously. In her words, we constitute them performatively by citation; we make them real by enacting the social scripts we learn from birth. The clothes I wear are supposed to conform to my genital arrangement, and so I'll wear a suit and tie rather than a dress. There are particular masculine ideals prevalent in our society, so I hit the gym in order to meet them. As a child, I was given footballs and trucks to play with, rather than dolls, and so forth. There are scripts that we all follow, even if we are not conscious of doing so. The repetition of these scripts imprints itself upon our bodies, and this is what creates gender and sex "identities." In this sense, these identities are more akin to learned habits rather than to natural givens.

Though these scripts are supposed to be seamless and mutually supportive of identities (my gender expression conforms to my genital, male configuration, which it turn produces a solid heterosexuality), this is not, in fact, the reality for many people; sometimes these identities do not reinforce one another as expected, but rather, challenge the way they are scripted to be performed. The way that one of them breaks down (for instance, in homosexuality), further challenges and transforms the others (for instance,

17. This is most famously laid out in her classic *Gender Trouble*. This work is notoriously difficult, however, and Butler has gone some way to greater clarity on the matter in her later collection of essays, *Undoing Gender*, especially "Introduction: Acting in Concert," "Beside Oneself: On the Limits of Sexual Autonomy," and "Gender Regulations."

my gender expression now includes sexual attraction to men, something that is *not* part of the social script for "true" manhood). Because of this, it is possible to enact these scripts differently, even against their usual flow, and thus expose how "unnatural" they really are.

Queer as a Strategy of Subversion

Since these identities are socially constructed and fluid, we can perform them in ways that expose this and show the artificiality of the whole construct. We cannot simply exit these scripts; they are both too strongly prevalent and also, in some ways, the means by which we can be recognized as human at all. We can, however, perform them "badly." By doing so, we highlight that we are, in fact, citing particular social expectations, and when one body performs in ways that are supposed to only be possible for other bodies, the artifice is shown and the "naturalness" of our performances challenged.

The most famous, if contested, example of this is drag queens: men who perform and exaggerate "classical" attributes of women, sometimes to such a degree that the "real" sex or gender of the performer is utterly occluded. For all im/practical purposes, they become women by their performances, showing that what we take to be natural is but an ideologically constructed enactment, and one that can be performed differently. Thus, queer is often associated with subversive strategies of camp, parody, or irony. We cannot escape the scripts we are given, but we can perform them in ways that open up new possibilities, new ways of seeing and living life, and ways that allow for the inclusion of more and more of our fellow human beings in all their grotesque and wondrous diversity. Subversive performances highlight the instability of our identity categories which open, in turn, the possibility for even more diverse ways of performance.

Queer as Boundary Transgression

Thus far, we have mostly discussed queer in the context of human identities, their formation, and their subversion. Deeply involved in this is the reality that the boundaries *within* these identities are unstable and thus sometimes transgressed (for example, one's sexual orientation may be experienced as basically heterosexual, but sometimes that line is breached and one may find a person of the same sex or gender attractive), and the boundaries *between* these identities are also breached (one's sexuality transforms her gender expression, which changes the meaning of her sex, which in turn impacts sexuality). But there are other, perhaps more important, ways that queer approaches expose and transgress boundaries that are presumed to be absolute.

The most important example of this sort of transgression concerns bodily boundaries. If one is asked where their body is, they will probably look blankly at the questioner and assume they are being toyed with. What could be more obvious? My body is this discrete, physical object that contains eyebrows arched in suspicion at the query as my hands point back to my torso. When asked if this is the same body that one has always had, the look and response will be similar. Of course it is; I've never been someone else. This is the body of common sense, the modern body: self-contained, autonomous, separate from the rest of creation.

But is it? Not a single cell of my current body was there when I first began to grow inside my mother's womb. How precisely then is this body typing at a laptop the *same* one that she gave birth to? I affirm that it is, but why this is so is less evident. Is it because the story of my body is continuous throughout its many changes, a narratival rather than strictly physical continuity? What might this say about our embodiment? When a mother breastfeeds a child, does not the body of the one enter and become the body of the other to sustain and form? When I communicate with another, isn't this somehow an extension of my body, an extension beyond the narrow confines of my physiological form? When a person has penetrative sex, is it really so easy to distinguish where one body begins and another stops? Can I simply point at my skin and thus show clearly the boundaries of my body? Could not the woman who has just nursed her child point to the sleeping infant as well to indicate where her body now resides? In other words, is it not true that our bodies are far more complicated than "common sense" would usually allow?

Queer theory helps us to think of the body beyond these boundaries of common sense. It emphasizes the way that bodily boundaries are constantly transgressed, where bodies cross, merge, join, and communicate. Just as gender, sex, and sexual identity are unstable, difficult to pin-down, and in constant flux, so too are our gendered and sexed bodies. By thinking about the ways our gender and sex identities operate and challenge our language and understanding, how they escape our easy categories, we are simultaneously led into ever deeper considerations of how our very nature as embodied does the same. In short, recognizing our gender and sex identities as fluid gives us grounds to think about the bodies that are gendered and sexed as more complicated as well.

By attending to these instabilities, we actually recover a much more ancient approach to bodies, one in which the personal body was seen as deeply implicated in the social and political bodies, which were in turn implicated in the body of nature, which were then caught up in the body of the cosmos. These were not seen as simple metaphors, but rather as genuine micro- and macrocosms dwelling within one another. The relationship of all to all was much more strongly emphasized. By showing the fluidity of not only identities, but also bodies, queer theory aims to expose the same relationships, and more besides.

Queer as "Simple" Strangeness

In all the ways we have discussed the word, "queer" contests the social construction of the normal and permissible. This has been done, though, with some degree of theoretical sophistication. There are times, however, when I also use the word "queer" to mean basically what it does in ordinary speech—perhaps less so in American, but certainly in British, English. The queer, then, can be used as a simple adjective or noun to highlight that something is usually perceived as bizarre or strange. I use the term in this sense in an attempt to remind the reader that "normalcy" is often an under-analyzed category, presumed to be an unalloyed good. Whether or not this is the case is far from evident, however, and "queer" serves to remind us of that. Thus, those who use the term tend to do so in a way that reverses it and challenges those who use it as disparagement: perhaps we are abnormal, but why is normalcy of such value to you? What makes normalcy something to be desired, especially if the costs of complying with its regime are broken bodies and shattered lives?

Like all other identities, that of the "normal" is constructed.[18] When I say that the queer stands in opposition to it, I mean that it stands opposed to the "ideal" normal that has been mythologized by society. For instance, within much traditional Christianity, for sex to be normal and respectable,

18. Though a "normal identity" here is used a bit more diffusely than in the cases of gender or sex, it is nonetheless true that many are quite invested in having an identity of "normal," and thus it can be used, at least, analogously to the other senses of identity discussed throughout.

it has to be between a married man and woman, and is usually construed as a rather sedate affair—some would even go so far as to suggest that it is solely to be used for the procreation of children. Anything kinky, rough, non-marital, same-sex, or between more than two persons is thus excluded. This is the norm as Western society has long construed it. But is this, in fact, how most people actually live their erotic lives? If it is not, as I suspect, then the "normal" is not about what a majority of people do, but rather about the constructed *image* of what people do. In this way, queer theory is not simply for gay and lesbian people, but for anyone who finds themselves off-kilter from societal norms. Thus, as Marcella Althaus-Reid observes, the "bizarreness" of the queer is not so much against actual practices as particularly constructed ideologies of "the normal:" "Queer is not oddity. Queer is precisely the opposite: it is the very essence of a denied reality that we are talking about here when we speak of 'Queering' or Indecenting as a process of coming back to the authentic, everyday life experiences described as odd by the ideology—and mythology—makers alike."[19] In terms of sheer numbers then, it may very well be more "normal" to be queer; queer theory simply wants to be honest about it.

It is nonetheless true, however, that seeing these norms challenged— even when we ourselves may not embody them—can be startling or disconcerting. The world is being written in a way other than we are used to seeing it. This is also part of the effect of the "usual" meaning of queer. The "weird" or "bizarre" makes us take more notice of that which we are prone to overlook. It makes us see that which we thought we knew in a different light, and this can be unsettling. Queer then helps us to escape a certain kind of complacency, and, accordingly, it is essential to the theological task.

What is Queer about Christian Faith?

Having given some account of my use of "queer" and my relationship to queer theory, it is now possible to discuss how both impact my theological thinking. Each of the senses that I have discussed have been long present in Christian theology, so claiming queer theology as a distinct sub-discipline is, in fact, inaccurate: *all good theology has always been queer*, even if this way of describing it is new. Christian practice and belief have always been somewhat bizarre—Roman Catholics, for example, worship God by eating him and from the very beginning Christianity has proclaimed a Messiah

19. Althaus-Reid, *Indecent Theology*, 71.

who triumphs by being brutally murdered. Bringing this weirdness to the fore can startle Christians into seeing anew what they may have become too comfortable with: at its best, theology breaks us out of complacency. Early approaches to gender and sex, especially in figures such as St. Gregory of Nyssa, also emphasized the fluidity and instability of these identities in the face of divine love; the church in the modern age has forgotten this, and part of the task of queer theology is to remind it of its own origins and wider tradition.

Further, Christianity has maintained from very early on that God became a human being in the particular, historical person of Jesus of Nazareth. This striking confession is about the transgression of what may be the most fundamental boundary in theology: that between God and humanity, between Creator and creation. Raymond Brown argues that this belief was developed over a period of decades: its full radicalness could not be immediately accepted. According to much modern interpretation, there is a "backward" trajectory to an ultimate recognition of Jesus as the pre-existent Logos made flesh. In this view, Jesus is seen at first as fully Messiah and Son of God primarily at his return in glory, which was assumed to be imminent (Acts 3:20–21). This Christological exaltation was then recognized as having occurred earlier, at the resurrection, in both Acts and Paul. In the Gospel of Mark, the belief in Jesus as God's Son is then moved back even further to his baptism in the Jordan and thus during his earthly ministry. In Matthew and Luke, Jesus is seen as God's Son from the moment of his virginal conception, and, finally in John, the pre-existence of the Logos, who takes flesh in Jesus of Nazareth, is affirmed.[20] Throughout this whole process of "backwards Christology," we can discern a grappling by the New Testament authors with the impossible idea that this man in their midst was uniquely related to God, indeed, *was God*. The very concept of the incarnation required years of discernment to embrace, precisely because it was so queer: the God of Israel was utterly distinct and different from creation. How then could the one revealed on Sinai take flesh?

A different account of the origins of belief in the incarnation is given by Richard Bauckham in *Jesus and the God of Israel*. Against this developmental approach, Bauckham argues that Jesus was recognized as God from the earliest New Testament writings. He believes that the earlier, more

---

20. For a brief discussion of this point, Brown, *Virginal Conception and Bodily Resurrection*, 43–44. A more developed account of this trajectory can be found in Fuller, *Foundations of New Testament Christology*. A newer account that furthers this developmental Christology is Dunn, *Christology in the Making*.

common account discussed above is anachronistic, trying to think about God's relationship to Jesus in terms of divine and human nature. The New Testament authors did not think in this way, though—it came later when Christian thought spread from a primarily Jewish context to a Greco-Roman one. Therefore, to impose that primarily Hellenistic framework on these texts distorts them. Instead, he argues that we can see from the earliest letters of Paul, the oldest New Testament writings, that Jesus was identified as involved in God's act of creation and is given God's name. These two aspects are, throughout both canonical and apocryphal Jewish literature, reserved to God alone: not even the angels or exalted patriarchs participate unambiguously in these. Thus, Jesus is seen as intimately involved in God's very identity from the beginning. Though Bauckham avers that belief in Jesus as Divine was not originally in conflict with Jewish monotheism, as the "backward development" approach often assumes, he nonetheless emphasizes the staggering newness of this development:

> An important point to make in this connection is that the identity of the God of Israel does not exclude the unexpected and surprising. Quite the contrary, this is God's freedom based on his revealed identity. He [sic] may act in new and surprising ways, in which he proves to be the same God, consistent with this known identity, but in unexpected ways. He is both free and faithful. He is not capricious, but nor is he predictable. He may be trusted to be consistent with himself, but he may surprise in the ways he proves consistent with himself. The consistency can only be appreciated with hindsight.[21]

In both of these different accounts of earliest Christian belief—differences I, as a non-specialist, will not attempt to adjudicate—God acts queerly to human eyes, from the very beginning. The boundaries of what we expect and think possible are transgressed, and all is made radically new.[22] Queer theology hopes to keep this ever in mind.

---

21. Bauckham, *Jesus and the God of Israel*, 51.

22. Needless to say, the controversies over these transgressions and identities do not stop with the close of the New Testament canon. The intense, and often violent, fights over early Christological and Trinitarian theology during the time of the earliest ecumenical councils attests to this in the past. Today, one need only to look at the controversy between Elizabeth Johnson and the U.S. Bishops in 2011 over her use of theological and gender languages to see that these borders are still highly contested and emotionally charged.

Christian belief and practice, at their best, also deploy the queer strategy of subversion, of parody, of irony. They are, as Elizabeth Stuart phrases it, "repetitions with critical difference." As Christians, we live out our lives in the world as does any other human being. We are subject to the same temptations, forces, powers, and principalities as anyone else in the communities in which we live. Yet we are called to queer that common life, to expose within it the Divine Life that is breaking through. We are called to see those around us, not as commodities with more or less utility, as late-capitalism encourages us, but rather as Christ walking in our very midst (cf. Matt 25). We are meant to be recognizable primarily by our love, and thus subvert those elements of society that are based on any other foundation. This is not, of course, to claim that Christians have been particularly good at this. Queer rituals like the Eucharist are there precisely to train us in this way of seeing, to look beyond mere appearances like bread or human flesh, and see there the Divine Love that pulses through creation. Our identities are relativized—shown as non-ultimate—apart from the identity we are being given: the identity of God.

These are just a few examples of the way that Christian faith and practice are already queer. One of the purposes of this book is to develop this insight and show how it is deployed in the thought of several queer thinkers. It is, in that way, an introduction to a new and under-appreciated kind of theology, but one that has as a primary goal the development of an ability to see what we have been doing all along with new eyes, to see the newness of God erupting forth. The works of the authors I discuss in these pages are not in any way limited to the subjects that I discuss with them, but they are particularly useful on those topics. In other words, though this is, in some sense, an introduction, it is a very selective and partial one. Most of the authors I engage with accept the purposes of queer theology and the queerness of Christian orthodoxy—as laid out in the ancient creeds—that I discussed above, but some, notably Marcella Althaus-Reid, contest it. Their selection should therefore be read as reflecting personal idiosyncrasies on my part, as well as my desire to maintain a certain thematic cohesion, rather than any judgment on those excluded or their work.

Plan of the Work

Christianity can be summed up by the queer dictum, in its multiple iterations, given by the early theologians at the beginning of this chapter: "God became human that we might become God." This claim sets the general structural paradigm that I follow throughout this book, even though the belief is not itself the main focus of conversation.

In chapter 1, I focus on the issue of "God becoming human" by attending to the body God takes on in the incarnation, that of Jesus of Nazareth. The main interlocutor is Graham Ward, along with Mark D. Jordan, to look more closely at how this body behaves in the Gospel narratives and what implications it has for our own thinking about bodies in general. The very idea of God taking flesh is queer, but by meditating more deeply on the particular body God takes, we are taught a great deal about what it means to be a body and how bodies are mutually constitutive of one another.

Chapter 2 engages the work of Elizabeth Stuart, Marcella Althaus-Reid, and Herbert McCabe to look more closely at how we are brought into this incarnate body of Christ via the sacraments. The sacraments, too, are queer acts with multiple instabilities, ironies, and tensions. Further, they teach us something about our living-in-the-world and how our participation in Christ's body should and does impact this. Finally, I look briefly at the church as itself sacramental and tensive.

After going through the incarnation and our sacramental incorporation into it, I turn in chapter 3 to the subject of eschatology. What does it mean to say that we are "made God?" What does this mean for our bodies? How does what has gone before impact the hopes that we entertain and nourish for the hereafter? How does the eschaton break-in already and how are we called to live it, queerly? These questions are explored in conversation with Gerard Loughlin's *Alien Sex* and James Alison's *Raising Abel*, and I conclude by offering an image (and the failure of images) for this queer hereafter from the film *Shortbus*: the Orgy of the Lamb.

Let us then begin, and attend to the body of God.

CHAPTER 1

Incarnation: Christ's Queer Body

For us and for our salvation, he came down from heaven: by the power of
the Holy Spirit he was incarnate of the Virgin Mary, and was made human.

—NICENE CREED

JESUS CHRIST WALKED SOME two millennia ago in the streets and byways
of Galilee and Judea. He was a particular person, in a particular place. He
didn't exist "Once upon a time," but in the days of Caesars Augustus and
Tiberius. He was fully human, having a body just like ours, but his healed
those who encountered it, challenged religious complacency, and died a
horrific death at the hands of the Roman Empire. This same body rose from
the dead and is made available to believers of all stripes in the sacraments,
particularly the Eucharist. Finally, this same body constitutes the church on
earth. This is the faith of the church. How is it possible, though, for these to
be the same body? What can this mean?

The way that best makes sense of this reality today, of these multiple
meanings and presences of the same body, is to think of it as queer.[1] It de-
fied solid conceptions and figurations of gender; sexual orientation; and the
atomistic, fully autonomous self-existence that mark the boundaries of our

1. For an account of the traditional understandings of this threefold body—historical, sacramental, and ecclesial—and the ways that the links between the senses of body
changed over time, see de Lubac, *Corpus Mysticum*.

"common sense" ideas of bodies and identities. The body of Jesus Christ reveals the fluidity of bodies, standing in solidarity with all those bodies that find themselves marked as queer today. Similarly, it interrogates those other bodies which fear such a designation.

The theologian Graham Ward has done a great deal to explore the cultural, political, sociological, personal, and ecclesial ramifications engendered by Christ's body. In this chapter, we will explore what the body of Christ means and reveals, how it defies easy gendering and definition, and how our own bodies are invited to unite with it, participating in the resurrected body of God.

Graham Ward and Christ's Body

Ward's General Approach

Before looking specifically at Ward's discussion of the body of Christ, we must take his method into account, which is laid out, among other places, in *Cities of God*. For Ward, the interpretation of the world and God's activity in it must be done analogically; that is, bodies must not be read as discrete objects standing alone, but rather as in constant and necessary relationship to others. In fact, following the early theologian Gregory of Nyssa, Ward denies that anything can even exist on its own, but that everything is constantly being gifted into being by God: "An object's identity, its intelligibility, only consists in its being an object of God's activity."[2] Rather than the God of rationalist deism—the clockmaker who sets all in motion and then exits the process—Ward sees God as constantly involved in the creation of the world *ex nihilo*. At every moment, in its every particle of existence, God is active in the world.

This constant activity does not, however, dissolve the essential difference between Creator and creature. Created reality is made by and for God. It is not God, but it is necessarily related to God. It is this relationality that Ward discusses using the language of analogy. Like an analogy, Ward means to show relationships that exist among things that are different, while also maintaining, not eliminating, those differences. God is ultimately active in every element of creaturely existence, but the two are not absorbed into one another pantheistically. Rather, God participates intimately in creation while remaining distinct and Other. Relation and difference will be key

2. Ward, *Cities of God*, 90.

poles for Ward, the creative tension between the two being the grid on which our bodies and their intelligibility are mapped.

Analogy, for Ward, is not limited to words, concepts, and ideas. On the contrary, it attests to deep and necessary relationships that are knitted into the very fabric of reality. Everything is related to everything else, while remaining distinct. Analogy permits us neither to deny difference (univocity) nor absolutize it so that communication is rendered impossible (equivocity). Analogy mediates between these two extremes. Ward recognizes that everything we know and perceive as humans comes to us mediated by signs. I am not consciously known even to myself in an immediate fashion, but for self-knowledge to exist I reflect on the languages, concepts, images, and experiences that I perceive. The only one for whom true immediacy is possible is God; to be a creature is to exist in mediation. Hence, all our knowledge and experience is necessarily partial and perspectival. Importantly, this does not negate the existence of objective reality for Ward, but rather indicates that we should be humble in all of our thoughts and pronouncements about it. Since we are limited in our capacity to understand, those understanding are always tentative, open to greater depths of nuance, correction, and truth.

Thus, all relationships involving humans are also mediated via signs, for only in these can we know anything at all, and the signs themselves are languages that we both receive and manipulate. Our bodies, and the meanings we attribute to them, are not exempt from this process. Rather than the solid, graspable, measurable body bequeathed by positivism and "common sense," our bodies are richly implicated in the transfer of signs—are constantly recreated and reinterpreted by the exchange of signs. Ward agrees with Gregory of Nyssa that our bodies are the totality of transformations, and that we do not yet experience our bodies fully. This can only occur at the resurrection/eschaton: in the language of Brian D. Robinette, "I will be my body."[3] The body which I "have"—not as possession but as gift in process, the gift of being-in-the-world—is but part of this matrix. Hence, our bodies are far more mysterious than we tend to think and it is in this mystery that they participate in the body of Christ. This participation in God through the body of Christ is the key to understanding all other participatory analogies.

---

3. Robinette, *Grammars of Resurrection*, 150. Robinette's account of the body is very similar to Ward's, though he attends less to questions of gender and sexuality.

The analogical relationship that exists between God and creatures—this participation in and of difference—also exists among us as creatures. The love, desire, eros that flows from God to creation should also mark us as the images of God. All bodies necessarily interact with others, but not according to zero-sum logic, which Ward calls the language of vampirism. My body does not receive itself simply by taking from another with no reciprocation. Rather, my body is *always* sharing in others and being shared by them—always exchanging bodily signs, always being recreated: "Communication is embodied giving, and what I give is consumed by the others to whom I give. [. . .] The body is always in transit, it is always being transferred. It is never there as a commodity I can lay claim to or possess as mine."[4]

Along with the Creator-creature difference, Ward sees sexual difference as essential to understanding our relation-in-difference to one another.[5] As embodied beings, we are also sexed beings. The two necessarily go together. In fact, our difference from others—and how we relate to them—is *usually* discussed using the language of "sexual difference" by Ward; such is its importance for his thought. It is important to be clear on what Ward does and does not mean by this, however. Sexual difference cannot be reduced to a simple matter of genitals, but rather deals with the entire gender/sex matrix of a person. These differences are not simply biological, but acted out in our lives—this is what makes them real. The whole of one's gender and sex are deeply embedded in complex grids of social intelligibility, which, in turn, are negotiated, parodied, repeated, and performed by persons.[6] This does not deny the differences, however, but expands them. Thus, sexual difference can exist not only between males and females but also between males and males, females and females, and those whose biological sex may not be clearly either. It is irreducible to an atemporal essence.

To clarify what Ward means by this, it may be helpful to look at his reading of Luce Irigaray, which he provides in "Divinity and Sexual Difference."[7] She is often accused of essentialising sexual and gender differences by her use of the vagina ("the two lips") as a feminine equivalent to

4. Ward, *Cities of God*, 91.

5. Another of these differences-in-relation that is essential for Ward is that which marks the Trinity. It is this relationship of difference that establishes all others. For our purposes we need not delve too deeply into this, however.

6. This is, of course, the language of Judith Butler, but also conforms well to Ward's understanding of gender and sex.

7. Found in *Christ and Culture*, 129–58.

the Lacanian phallus. Ward reads this move as taking place at the symbolic level of subjectivity, however, not the biological. As many scholars of Lacan argue that the phallus is irreducible to the male penis, so Ward argues that the two lips are irreducible to the vagina. Thus, the attributes that make up "masculine" and "feminine" are indeed real and can be discussed as such at this symbolic level, but they cannot simply be mapped onto the sexed body univocally—male equating masculine and female feminine. Similarly, the classic distinction between sex and gender bequeathed by "Second Wave" feminism is troubled: "Irigaray does not reduce being sexuate to the categories of physical sex or gender. Sex is already gendered as gender is already sex."[8] In other words, there is no point of pure nature or biology that precedes our gendering; gender cannot be a simple cultural mapping onto pre-existing sex and genitals. For Irigaray, the phallus and/or the two lips allow us to enter symbolically into subjectivity, but there is no necessary reason why the phallus is for boys and the lips for girls. As she states, with Christ as an example, both can exist in the same person: "'In the body of the Son of Man there appears, in the form of a wound, the place that, in women, is naturally open.' In other words, this 'Son of Man' bears both phallic and two lip markers."[9] This is a symbolic reading of a physiological reality, one that is quite in keeping with Christian exegesis of the wound in Christ's side being the womb from which the church is born. John Chrysostom, for instance, avers, "Since the symbols of baptism and the Eucharist flowed from his side, it was from his side that Christ fashioned the Church, as he had fashioned Eve from the side of Adam."[10] Though Chrysostom uses a traditional gender mapping (Christ/Adam/male, church/Eve/female), the gendering is much more ambiguous, as the wound in Christ's side is often reckoned as a place of entry and reception from the divine womb.[11] Sexual difference is in fact essential to our humanity, and relating across it while maintaining it is a necessary part of embodied living. Our personhood is constituted only by "participation in an economy of desire for and by the other," and otherness that is sexed, but irreducible to uncomplicated male/female difference

---

8. Ward, "Divinity and Sexual Difference," 143.

9. The quoted citation is from Irigaray, *Marine Lover*, 181; cited in Ward, "Divinity and Sexual Difference," 140.

10. John Chrysostom, *The Catecheses*, 3; quoted in *Liturgy of the Hours IV*, 474–75.

11. See, for instance, the discussion of these matters in Rogers, *After the Spirit*, 119–25 and 133–34.

only.[12] This participatory economy is only properly discerned when the key relation between Creator and creature is acknowledged, however.

Only in the right relation of divinity and creation, mediated in the body of Christ, do other relations exist and find their meaning. We observe how this fundamental economy is governed by the passionate love and desire of eros.[13] It is a desire that seeks union with the other. Eros presumes genuine difference, so that real union with another—and not simply the same—can occur, and the Christian economy sketched by Ward reflects a desire that does not seek to assimilate the other or fill a lack in itself, but rather to unite with the other *as* other, celebrating the difference that eros bridges. God does not relate to creation by trying to assimilate it into Godself and control it, but rather to delight in its freedom and the love that is returned. The God of orthodox Christianity is not the God of Hegel, who uses history and creation primarily as a means to "achieve" itself.

Christian eros, then, is not the libido of Freud or the lack of Lacan, endlessly searching for an impossible fulfillment. Rather, it is excessive, pushing beyond boundaries and seeking to participate fully in the gifting of which it is a part from God: "Christian desire moves beyond the fulfillment of its own needs; Christian desire is always excessive, generous beyond what is asked."[14] It is not a desire to consume, own, or accumulate, but rather to participate in the divine desire which creates us from nothing. Ward calls this whole process/matrix Eucharistic—we are given, receive, and return praise, worship, and love.

It is this fundamental relationship—between Creator and creature—that prevents our human interactions from becoming those of domination and lust. This is an important point to recall, because the risks of the

---

12. Ward's reading of Irigaray is very similar to the thought of Halberstam, *Female Masculinity*. Without using the Lacanian vocabulary, Halberstam also permits feminine/masculine to retain their usual meanings and connotations, but separates them from male and female bodies. Therefore, as a body sexed male can bear both the phallus and the two lips for Irigaray—rendering it complexly gendered—so can Halberstam read a body sexed female as embodying masculinity.

13. In the Christian debates on erotic vs. agapic love, Ward correctly recognizes that the breaks between the two are not only artificial, but dangerous. His view of eros, like much else, reflects the thought of Gregory of Nyssa, who affirms, "love (*agape*) that is strained to intensity is called desire (*eros*)." Eros, then is the intensification of agapic love, not a difference in kind: Nyssa quoted in Ward, *Cities of God*, 116. For more discussion of this, especially in connection with Anders Nygren and Karl Barth, see *Cities of God*, 183–87.

14. Ward, *Cities of God*, 77.

boundary transgression that Ward details are only too apparent. If there is no solid "I" or "my" body, then the potential for abuse is rife, especially for women who know far too well what it is to have their boundaries violated. But, since all analogical connections only operate properly within the larger divine matrix of giving and receiving, we cannot properly speak of them outside it, or at least divorced from it. Removal from this matrix—the violation of boundaries for their own sake or for the sake of domination—is never permissible in the Christian economy. The relations may be queer, but they are not detached from a fundamental ethic. Rape, physical and otherwise, is never justifiable in the Christian economy; any theoretical reading which would seem to allow it is incomplete, misunderstood, or outrightly diabolic.

Since all bodies necessarily participate in others for their intelligibility—specifically the constant participation in the divine gift of creation—when God assumes a body in Jesus of Nazareth, that body becomes a mediating site and source of revelation. In fact, as Ward observes, the body of Christ becomes *the* human body, from which we learn all others. It is the only self-defining sign: "In the analogical account of bodies, within an account of incarnation and creation, only the body of Christ (hidden, displaced and yet always pervasive for always disseminated) is the *true* body and all these other bodies become true only in their participation within Christ's body."[15] Christ's body is the true one because it participates fully in all the divisions of the analogical economy—Trinitarian, ontological (Divine/human), and sexed. Christ's existence as fully God and fully human—affirmed in the creeds—permits this, and by joining with the God-man, we enter as well into full participation in the other aspects of the economy: right relation of sex differences, right relation to God, and entry into the very life of the Trinity itself. This is salvation for Ward.[16]

This summary of Ward's basic approach sounds very theoretical, and it is, but—like all good theory—it is this way because it is trying to be as precise as possible about some very complicated aspects of our lives

---

15. Ibid., 93.

16. Ward's interest in gender and sexuality tends to root the implications of the incarnation in our relationships with other people, and sometimes with an abstracted "creation." Though he does not spend much time on it, and I cannot go into it here, there are numerous ways that his reading of Christ's incarnate body can also impact views of ecology and the wider cosmos. His idea of a queer body is, it seems to me, rife with possibilities for engagement with the wider evolutionary and cosmic Christology of Pierre Teilhard de Chardin.

that are difficult to verbalize and bring into speech. Essentially, all Ward is saying here is that our desires, our relationships with one another, our relationships with our own bodies, our lives in creation itself, are all ultimately anchored in the life and constant, eternal activity of God. The way we properly understand these relationships with God and one another is through the incarnation of Christ. In some respects, his view of reality is more "mystical" (and I mean absolutely no denigration by use of the term) than is often times thought, where we are constantly being made and recreated not only by God, but in all our interactions, even the most mundane and menial. This constant interplay of sameness and difference, of closeness and distance, of making and unmaking, is discussed by Ward using the language of analogy. In all of this, the queer, disseminated, deeply present body of Christ is the lynchpin of understanding and our participation in the Divine. What does it mean, though, to call Christ's body displaced yet pervasive? Let's look more closely at the account Ward gives of Jesus' body.

The Displaced Body of Jesus Christ

In *Cities of God*, Ward discusses the body of Christ as presented in the Gospels.[17] In order to show how the body of Jesus is elastic—ultimately expanding to include all other bodies—Ward gives careful account of six "icons" of Jesus' life. The word, though used by Ward, is proposed by Mark D. Jordan as a way of understanding the function these moments of Christ's life serve. In describing these key events, Ward shows how they implicate bodies in the eternal and how God's redemptive activity for humans are shown forth in them. This is what renders them iconic, like the images that adorn Orthodox churches. It also shows a movement from the "simply" or "normally" sexed/gendered body to a complexly gendered, but no less real, embodiment: "What happens at the ascension [the final icon], theologically, constitutes a critical movement in a series of displacements or assumptions of the male body of Jesus Christ such that the body of Christ, and the salvation it both seeks and works out [. . .] becomes multi-gendered."[18]

17. This chapter is also included, in modified form, as "Bodies." In this form, the essay has been very influential and debated among theologians. For a useful feminist appropriation of it, see Johnson, "How is the Body of Christ a Meaningful Symbol?"

18. Ward, *Cities of God*, 97.

Circumcision (Luke 2:21)

The first of these icons is that of Jesus' circumcision, which Ward reads as an icon of the incarnation as a whole.[19] The body of Jesus, though fully human, is also a new creation. Ward, quoting Tertullian, speaks of Christ being created from the Virgin's womb: just as the first Adam was made from the earth, so is the second in the "earth" of his mother. This is a very traditional reading that shows that Christ's body is made of the same material as ours, while also affirming its miraculous nature, but I think the image can be pushed further to bring out the gender and sex ambiguity that Ward seeks to demonstrate. We can do this by associating the infant Jesus Christ not with the first man in this instance, but rather with the first woman. Eve is made from the already-existing body of Adam, as Christ is made from the already-existing body of Mary. Both are miraculous, but the standard typology is here reversed. In this respect, at least, the parallels become Adam-Mary, Eve-Jesus. I do not intend to deny the traditional typologies, but simply to demonstrate that, like the gendered bodies they figure, they too can be subverted and expanded.

Whichever way it is read, the infant Jesus' body is linked to that of the first creation. The circumcision, as traditionally interpreted, is the first letting of Christ's blood, thus symbolically linking the infant to the crucifixion and resurrection.[20] Jesus' body is completely material, but also already displaced, which is to say, expanded. His materiality is eschatologically informed: "From the moment of the incarnation, this body then is physically human and subject to all the affirmities of being such, and yet also a body looking backward to the perfect adamic corporeality and forwards to the corporeality of resurrection."[21] These symbolic readings of Christ's body are no less "real" than the materiality of it. They are mutually implicated and written into one another. The body is expanded from a historical fact to

---

19. Properly, this may be more of a prolegomenon to the icons, rather than the first of their number for Ward, since he consistently refers to five, not six. Still, seeing as how it serves the same function and for ease of analysis, I will include it with the others. There will be further discussion on the specifically political implications of Jesus' circumcision at the conclusion of this chapter.

20. It is also worth noting that in many medieval paintings, the nativity of Christ is often depicted with the babe lying not in a manger, but upon an altar. The proleptic linking of the Christ child and his death is not limited to the icon of the circumcision.

21. Ward, Cities of God, 98.

encompass and figure the whole of salvation history. The boundaries of the body are temporally transgressed.

As stated above, one of the boundaries that Christ transgresses is that of sexual difference. From the beginning of his earthly existence, Jesus' sex is rendered both specific and unstable. As the act of circumcision shows, Jesus is a male with male genitals. Yet his maleness is miraculously formed from female matter. The XX chromosomes of Mary produce the XY of Jesus. He is male, but that maleness is unique, and will continue to be queered throughout his life.

Finally, Jesus' body is symbolically shown to confound various sexual norms and taboos. In much traditional exegesis, Mary's womb is both bridal chamber and site of maternity. It is a womb in the obvious way, but bridal chamber in that divinity and humanity are united within. Mary, herself, is giving birth to her creator—uniting with the body that gives meaning to all others, including her own. The sexualized symbolic, long recognized by the church, "confounds incest and the sacred."[22] The most primal and universal of taboos is rendered unstable by the body of Christ. All others must be cast into similar relativity.

Transfiguration (Mark 9:2–8; Matt 17:1–9; Luke 9:28–36)

From here, Ward moves the discussion to another of Jesus' displacements: the transfiguration. This is when the physical body of Jesus becomes charged and redolent of the Divine, manifesting it even to sight. Like the circumcision, it figures a temporal displacement in that it shows forth the glory of the pre-lapsarian body, but also points towards the resurrection that has not yet occurred. It is also an object of desire—of sublime, terrible beauty—but one that opens up eros. This body is truly attractive and desirable as transfigured, but this is due not to the physical form of the body itself, but rather the Divine which animates and glorifies it.[23] It "performs our resurrection

---

22. Ibid., 99. It should go without saying that this is not intended by myself or Ward as a defense of incest on the physical level, but rather meant to highlight the transgressive nature of Christ's body and the way that it is necessarily implicated in a much wider symbolic—as all bodies are. Christ renders the language of "common sense" and decency ambivalent.

23. It is intriguing in this sense to reflect on the Christian tradition that Christ was physically ugly, fulfilling Isaiah 53:2. If this becomes our interpretative lens, the eros of the transfiguration is even more clearly not merely physical, but also not disconnected from it. For more on this tradition, and how it has been abandoned by the modern

hope" and opens the space of yearning in us.[24] Yet it is displaced because, though the body is desired, it is desired not as a commodity to seize and use, but rather as a means to unity with the Divinity that is figured. The glorification of this body awakens in us a yearning for our own glorification with this one beloved of the Father. In other words, the desire for this body is real and erotic, but cannot be reduced to the realm of the sexual: eros is shown to exceed the activity of the genitals. The body of Jesus becomes an agent to drive us in our desire beyond the merely physical. This is not to claim that the sexual is erased, judged negatively, or abjected, but rather exceeded and fulfilled; sexuality simply cannot account for our desire at this point, for it is in this transfigured body that sex finds all of its meaning. Desire for this body need not become encumbered by questions of sexual identity. Peter, James, and John yearn for and are terrified by this body, but are not rendered "gay." The suggestion itself seems absurdly reductive, and sexual identity/orientation is shown to be a tenuous category that cannot account for or incorporate our deepest erotic desires and hopes. Jesus' body both evokes and goes beyond the simply sexual.

This transfigured body reveals another economy altogether. It is one predicated not on lack, but rather on loving and being beloved—shown by the voice from the encompassing cloud. Our desires are fired, not to possess or dominate, but to join in this matrix of the Beloved, to become also those whom the Father will so describe. This desire is not at the expense of Christ, but *with* and *through* him, since he—as the transfigured—is the only one who can lead us to the Father who loves him.

Eucharist (Mark 14:12–26; Matt 26:17–30; Luke 22:7–39; 1 Cor 11:23–26)

The Eucharist—the next icon—brings us ever deeper into this economy of loving and being loved. This displacement is "more abrupt" in that the body is quite clearly seen as spatially, and not only temporally, dislocated.[25] Jesus' body is *both* speaking and sharing at table, *and* also the food being passed. As Ward states, "The body of the historical man begins its withdraw from the narrative, from direct [that is, sensory] representation."[26] The body is

church, see Moore, "On the Face and Physique of Jesus."

24. Ward, *Cities of God*, 99.

25. Ibid., 102.

26. Ibid.

becoming no less "real," but it is beginning to exit the mode of "common sense." It is here that we begin to perceive more clearly the reality of bodies, marked as they are by figures and signs. The body is not limited to what was perceived as itself, showing that "this physical presence can expand itself to incorporate other bodies, like bread, and make them extensions of his own."[27] Furthermore, this goes beyond the ancient way in which bodies were seen as permeable and fluid by nature.[28] Our positivist sense of autonomous, separate bodies was not that of the ancients, but the Eucharist effects an even deeper queering "such that one can be a body here and also there, one can be this kind of body here and that kind of body there."[29]

This, of course, is only possible to this degree because the one disseminating his body is also God. I cannot displace my body into that of bread as Christ did, though my body is nonetheless continually displaced both figurally and physically. Christ's ability to make this bread into his own body demonstrates both his lordship over creation and his deep, abiding unity with it. All the analogical levels of the economy of bodies (Trinitarian, ontological, and, we shall see, sexual) are implicated here and implicate both Christ's body and our own.

Similarly displaced is the sex of the body. Eucharistically, the body of Christ cannot be said to be male in a simple way. It is now also bread, which has no sex; it is neuter. The body of Christ is both sexed and not sexed. Further, the extension of the body that we are observing is not limited to that of the bread alone. The disciples who eat it are also taking in the body of their Lord, and in the church's understanding, this act is the reverse of normal eating. Instead of the material of the bread being broken down and incorporated into the body of the eater, the one who consumes is instead taken into and united with the body of Christ. They, and all their human specificity, including sex, are brought into the now multi-sexed, multi-gendered body of Jesus. At this point in Ward's narrative, however, this is only for the very few present at the Last Supper. We will return to this point more when we discuss the final icon of the ascension, but it is important to note the time frame of this first Eucharistic feast. It is held just before Jesus is to leave his disciples forever, at least in the way that he has been with them. He will go on to die, rise, and ascend, but no longer will he be their companion

27. Ibid.

28. For more on this ancient idea of body, and its significance for St. Paul, see Martin, *Corinthian Body*.

29. Ward, *Cities of God*, 103.

in the ordinary sense of the word. It is only through the disappearance of the physical body that it can be disseminated, allowing the incorporation of others. This incorporation allows the crossing of multiple boundaries, without erasing them completely, boundaries of ethnicity, gender, class, and much else. These boundaries are transgressed and shown as unstable, fluid, and queer. Yet the absence of Christ's body is not final, and the gift of it sacramentally foreshadows the eschatological reunion of all bodies; the Eucharistic undoing of gender marks an even greater intimacy than is possible when Jesus walks on the earth. Thus, even categories of absence and presence are transgressed.

One final point needs to be emphasized about the body here. The fluidity of the body renders it deeply vulnerable. This vulnerability is necessary when boundaries are transgressed, if not erased. Jesus surrenders his body to his disciples at the first Eucharist, and these same disciples will take it and either hand it over to the authorities, deny it, or abandon it. The moments of deeply erotic intimacy shared at table will pass into those of pain, abandonment, and loss. As Peter knew all too well, the closeness and overlap of bodies makes each of us responsible for the other. By denying Jesus, Peter was also denying himself, for once he had partaken of body and blood at table, where the one began and the other left off was impossible to discern.

Passion and Crucifixion (Mark 14–15; Matt 26–27; Luke 22–23; John 18–19)

This brings us to the icon of the crucifixion. The breaking of the body as bread is relocated to the breaking of Jesus' physical body, first by torture and then by death. Jesus is brought into a power struggle in which his body becomes the site of utter passivity. The acts of violence afflicting his body "are all manifestations of various desires in conflict, [which are also] sexually charged."[30] Pilate's absolute power over life and death is twinned with the passivity of the one to die; the frenzy of the soldiers' violent touch manifests the domination of empire over that of the helpless "King of the Jews." All these forces come into play at the locus of Jesus' body, the symbolic action played out upon him only far too real.

Regarding physical sex, Ward argues that a further displacement occurs here. In the power play and vast conjunction of intense bodily

30. Ibid.

symbolics, the maleness of Christ's body is lost—he is no longer a man, but rather meat. He is here neither woman nor man, though as was discussed above this body still evinces both masculinity and femininity. Though this furthers Ward's point about the irreducibility of gender to sex—Jesus is not castrated, but is still not male—I am not convinced by Ward's argument. Though the body is indeed treated as raw flesh—not the body of a human—the maleness of the body is not lost in the crucifixion. It also seems a dangerous reading, for to fail to see the body as human is to accept the very logic of empire that brutalized Jesus. His body is, however, humiliated. According to most historians, the crucified were executed nude, as a sign of complete powerlessness and exposure. For the Romans, executing a Jew this way would be doubly shameful, since his circumcised genitalia would be exposed to the judging gaze of those who found the practice barbarous. The man is rendered passive, treated as a woman to the ancient mind, and it is not accidental that the Gospels portray Jesus as passive throughout the passion narratives. This "feminization" needs not be taken with the negative connotations that it would have held then, however, nor—if Ward is correct—need it make any necessary comment on women. Christ is passive, but that passivity is testament to the power of God, the God who both dies on the cross and rises from the dead. Jesus' feminization is a source of glory, not shame. Indeed, the very concepts are troubled because it is through his passivity/passion (femininity) that he conquers (masculinity).[31] His masculinity and the maleness of his body are indeed troubled, but they are not effaced completely, as Ward reads them to be. His body is indeed objectified as Ward observes: "The body as object is already being treated as a dead, unwanted, discardable thing before Jesus breathes his last."[32] This objectification does not, however, strip the body of its already-complex sex, but only serves to further that complication.

More interesting than the status of Christ's sexed body in this icon is Ward's reading of eros. Desire is operative throughout the passion accounts, and to this point it is shown largely as frenzied and libidinal: the madness of Dionysus poured onto the body of Jesus. Desire does not cease when Jesus dies, but it is transformed. Rather than libidinal and deadly, eros is now indistinguishable from pathos. The desire for the body of the crucified is still present, but it is transfigured as mourning and loss.

31. For a challenge to this line of thought, and deeper analysis of how the male body-in-pain can be read as redemptive, see Brintnall, *Ecce Homo*.

32. Ward, *Cities of God*, 104.

This shift to pathetic desire is particularly evident when looked at in contrast with the transfiguration. Both are iconic moments when the body of Jesus is held up and gazed upon. On the Mount of Transfiguration, the physicality of Jesus is suspended, that is, it becomes a transparent conduit to the glory of the Divine, without being itself erased. The physical is similarly pointing beyond itself here, but in a different way. The sheer weight of human brutality overwhelms the physicality of Jesus, reducing first his humanity to mere *bios* and then to death. As the transfiguration displaced both Jesus and the viewer—by enflaming a new desire—so does the cross: "We are the ones displaced; that is what the crucified body of Christ recalls us to—a primary relationship to God from which we are estranged."[33] The bleeding, violated physicality of Jesus brings us and our bodies to a more primal experience: the dependence that we try to evade.

The loss of Jesus' body and our continuing desire for it brings us into a larger economy of relationship. We are forced to recognize our own contingency—our inability to sustain ourselves. Our dependence and interconnectedness are made only too evident—we too cannot stop from dying and are vulnerable to violent touch—and yet this displacement is not from some preexisting wholeness, but the exposure that wholeness never existed.[34] Our desire is enflamed by Jesus' body as it is lost, but this loss is not tragic, because it allows us an even greater participation in Christ's body. This is the significance of the trope mentioned above, of Christ's wounded side being the womb from which springs the church in the water and blood, figuring baptism and Eucharist. The opening of Christ's body permits us to enter into it as church, dying with him that we might also rise. The brokenness, however, is key. It is, in fact, required. The opening within us—the displacement of our illusions of autonomy—becomes a *sine qua non* for our salvation, for it allows us the space in which we can be filled: "Recognition of lack of foundations within oneself [. . .] requires and enables a reception of divine plentitude."[35] Our bodies are displaced into the crucified, and this

33. Ward, *Cities of God*, 106.

34. Brian D. Robinette, following Drew Leder, speaks about this experience as that which creates the sense of alienation from our bodies, being jolted from our normal lives where we hardly notice our bodies at all—where we seem to stand outside, beyond, or unbound by them: the ecstatic body—to the perception of the body's otherness, the body as an obstacle; our being reminded of our boundedness, vulnerability, and connectedness: the recessive and dysfunctional body. See *Grammars of Resurrection*, 136–45.

35. Ward, *Cities of God*, 108.

becomes our life. Obviously, this displacement is also connected with the icon of resurrection, to which we now turn.

Resurrection (Mark 16; Matt 28; Luke 24; John 20–21)

At the resurrection, Jesus' body appears in a glorified, mysterious form. As Ward says, "It opens up a spiritual topos within the physical, historical, and geographic."[36] Christ's body is no longer simply bound by these created realities, but imbues them with new significance and power. The body is not contained by space and time, but it also does not remove itself from them. In so doing, Christ shows the truth of all bodies, which also cannot be reduced to these categories. Our bodies bear the past as they proceed into the future; our physicality cannot be reduced to physiology since the physical activities of our bodies unfold to countless others. The resurrection unveils this at the extremity by showing what our bodies, and thus ourselves, are to become—what they are being gifted into by God. When the disciples first see Jesus, they cannot immediately recognize him.[37] Our usual identity markers—those by which we commodify and group bodies—are troubled. This inability to identify is "part of an unfolding logic of displacing bodies, bodies which defer or conceal their final identities; bodies which maintain their mystery."[38] Ward does not claim that the body *has* no identity, merely that it cannot be easily perceived—it is caught up and hidden in the mystery of God, from whom all true identities flow.

Jesus' body is mysterious; it is not bound by the usual human limitations, but also does not annul them. He can pass through locked doors, but can also eat and be touched. His body exceeds our capacities to categorize and limit. It cannot be "grasped, catalogued, atomized, or comprehended."[39] Yet it still, profoundly and powerfully, *is*. By being so, Jesus does not end or destroy one kind of embodiment and usher in another, but rather highlights the lurking mystery of all bodies by showing what these bodies will

---

36. Ibid.

37. Ward makes an enigmatic suggestion as to why this might be so. He writes that Jesus can "occupy other bodies (which causes so many misidentifications of who he is)." Ibid. This seems to imply some sort of Christic "possession" of bodies, which would of course be another instance of displacement, but would also cause problems pertaining to free will, among others. He neither develops nor returns to this idea elsewhere, so far as I can find.

38. Ibid., 109.

39. Ibid., 111.

be and, in some way, already are: imbued with a "materiality which can never fully reveal, must always conceal, something of the profundity of its existence."[40] The body of the crucified, like our own bodies, is caught up in analogical relation to God. The divinity shown at the transfiguration in a glimpse is here redolent in the flesh. Jesus is completely Lord, and also completely part of a creation made gloriously new.

Ward sees in the icon of the resurrection a critique of physiological fundamentalism when discussing sexual difference as well. In "There is No Sexual Difference," Ward provides a close reading of two of the resurrection narratives in John 20: those of Mary Magdalene and Thomas.[41] He notes that both have the same fundamental structure, and are both deeply sexualized. This eroticism arises from their relationships, attractions, and encounters depicted. Sexual difference only makes sense for Ward when read in terms of the larger differences and distances between persons, as well as their similarities and fluctuating closeness. It cannot be reduced to genitals, as many conservative Christians wish to do, where sexual difference can only exist between one with a penis and another with a vagina as an assumed *a priori* to all relationships. Sexual difference arises within a matrix of other differences, and only exists within this matrix.

The eroticism of the encounter with Mary Magdalene is well attested. Not only is there the exchange of physical touch in the narrative, which Jesus must break, but also the history of its interpretation. From the gnostic gospels to *The DaVinci Code*, the eroticism between Christ and Mary has been affirmed and imaginatively developed. Moreover, the scene also recapitulates the eros of the first man and woman in the Garden of Eden. Those relations, marred by the fall, are here restored. The displacement of bodies is also in evidence. For Ward, the desire that Mary shows when she asks Jesus—mistaking him for the gardener—for the body of her master is elicited by the fact that she still carries him within her. Her memory of their encounters, of his teaching, creates a "pseudo-presence," that is internalized within her. They are neither one, nor separate: "Jesus' presence is part of Mary's presence, and it is the physical absence of that presence that remains within her, displacing both a sense of herself and him, that installs

40. Ibid.

41. Found in Loughlin, *Queer Theology*, 76–85. This essay is a modified version and combination of two pieces from *Christ and Culture*: "Redemption," 113–28, and "Divinity and Sexual Difference," 129–58.

her desire."[42] Her yearning for him is not simply a matter of his being gone, but also of him still being present to her. She is not herself without him, nor he without her. There is proximity and there is distance, sameness and difference.

Similarly, there is a movement in this encounter from sight to touch. Mary sees the emptiness of the tomb, and then the Lord whom she misrecognizes. Her name spoken by him—connecting to the knowledge carried within her, the knowledge of their relationship—allows her to recognize and embrace him. Ward does not want to overstate the difference between sight and touch because, as he rightly points out, there are looks that can heal and those that can wound, yet he does see that somewhere in the matrix between the two, what we call sexuality arises: attraction, yearning, and movement to unite. The *distance* between bodies which desire seeks to overcome is analogically mapped onto the *difference* between the bodies which enflames desire. Yet, what is important is that this difference does not *precede* the encounter and relationship. Sexuality arises between the two; it is not an *a priori*. Their sexual difference—the otherness, the distance, that desire seeks to bridge and yet lovingly maintain in order that the other can be herself even as she is transformed—comes from the encounter, from the glances, the touch, the movement: "Bodies, I suggest, become sexualized through a consciousness of being-in-relation of various kinds, through attentive rationalizing and responsive readings of body language. In being sexualized[,] bodies negotiate both difference and affinity, distance and proximity—they do not just encounter difference/distance."[43] As there can be no difference as such among creatures—this is unthinkable and meaningless, for all difference is relative between things that have some kind of similarity—there can be no sexual difference abstracted from the encounters between actual bodies. Difference only exists in relationship and encounter, and so does sexual difference. And, as we shall see, this sexual difference does not depend on the biological sex of the persons involved, but rather can exist between those of the same sex as well.

Since sexual difference and desire (*eros*) lies in the whole matrix of encounter between responsive beings, it cannot be reduced to the genitals one bears. This is evident when we examine the erotic and sexual charge of Jesus' encounter with Thomas, an encounter that closely mirrors that of Mary in the pattern of absence/distance, recognition, and drawing near to

42. Ward, "No Sexual Difference," 79.

43. Ibid., 83.

unite. Thomas, too, has internalized the body and presence of his Lord, but in a different way

Thomas' need to see the wounds in Jesus' side and hands for proof that he has risen is evidence of how he views his Lord: he is now the one who has been crucified. His sufferings and death are what identify him. As Ward observes, "Jesus' death lives in Thomas; lives in his memory, his language and his understanding of who this man is/was."[44] As Mary has internalized her master's presence so that it creates a longing in her, so has Thomas. He too wishes to be back in the physical presence of the one whom he carries in himself. Ward does not read Thomas' incredulity at the initial testimony of the other disciples as some sort of proto-atheism or agnosticism. It is not the mere demand for physical evidence which alone can attest to the real. Rather, it is because Thomas' wounding is one that dares not hope that its most ardent desire can be fulfilled: that the Beloved is not truly gone.

The matrix of movement from sight to touch also animates the story of Thomas. He indeed does see Jesus' wounds, but in Ward's reading, this is insufficient.[45] The intimacy that he is invited to by Jesus is even greater than that of the Beloved Disciple who reclined on Jesus' chest at the Last Supper; Thomas is invited to enter carnally into the tortured body of the Lord, the body he has internalized: "Put your finger here and see my hands, and bring your hand and put it into my side, and do not be unbelieving, but believe" (John 20:27). Thomas, unlike the other disciples, is invited to enact his desire for union. The distance between Jesus and Thomas is crossed and contact is made in encounter, even if only briefly. The difference between the two is overcome, blurred, and yet also maintained.

That this difference is erotically and even sexually charged is evident not only through the matrix of distance/proximity, sight/touch, difference/identity, which all enflame and power desire, but also through the interpretative tradition of this story. Ward reads the Johannine account through the lens of Caravaggio's famous painting of this encounter. In this, the intimacy and eroticism are manifest. Jesus himself is guiding the hand of the

---

44. Ibid., 80.

45. There is, of course, no clear indication in Scripture that either Thomas or Mary actually touch Jesus. It is neither confirmed nor denied, simply omitted. Ward, believing there to be nothing to preclude his reading, believes they did, following as well centuries of artistic interpretation of the various scenes. Considering his unwillingness to make too sharp a distinction between sight and touch, it could be argued that his analysis stands even if physical contact is not established. For an extended discussion of his rationale, see footnote 26 in "Redemption," 121.

fascinated Thomas toward his side. He is guiding the penetration of his wound, of the womb from which the church is born. Strictly (and anachronistically) speaking, this encounter is homosexual: it involves deep erotic intimacy between two people of the same sex. Yet this description of the event tells us precisely nothing. It tells us nothing about why the encounter is so erotically charged. It tells us nothing of the relationship between these two. It tells us nothing of the profound desire enflamed and maintained between them. In other words, the sexes of these men tell us nothing that significantly illuminates the encounter.

Mary and Jesus are different, as are Thomas and Jesus. These differences are sexually and erotically charged through a complex matrix of distance/proximity, sight/touch, and the mutual presence of the other that each bears. This is where the sexual difference arises, from the encounter and relationship, not from the genitals or biological sex of those involved. This is why Ward can say, as mentioned above, that sexual difference exists between male and male, female and female, and male and female. The encounters with the resurrected Lord intensify the limitations and reductions of modern conceptions of sexual difference and sexual orientation, limitations first seen at the transfiguration. Jesus' body is not only queer in its fluidity, openness, and excess; it is queer by how it relates to other bodies erotically, drawing them towards the Divine.

Ascension (Mark 16:19–20; Luke 24:50–53; Acts 1:6–12)

This brings us to the final displacement that Ward discusses and it is, for him, one of the most significant. At the ascension, the displacement of the body of Jesus of Nazareth reaches its farthest by being displaced into the community of the church. Once again, this is not to erase Jesus' body, but rather to expand it into all bodies. The physical body of Jesus is now absent, but his body is not gone: it is present in the church which is now the body of Christ on earth.

Ward's notion of the church as body of Christ is *not* a metaphor if by that we mean simply a likeness or extrinsic image. It is always much more than that. Ward means the church as Christ's body quite literally, as he quotes John A. T. Robinson's reading of St. Paul: "It is almost impossible to exaggerate the materialism and crudity of Paul's doctrine of the church as literally now the resurrected *body* of Christ."[46] This is how Ward rightly

46. Robinson, *The Body*, 51; quoted in Ward, *The Politics of Discipleship*, 248.

reads the body of Christ tradition, though the "crass" materiality is very complicated, indeed. Ward claims that the ascension does not create a rift between Jesus on earth and Jesus glorified. Rather, he sees it as allowing the full dissemination of his body into the bodies of all those who follow him and are baptized in the church.

This displacement also challenges, once again, the simple reading of Jesus' body as male. Once this displacement occurs, the body of Christ becomes multi-gendered. It becomes a body that bears the bodies of men, women, and those who do not easily fit in these categories. The body of Christ constitutes every imaginable performance of gender, as much as church officials wish to deny it. This tells us something not only about ourselves as persons, but also something about the body of Christ. Once again, Christ's body confounds our attempt to categorize via gender.

The church is now mandated to carry out the mission of its master on earth. It is a body dedicated to proclaiming the salvation of creation found in Christ, but also the body dedicated to tending to the bodies of those now suffering and in need. Since it is the queer body of Christ, it should be no surprise that the boundaries of the church are as difficult to map and place as those of Jesus discussed above.

By reflecting on the fraction rite in the Anglican liturgy, Ward discusses the church as the erotic community—as a community constituted and living in desire for one another and for God in Christ. As the body of Christ on the altar is broken, shared, and distributed, so are we caught up in an action of expansion and participation in one another and the world. The "we" here is significant. Following from the notion of the body as always unstable and mapped onto other bodies—and receiving other bodies in turn—Ward challenges the notion that "I" is the central designator of personhood. For him, this furthers the atomization of the individual that is endemic to the modern age. Rather, "'we' is the proper human subject, 'we' is an indication of personhood, not 'I'—'we' as physical and psychological beings, as particularized male and female, sinner and saint, able and disabled, of this race and that, of this social class and that."[47] This "we" is bound together erotically in the church; to participate analogically is to become one flesh.

This "we-ness" is located and constituted in and as the body of Christ. As we have been discussing, however, the body of Christ is a body which constantly displaces itself and defies reification or simple location. The

47. Ward, *Cities of God*, 153.

church participates in this dislocation as it participates in the body of the master. The community is gathered together at the Eucharistic banquet, and is dispersed throughout the world. It is one, but is made up of many. This allows the body of Christ to transgress boundaries and to be found beyond the borders of institutional churches. The body as community is caught in a constant rhythm of gathering and scattering: "It is itself a fractured and fracturing community, internally deconstituting and reconstituting itself."[48] The body of Christ, displaced into the church, is a queer body that cannot be limited any more than the body of Jesus of Nazareth could be when it walked upon the earth.

This community is not only present in space, but also in time. When we participate in Christ's body, we participate in the temporal plenitude that is immediate to God. This is most evident in the Eucharistic liturgy. In the Eucharist, the church is not "seizing" some sort of immediacy that is absent at other times. We are not reifying God or attempting to experience all time immediately as God does. Rather, we participate by remembering and by enacting our hope. "Now" cannot be grasped; it is always but a constantly moving target in the inexorable flow of time. This is how we experience eternity, as creatures: "For the Eucharist participates in a temporal plenitude that gathers up and rehearses the past, while drawing upon the futural expectations and significations of the act in the present."[49] This act of the body of Christ belongs "both to all times and to no one time" and hence allows us to participate in the eternity that is Christ's in God.[50]

This reality furthers the amorphousness of the body of Christ and the inability to set its boundaries, precisely because the community cannot be limited only to those who are alive today. As the church shatters the boundaries of location—by being displaced throughout the earth—it also shatters those of time by being displaced into eternity. The liturgy—the ultimate visible sign of the church—highlights the oneness, not only of those gathered in a given place, but also those who have so gathered and will so gather. In other words, the liturgy brings together the entire communion of saints who make up Christ's ecclesial body. In its fullest sense, this is the body of Christ and will remain incomplete until all those yet to come are joined to it, not merely in hope, but in reality.

48. Ibid., 154.
49. Ibid., 171.
50. Ibid.

What, precisely, makes this body of the church an *erotic* community, though? The answer to this has already been seen, and it involves Ward's insistence that, in the body of Christ, difference is not eliminated, while real unity still exists. Difference, and the desire for union across it, creates eros. At the risk of being trite, the body of Christ in the church is a body of difference in unity. The "we" that is the church is essential, because it means that the multitude cannot be assimilated into an undifferentiated "I," even if that "I" is God. Ward bases this view ultimately on the Trinity—the essential unity in difference—which we participate in through the body of Christ. This very incorporation with God, however, is always already based on a preceding desire, that of God for us: "Our desire for God is constituted by God's desire for us such that redemption, which is our being transformed into the image of God, is an economy of desire."[51] This desire for God is what brings us into the body of Christ, and it is inseparable from, though irreducible to, our desire for one another.

Desire depends, however, on the existence of difference. We only desire that which is different from us, but it must be a difference that is not absolute. As mentioned above, absolute difference has no meaning; difference can only exist among relations. If there is no relationship at all, there is nothing that can be recognized meaningfully as difference—simply a void. The church, therefore, must be a body of desiring bodies that are not absorbed into one another—for then desire would cease. And salvation itself is a matrix and network of desire and being desired.

Due to this insight, it is also important to recognize that love of neighbor is necessarily correlative of love of self. There must always be a space where the desire of others can be received and incorporated. This is an analogy to the very constitution of ourselves by the desire of God. In any "we," the "I" always remains (though transformed by its wider communal participation), but never for itself alone: "The I is born *in relation to* and that is intrinsic to its being made *in the image of*, for God is also always and only in relation to," among the persons of the Trinity, humanity, and the very cosmos.[52] There is no atomistic "I" that can either live only for itself or abandon itself completely for the sake of others.[53] Reciprocal de-

---

51. Ibid., 172.

52. Ibid., 176.

53. This is Ward's critique of thinkers like Levinas, who speak of our obligation to the other at the expense of the self, precisely because Levinas fails to recognize that there must always be a pattern of reception and giving: an other must exist for the other.

sire—though incommensurate, for God's eros is infinitely stronger than our own—constitutes the relations between ourselves and others in the church, and that body to God. The church is an erotic community.

This very desire is what makes the church as body of Christ exceed the boundaries of institutions. Institutional churches help define and particularize the body of Christ, giving it specificity, but they cannot confine it. The desire for difference—to lovingly give and receive—always extends to those outside of institutional boundaries, because the bodies that are incorporated into the body of Christ are not found only there. Each person exists in other bodies as well, where the desire of God found in the church also operates: "The one body of the We, made up as it is of so many singular bodies, each, according to its desire, extended into and operating within various social and political bodies, produces a space which is excessive to these institutional ecclesial places."[54] The body of Christ that is present in the church desires its consummation and completion in God, and this desire is not only for itself, but for all other bodies as well: "The body of Christ desiring its consummation opens itself to what is outside the institutional church; offers itself to perform in fields of activity far from chancel and cloister."[55] The church performs outside the churches.

Ward is obviously committed to maintaining that the desire that creates the body of Christ exceeds institution, and therefore those who are outside of the institutional church can themselves be members of Christ's body. This does raise the question of how one becomes a member of this body, however. There is, for instance, this curious passage from *Cities of God*: "To be bold: God founds society as those who are called to be in this time, with this particularity, for this purpose. Those called to be constitute the *ecclesia*."[56] This appears to make the church and society co-terminous.[57] In its context, this passage is referring to how only the analogical relationships discussed above (Trinitarian, ontological, sexual) can create and allow true community, genuine unity in diversity. Ward is critiquing what he sees in most contemporary societies as parodies of the church that create

54. Ward, *Cities of God*, 180. The use of "place" and "space" is technical language taken from de Certeau, *Practice of Everyday Life*. For Certeau, "space" exceeds merely geographical or topographical "place," while also enacting it.

55. Ward, *Cities of God*, 180.

56. Ibid., 117.

57. This problem is pointed out as well by James K. A. Smith, where he alleges that Ward identifies the church with all humanity, even going so far as to question why Ward remains Christian: *Introduction to Radical Orthodoxy*, 257.

merely virtual communities, while real ones disappear. What does it mean to say that God "founds society?" Clearly, Ward cannot mean simply any society, for this would include also the virtual communities that he wishes to critique. Could he be pointing to the eschatological community, where the body of Christ—the *ecclesia*—and all human society will in fact become one in the redeemed kingdom of God, the Heavenly Jerusalem? Might it merely be rhetorical overstatement, intended to drive home the difference between the true society founded by God and all those that we see around us? Perhaps that true sociability has its basis in the church? It is unclear.

Ultimately, it seems that there is some kind of distinction and boundary between the church and society writ large for Ward, though it remains a very fluid boundary. In a later work, *The Politics of Discipleship*, Ward asserts that baptism is required for incorporation into the body of Christ, for it is via the Spirit that we participate in this body, not via nature. A genuine ontological shift occurs, but this is an intensification of our life in the world, not our removal from it, just as the displacement of Jesus' body at the ascension ushers in not the absence of Christ, but more intensified participation in him: "Baptism 'by [*en*] the one Spirit' marks an ontological shift from being in the world to being *en Christo*. [. . .] But neither members nor even Christ are translated out of this world; the use of *en* suggests, rather, another level of ontological intensity available in this world but not concurrent with it."[58] The Spirit of God brings us into the body of Christ, and this is true baptism, but this cannot be limited to the ecclesial rite, even as that rite clarifies the meaning of this activity, renders it visible, and genuinely brings it about.[59]

Difficulties with Ward

One might note that the conversation has become a consideration of the church, and this in a chapter purportedly devoted to the incarnate body of Christ. Christology seems to have passed into ecclesiology, even as the borders between the two remain permeable. The difficulty of distinguishing between the church and society demonstrates a key problem in Ward, however, on both ecclesiology and the body of Jesus. Both are ultimately

58. Ward, *Politics of Discipleship*, 249, discussing 1 Cor 12:12–27.

59. More will be said on the question of baptism and queer incorporation into Christ's body in chapter 2 below.

rendered troublingly amorphous; they lack specificity.[60] The conversation about the church easily replaces the conversation about Jesus, and he seems to be simply absorbed into the ecclesial body.[61] Ward is adamant that this is an extension of Jesus' body, not its loss, but nonetheless the person of Jesus Christ seems occluded. The way these bodies seem to become coterminous likewise oversimplifies the relationship between them. As Kevin Hart states in his critique of Ward on this point, "We may participate in the Church but eschatologically we belong in the Kingdom, and that is why Christians call forth the judgement of Christ endlessly upon the Church and ourselves."[62] How can Christ be the judge of the church when he seems so utterly absorbed in it, when there is no distinction between him and it any longer? And if that image is, for various reasons, troubling, how can Jesus be even a friend or lover? Ward supplies no answer.

60. This amorphousness is not Ward's alone, but is a feature of many other thinkers associated with "Radical Orthodoxy," like John Milbank and Catherine Pickstock. It may be, in part, due to what Lawrence Paul Hemming calls "Anglican fuzziness" regarding ecclesiology: Hemming, Radical Orthodoxy? 103. Though it would take us too far afield to delve into it, one approach that could solidify the church—but also allow it the participatory and perichoretic structure envisaged by Ward—would be that of the ecclesiology of communion, which has inspired much productive work among Roman Catholic and Orthodox thinkers. For just a few of the studies in this increasingly voluminous literature, see Doyle, Communion Ecclesiology; Gaillardetz, Teaching with Authority, esp. 3–30; Tillard, Church of Churches and Flesh of the Church; and Zizioulas, Being as Communion.

61. With a slightly different emphasis, Virginia Burrus also critiques Ward on this point. She fears that the way Ward moves to displace Christ's body onto the church too easily loses the specificity of gendered bodies and their experiences in what she dismisses as "doctrinal sleight of hand": Burrus, "Radical Orthodoxy and the Heresiological Habit," 42. This tendency is not unique to Ward, however, and Robinette insists on the importance of the empty tomb tradition to avoid just this temptation: "By saying, 'He has risen, he is not here,' resurrection faith most certainly affirms that Jesus has been transformed into an eschatological mode of existence that enables him to be 'present' in a qualitatively new way; but it says this precisely while acknowledging the freedom of the risen Jesus who remains eschatologically Other and thus 'absent' from any and every effort to manipulate or subsume into an agenda." See Grammars of Resurrection, 92–93. Karl Rahner called this attempt to absorb Jesus into the church, and thus have the church—especially its teaching office—somehow replace Christ "ecclesial monophysitism:" quoted in Ruggieri, "Beyond an Ecclesiology of Polemics," 312.

62. Kevin Hart, "Response to Graham Ward," 210. Ward does recognize the distinction between church and kingdom that Hart refers to, though he leaves it rather underdeveloped. It is also possible that this later passage is intended as an answer to Hart's critique—"When the kingdom is fully come, then the church and its sacraments of grace are no longer necessary, for there the relationship to Christ is immediate:" Ward, Politics of Discipleship, 182.

In one sense, Ward can be forgiven this amorphousness, because when we start speaking about the resurrected body we are on terrain that is even shiftier and more uncertain than we are when speaking about the bodies that we supposedly know so well. And Ward has admirably demonstrated their complexity! Still, the trouble remains. I do not intend to offer a "more solid" version of the resurrected body of Christ and its relationship to the church than Ward does, precisely because I have no more access to this body than he. I do, however, want to discuss two aspects of embodied human personhood that I think must be present in any discussion of the resurrection and the relationship of Jesus' risen body to other bodies. These are not the only possible aspects, but they do seem to be criteria *sine qua non*. It is in some of these areas that I find Ward problematic.

The first is materiality. In order to be faithful to the tradition that it is the body, and not simply the soul, that rises from the grave, the materiality of that body has to be maintained. It is glorified, transfigured, and rendered into a new kind, yet it remains somehow material. The resurrection does not make humans into angels existing as pure spirit.[63] This aspect may be the least problematic in Ward, because he is quite clear that Jesus' resurrection is corporeal and that, after the displacement of the ascension, that corporeality is maintained through the physicality of those who make up the church. Whether or not Christ's body "resides" somehow in heaven as Calvin thought, it is clear that the physicality of it is not completely erased in the corporeal expansion.

Hart's critique, however, illustrates my second point of concern, on the agency of the risen Jesus. If Jesus and the church become so completely united that all distinction melts away, then the question not only of Jesus' traditional capacity to judge is thrown into question, but also the capacity of Jesus to continually give himself and receive the other. For when I speak of agency, this is primarily what I have in mind. I do not mean that Jesus holds onto some center of subjectivity that remains only "his," as if he were a petulant child unwilling to share. Rather, it seems that in the rich fabric of interpersonal relationship that Ward lays out and is discussed above, there must be an "I" that can give itself to the other and receive the other in turn. Again, this is not an isolated subject who exists separately

63. Ultimately, that is. I do not have the space to discuss, and Ward does not deal with, the question of an "intermediate state" between the death of a person and the general resurrection/judgment. Though common in most traditional Christian eschatology, the concept of such a state has been troubled by many contemporary theologians across the ideological spectrum.

and autonomously, where self-donation is some act of condescension. As Ward rightly argues, the "I" is always already informed by and constituted by the "we."[64] Yet, it also remains free. This freedom to donate and receive is constitutive of love. Yet, if the "I" of Jesus becomes so utterly absorbed into the "we" of the church, then can Jesus continue both to love and give himself to us, and we to him? Similarly, is Jesus now simply active only in the church in history? Can he somehow go "ahead" of the church, calling it to what it is supposed to be? If he can, and I and others want to affirm that he can, it is difficult to reconcile with Ward's presentation of Christ's body. At the very least, Ward needs to make greater distinction than he does.

These questions are pressing, not simply because of their treatment of Jesus' risen body, but also because they are deeply implicated in our own hopes for resurrection. The only hints towards our own destiny in the general resurrection are the accounts of Jesus and his body. If Jesus of Nazareth, who lived, suffered, died, and rose is so absorbed into the "we" of the church that he loses his own specificity and unique personhood, is this the same thing that will happen to us as well? Will my body be raised—my full humanity restored to even more than it had been before—only to be lost again into some sort of celestial soup? Will this mean that I can no longer love in a meaningful sense, or be loved, because there is no "I" who any longer exists distinct—not separate—from the whole? Is this adequate to either our hope or to the Christian tradition? Is it adequate to the rich account of difference and its proper maintenance that Ward lays out and is discussed throughout this chapter? I fear that Ward's discussion of Christ's displacement into the church fails on each of these points.

At the risk of being overly personal, I have a confession which, though perhaps unpopular or dismissable as overly pietistic, is nonetheless true: I do not want to die.[65] Or, more accurately, I do not want to *be* dead. The

---

64. In the case of Christ, this includes not only those who encountered and shaped Jesus of Nazareth, but more importantly, the prior "we" of the Trinity itself.

65. The anxiety caused by this statement, made by a Christian to other Christians, is itself testimony to something important in contemporary Christian theology that I cannot go into here. Perhaps it is our desire to disprove Marx's claim that religion is but an opiate that causes us to stifle our ultimate hopes. Whatever the reason, queer persons—and especially gay men afflicted by AIDS—seem to be more comfortable with this affirmation of hope in a very concrete eschaton than many others: "an Anglican priest, Malcolm Johnson, was struck by just how comfortable gay men were with discussing death, funerals and the afterlife. Another Anglican priest, Andrew Henderson, felt that he was never expected to confirm belief in the afterlife precisely because that belief was already so strong in the men he ministered to. Other ministers noted a strong belief in

death of the body is an inevitability that Christianity does not allow us to escape, but its finality is utterly undone by the resurrection. As Woody Allen quipped, "I don't want to live on in the hearts of my countrymen; I want to live on in my apartment." His apartment being, no doubt, much finer than mine, I will settle for the City of God. Yet, like him, it is still *I* who wish to live. Not me as I am now, but also not me as so different that my life loses all significance and meaning. The resurrection is about continuity *and* transformation; the fulfillment of our earthly lives, not their annihilation. I want to be able to experience the love of God, the love of neighbor—both in a degree of intimacy that I cannot yet begin to even fathom. Yet there must still be an "I" that can do this, an "I" that can be a real part of the more fundamental "we." I readily grant that I have no idea what I will be like then, what I will look like, how my body will be, and how it will interact with other bodies. But the life that I've lived on earth cannot simply be eliminated and absorbed into something else. Likewise, the sufferings of queer persons must be healed, but those witnesses of God's queerness themselves must not be annihilated. If Jesus' person is lost into the "we," will not the same happen to us? If so, then my hope will not be fulfilled, the promises made by Christ will be for naught. Fortunately, there is evidence that this is in fact not the case.

There is scriptural evidence that challenges the absorption of Jesus into the church. These texts also emphasize his fundamental unity with the church, but without making them so identical that the differences which allow for real love vanish. One is the appearance of Christ to Stephen at his martyrdom (Acts 7:54–60). In his trial before the Sanhedrin, Stephen's martyrdom and words closely mirror those of Christ as depicted in the Gospel of Luke. Stephen's body is somehow also Christ's body—that which was inflicted on the latter is repeated non-identically on the former. The true displacement of Christ into the church and its members is established. But Stephen also sees Jesus in a vision, standing at the right hand of the glory of God. The body of Christ can be, at the same time, displaced into the church as well as be a non-reified "object" for the adoring gaze. That is to say, Jesus can be both united inseparably to the church and also act for and towards it. The actions of Christ and the church are not utterly different, but they are also never reducible to each other, just as Christ's agency is

bodily resurrection." See Stuart, *Gay and Lesbian Theologies*, 65–77, esp. 65–67, quote from 66. See also the hope-filled reunion that concludes Norman René's film, *Longtime Companion* (MGM, 1989).

never separate from the Father's and Spirit's, yet remains always, somehow, his. Jesus is shown as being himself, but not only himself.

Another scriptural occurrence of this paradigm is the appearance of Christ to Paul (Acts 9:3–6; 1 Cor 15:8). In Acts 9, when Paul is struck blind on the road to Damascus, he hears the voice of Christ asking why Paul is persecuting him. Not his church, not those to whom he is especially bound, but *him*. The persecution of Christ's church is a persecution of Christ's body.[66] That displacement is maintained. When Paul recounts this in 1 Corinthians 15:8, however, he speaks of having seen the Lord, just as all the others who witnessed the resurrection saw him. Christ was at once one with the church, so that persecutions attacked him, yet he was also able to be seen and encountered by Paul.[67] I do not mean here to get into the debate over what Paul exactly "saw," but simply mean to demonstrate that Jesus is able to act as distinct, but not separated, from the church. The complete identity between the two that Ward implies does not seem to fit in this account.

Examples could be multiplied, but the end result is that the resurrection of the body affirms both the complete union and intimacy of bodies one with another *as well as* their difference and irreducibility. They are specific, even as they are not separate. Before moving on to how we are incorporated in this queer and troublesome body of Christ, it may be useful to return briefly to the specificity of his body—at least in its political ramifications.

The Sacred Penis[68]

Having engaged in critique of the amorphous space where Ward leaves the body of Christ, it seems appropriate in concluding this chapter to return once more to the specific body of Jesus of Nazareth. This body has been garnering queer attention of late, paradoxically in conversation about that

66. Another important example directly related to these cases is the Parable of the Sheep and Goats (Matt 25).

67. This would be true regardless of whether or not one accepts the Lucan depiction of the ascension forty days after the resurrection or the Johannine account whereby resurrection and ascension are more closely united, perhaps even simultaneous.

68. My intention with this heading is not to fetishize Christ's sex or make some general statement on the phallus. I am, instead, utilizing traditional Catholic language of devotion to Christ's body, such as that referring to the Sacred Heart.

which makes Christ most "normal," perhaps even banal: since he was sexed male, Jesus had a penis.

We have no more access to the penis of Christ than we do to any other part of his physical body. We do know, however, from the account of his circumcision in the Gospel of Luke that he seems to have been a "normal" male in his genital embodiment. Yet this very basic fact has been the cause of much political maneuvering, both culturally and ecclesially. It is this queer politics—a politics built around this most mundane of male qualities—that I wish to discuss. This is both because of its importance for queer theology and its ideas on embodiment, and also because of the way it reveals our anxieties about the human body.

In his essay, "The Politics of Circumcision (and the Mystery of All Flesh)," Graham Ward discusses the political ramifications of our depictions of Christ's penis.[69] Particularly, Ward wants his readers to analyze the presumed knowledge we possess (or think we possess) when we enter into discussion of Christ's body. He is not trying to claim that we must assume nothing—this is impossible—but rather allow our assumptions to be questioned and recognize how they might change over time. To illustrate this project, Ward looks at two cultural representations of Christ's sex: Luke's depiction of the circumcision and Michelangelo's statue of the Risen Christ. In both, he emphasizes the political significance of the depictions, as well as what they communicate about ideologies of embodiment.

Two things are especially important in Jesus' circumcision. The first is that it is "proof" that Jesus possesses a fully human body—it is a mark of the incarnation.[70] This is no docetic account of the human embodiment of God. Secondly, it shows the ethnicity of Jesus—he is a true Jew, and a Jewish male at that. The ritual not only marks Jesus' physiology, but is also a political action, placing him in *this* group, not that.

Ward asks the intriguing question of why it is in Luke, and not Matthew, that we get an account of the circumcision. These are the only two Gospels to give accounts of Jesus' infancy, yet Luke is, by scholarly consensus, believed to have been written for a largely Greek, Gentile audience and Matthew for a Jewish one. Why should the one writing for non-Jews emphasize this practice and the one aimed at Jews omit it?

69. Found in Ward, *Christ and Culture*, 159–80. This essay is also presented in substantially the same form as Ward, "On the Politics of Embodiment," 71–85.

70. For more on how this connection was made in Renaissance art, see Steinberg, *Sexuality of Christ in Renaissance Art.*

Ward argues that to understand this inclusion, we must look at its cultural effects, as well as its theological properties. To many in the Gentile world of Luke's day, circumcision was, at best, an embarrassing rite of a backward people and, at worst, a brutality inflicted on the human body. This was the presumed ideology of the body that Luke's readers/hearers would have had in mind. There is even evidence of diaspora Jews having foreskins surgically restored so they wouldn't look "ridiculous" at the baths or in athletic contests.[71] The circumcised body was seen as incomplete, deformed, by the wider Greco-Roman world.

So why did Luke choose to emphasize the fact that Jesus was circumcised? Ward argues that it was an exercise of resistance to the culturally-constructed ideas of bodies circulating in his day. Ideology could not trump Luke's commitment to a different understanding of body. Not only this, Luke uses the scene to highlight key points of his understanding of who Jesus was within the history of his people:

> The circumcision links salvation to naming, weaving a complex relation between Mary's body and Christ's. For the cutting Jesus undergoes Mary herself will undergo when "a sword will pierce through your soul *also*" (*de*; Luke 2.35). The present event of circumcision dissolves into the future prophecy while it floats upon a past resonant with connotations of shepherd kings and sacrificial lambs.[72]

Jesus' body is inseparable from that of his mother and the Jewish people whose law he had come to fulfill. Even when discussing the penis of Jesus and the specificity of his body, its irreducibility to the purely physiological remains.

The account of Jesus' body goes even further than this, though, because the ancient body was not seen as the medicalized monad we think of today. It was always porous and implicated in numerous other bodies. The body was a microcosm of the cosmos itself, wherein "the perfection of the physical was an aspiration towards the realization of political harmony and cosmic beauty."[73] In emphasizing the circumcision, not only does Luke gesture at Christ's full humanity—he also challenges the presuppositions that were assumed behind concepts of beauty and wholeness.

---

71. For more on the procedure and its significance, see Hall, "Epispasm."

72. Ward, "Politics of Christ's Circumcision," 169, emphasis in original.

73. Ibid., 172.

How does Luke's account differ from that of Michelangelo?[74] The artist's risen Messiah—like his David—is depicted in the nude. Yet, it is also quite clear that the penises of both figures are uncut: "These bodies are not Jewish bodies and neither of them shows a circumcised penis."[75] Why might this be?

Ward argues that Michelangelo lived at a time where the Greco-Roman young male was seen, once again, as the figuration of beauty and wholeness. These ideas were very similar to those held in ancient Rome, since Renaissance art was often self-consciously based on these earlier works. But while in Luke we find resistance to this cultural hegemony and denigration of the Jewish body, in Michelangelo we see capitulation to it. The Jews are a despised people, and thus cannot bear in depictions of their bodies the cosmic and soteriological weight of Christ's body. These are the political implications that Ward draws from attending to Christ's penis. I wonder, though, if there might not be another possible reason for the difference between the two depictions, a more theological one.

Though I suspect Ward is correct in his appraisal of why the Risen Christ is uncircumcised in Michelangelo's statue, it is possible that this is less a statement of the artist's view of the Jews and more about the resurrection (this, of course, does not apply in his depiction of David, who is not shown as risen or glorified). If, in the resurrection, our bodies are restored to their wholeness, it is not necessarily anti-Jewish to argue that the foreskin would be restored as well. Yet this would certainly undercut for Jews a very important aspect of their identity, not simply as persons, but as the people of God. Ward gestures to this problem, but does not directly engage it in his essay. Is it perhaps possible, however, that the resurrected body could be circumcised and uncircumcised? What follows is entirely speculative, but I believe it helps to further establish the queerness of Christ's body, while also maintaining its specificity as sexed.

The risen body of Jesus, as discussed above, behaves very oddly in the Gospels. Particularly, it seems to adjust itself to the needs of those it encounters; it is truly a body-for-others. Mary Magdalene cannot recognize him until Jesus says her name. She replies "Rabboni." Jesus, for her, is primarily a teacher, and until she can see him in that capacity, she cannot recognize him. Similarly, Thomas can only believe and "see" Jesus by being

74. Ward uses other artists as examples as well, but I will deal with Michelangelo for the sake of clarity and brevity.

75. Ward, "Politics of Christ's Circumcision," 174.

directed to the wounds in his hands and side; for him Jesus is the crucified, the one he mourns and dares not hope to see again. Finally, at Emmaus (Luke 24:13–35), the disciples recognize Jesus only through the breaking of the bread, that which they associate with the master due to both his most important miracle (the Multiplication of the Loaves, which is the only miracle recorded in all four Gospels) and with the last time they saw him at table the night before he died.

What is interesting about these accounts it that each encounter with Jesus brings with it a different form of recognition. Jesus is ultimately recognized because he is seen as the disciples need to see him. Thomas may not have been able to recognize him if Jesus spoke his name. Likewise, the breaking of the bread may have been insufficient for Mary to discern the body of her Lord. Only the account with Thomas mentions the wounds, which one would have to think would be rather noticeable. In the same gospel, Mary seems to take no notice of them, which is difficult to imagine; surely, wounded hands and feet would have been ample evidence that this was not simply any gardener. What if this textual absence is due to their physical absence, precisely because Mary does not need them to be present? Yet Thomas does, and so the body of Jesus is marked accordingly. Jesus' body is not reducible to the "usual" signifiers of bodies—it exceeds them—yet it is also truly a body for others that appears as it must so that intimacy might be created or restored.

If this logic is accurate, then Jesus' penis might indeed be uncut to the gaze of those who have that estimation of bodily integrity, like Michelangelo. For a Jew after the resurrection, however, the penis may be circumcised as an eternal taking up of their distinctive way of being the people of God, even as that category is universalized. This is of course speculative, but it seems to be in keeping with the way that Jesus' body behaves after his own resurrection. It also may allow our discussions to transcend the political dimension that Ward rightly points out: that the risen Christ, even in artistic depiction, exceeds its representation. The body can accommodate us and our expectations, even as it exceeds them and pulls us along to a new understanding.[76]

---

76. Another, if more problematic, example of body-for-the-other is the famous apparition of Mary to Juan Diego, known as Our Lady of Guadalupe. In this vision, Mary appears as a pregnant Aztec princess. Though it is a vision, not a resurrection appearance, the malleability of the body is striking. The distinctions between vision, image, and relic are also rendered ambiguous: "The Virgin of Guadalupe in the New World *became* to many adherents the supposedly miraculous picture of her that appeared on the cloak

The "wounding" of Christ at his circumcision has frequently been read as a first spilling of his precious blood as a precursor of his death. The way I have just discussed the circumcision of the risen body is also useful to understand these wounds in the resurrection. Many people, like James Alison, find the idea of these wounds being borne by the risen body—even through all eternity—as a sign of the deep continuity between now and then.[77] That our personhood, our lives, our stories are not annulled at the resurrection, but are rather taken up and glorified. This includes even our sufferings and death.

In many ways, this is an appealing notion, especially for queer persons. It indicates that the sufferings we have endured are not meaningless, but themselves shape who we are and who we will be when transfigured. The glorified wounds emphasize that our pain need not be a cause of shame or scandal. But the risk of this approach, I fear, is that suffering becomes in some way eternalized. After all, the resurrection is not simply about glorifying our wounds, but about healing them. Can that healing truly occur if they are with us eternally?

If the idea of the risen body as a body-for-others is accurate, then there may be no need to choose. Our sufferings, our wounds, are not rendered glorious for their own sakes, or even for ours. Jesus does not need to bear his wounds after the resurrection, Thomas does. The wounds are a source of identification—a place of compassion—but they do not exhaust who Jesus is. The same can be said with ours as well. Our own sufferings are not glorified in order to be dwelt on eternally, but rather to be sites of compassion and intimacy in the glory of the collective resurrection. They may be there, or not. They may be remembered or not, not as a source of resurrected neuroticism, but as places of contact with others who need them. The descriptions of Christ's wounds after the resurrection, both circumcised and crucified, suggest this idea. They are there when they need to be for others, but they do not define or limit the body *in toto*. The risen

---

of the peasant who received the apparition in 1531." Bynum, *Christian Materiality*, 22. This text gives a rich account of the relationship between materiality and bodies, and the uneasy borders between representation and reality that fueled much late medieval piety. For more on the Virgin of Guadalupe and its theological ramifications, see Elizondo, *Guadalupe*. Marcella Althaus-Reid, on the other hand, finds the *Guadalupana* to be, at best, an ambivalent and often harmful image for Latin American women, see *Indecent Theology*, 47–86, esp. 50–57.

77. See Alison, *Raising Abel*, 31–33.

body always exceeds and moves beyond that which was there before, even as it retains it.

A different, but related, political analysis of Jesus' penis is given by Mark D. Jordan in his essay, "God's Body." Jordan characterizes the essay as a meditation—it critiques while also enacting a particular form of piety. This genre choice is not accidental, for it is precisely the image of God incarnate as object of meditation that draws Jordan's attention. The implications of our ideas of Christ's body on Christian belief are at issue. The primary image of Christ in Catholicism is that of the crucifix, but this image is usually presented in an ambiguous manner due to a particular absence: that of Jesus' sex.[78] Yet, despite the profound reticence and anxiety surrounding Jesus' genitals, the church makes much of Jesus' gender and masculinity; in fact, it insists vehemently on them.

Jordan considers most of the images of Jesus, particularly depictions of his crucifixion, as "Jesus' corpses."[79] This is not only because the scene is of Jesus' death, but also because these images cannot convey a "real" man, precisely because of their anxieties over Jesus' male body. As is accepted by most historians, Jesus was mostly probably executed naked, in order to expose his body—particularly his Jewishness—to shame. Yet God has no shame in the body of Jesus and permits the display. Our own depictions are not so comfortable, however. Jesus' body must be sanitized and covered even at this moment which highlights vulnerability and exposure. Theology's refusal to look under the loincloth has only helped the creation of this corpse, a corpse repudiated by God at Easter: "The big business of theology has been to construct alternate bodies for Jesus the Christ—tidier bodies, bodies better conformed to institutional needs. I think of these artificial bodies as Jesus' corpses, and I consider large parts of official Christology

78. Jordan, like Ward, is not trying to create a fetish of Christ's genitals by this reflection. Rather, he simply wishes to give them their due as a part of the incarnate body that troubles us. In a "complete" depiction of Jesus on the cross, "[t]he genitals would be considered—as they were in some periods of Christian painting—a powerful sign of the fullness of incarnation. The penis would be circumcised in conformity with scriptural evidence and as a sign of Jesus' obedience to Jewish law. But it would be neither exaggerated nor minimized, fetishized neither as a commodity to be chased nor as a disgrace to be repudiated:" "God's Body," 284. Still, even if there is danger of fetishization, it is not clear why this should be more problematic than other reflections on particular body parts in Catholic theology, from the hearts of Jesus and Mary to the relics of saints.

79. Jordan, "God's Body," 283.

their mortuaries."[80] But what institutional needs are served by covering that which was exposed, by negating what God has affirmed?

One of the concerns that leads to this reaction is the ancient ambivalence—and often outright hostility—of the church to the erotic and the embodied. After all, what might be going through the mind of a sculptor as she loving created and molded the genitals of Jesus for an accurate crucifix? It would be, one might assume and hope, an act of devotion on her part, of intimacy, of love. The devoted adorer is a sexed being—she has the same fullness of humanity that Jesus had and that makes the church uncomfortable. Might the reluctance of the church—and those that make it up—to embrace the full consequences of the incarnation stem from our own inability—or fear—to think through the relationship that these bodies bear to one another? Not only, "What am I thinking about this nude man on the cross?" but, "What does he think of me?" Jordan asks, "How does his gaze on my body affect my gaze on his? How does the intimacy of our relationship trouble my relation to him as someone who has a sexed body? Must I hide his sex in part because I can't figure out how to think of his sex in relation to our intimacy, my devotion?"[81] How do I as a sexed being relate to him as a sexed being?

What if the worshipful gazer is a straight man, for whom Jesus *must* be, at most, a kind of buddy—in order to maintain the devotee's own solid heterosexuality—yet, somehow, more than that as well? What if the one who gazes is a straight woman or gay man whose desire might be enflamed by this image? Isn't this dangerous territory? But isn't the creation of desire precisely what this image is meant to do? Enflame us with love and the yearning to unite with the one who shows his love in outstretched, pierced arms? Are we not invited, like Thomas, to enter his body through his wounds? How do we think of this body—this body of God—and our relationship to it?

The shame—the embarrassment—that we think obligatory in this scenario reveals something to us about ourselves, but nothing about God. God has no shame in Jesus' body, just as Adam and Eve were shameless before sin. Jordan avers that the loincloth is there not for Jesus' sake—or even that of piety—but our own: "We need that loincloth to keep ourselves from being ashamed. The cloth covers part of Jesus, which means that it

80. Ibid.
81. Ibid., 287.

helps us not to look at ourselves. His loincloth is made to cover our eyes."[82] Do we dare to let this part of ourselves be redeemed as well by the man who is God, in all his shamelessness?

A further issue that reflection on the body of Christ raises is that of his masculinity—his gender.[83] As silent as the church is, and wants us to be, on Jesus' sex, it is ferocious on his gender. That Jesus Christ was a man is constantly commented upon, especially in the Roman Catholic Church. Jesus was a man and chose only men as his apostles.[84] The Vatican is vociferous on this point and it is the main rationalization for why women cannot be sacramentally ordained in the church. Though the Catholic Church tries to ensure that we do not think about why, it is absolutely necessary to remember that Jesus is a man. But Jordan looks further than this and asks, "What kind of man was Jesus?"

Jesus' masculinity does not seem to conform to what we are led to think men should be, in the stereotyped sense. In fact, Jordan calls it a "eunuch masculinity."[85] It is a strictly celibate masculinity, since ideas that Jesus might have had sex are as disturbing—if not more so—than him having the organs that rendered this possible. This, in turn, highlights the odd masculinity of those who stand *in persona Christi* at the altar in Catholic churches: the male-only priesthood. These men have often been treated as a third sex or some sort of intersex. They must be male, but both their roles and their presumed celibacy render their masculinity somehow different from that of other men. Jesus' eunuch masculinity both legitimates that of the clergy and raises questions about the very need for maleness in the ministry. After all, if one must have a penis, yet need not perform masculinity as usually understood, why the first requirement? A woman could just as easily perform Jesus' eunuch masculinity, or in another sense, his femininity. Perhaps the reason that Jesus' manhood is so firmly insisted upon is precisely to shore up that of the priests who stand in his place, whose own manhood is never quite evident in an untroubled fashion. All

---

82. Ibid., 284.

83. Jordan makes clear that, though he uses the classic distinction between sex and gender, he finds it ultimately provisional and unstable in itself: ibid., 285.

84. Most contemporary biblical scholarship observes a distinction between the Twelve and the college of apostles, of whom there were most likely women. This argument is consistently ignored by defenders of the ordination ban. See, among many others, Sullivan, *From Apostles to Bishops*, 17–53.

85. Jordan, "God's Body," 286.

these thoughts are triggered by reflecting on the penis of Jesus, the sex that he bears and also renders problematic.

This chapter has been a queer discussion of the body of Christ, largely through the work of Graham Ward. Though I have great respect for Ward, I have also pointed out some troubling aspects of his work, particularly the amorphousness of any distinction between Christ and the church as well as the danger of losing a truly personal resurrection. Returning to a more concrete reflection on Christ's body at the conclusion, I have discussed the value of reflecting on Christ's penis, Christ's sex, in order to think through the political implications—cultural and ecclesial—that such reflection manifests. This, in turn, raises questions about us as church and our comfort with the full implications of the incarnation, into which we are also incorporated. But how does this incorporation take place? How does one enter into the displaced body of Christ? It is this that the next chapter will examine.

CHAPTER 2

Sacraments: Queer In-corporation

The only thing that makes the Church endurable is that it is somehow the Body of Christ and that on this we are fed. It seems to be a fact that you have to suffer as much from the Church as for it but if you believe in the divinity of Christ, you have to cherish the world at the same time that you struggle to endure it.

—FLANNERY O'CONNOR[1]

Christ lives on in the Church, but Christ Crucified. One might almost venture to suggest that the defects of the Church are His Cross. [. . .] And he [*sic*] who will have Christ, must take His Cross as well. We cannot separate Him from it.

—ROMANO GUARDINI[2]

WE HAVE SEEN THAT not only is the concept of the incarnation queer, but that the body God took on—that of Jesus of Nazareth—was as well. Pivotal to this understanding of queerness is the ability of Christ's body to expand and include all other bodies after the ascension, to become more intensely embodied in the bodies that make up the church. How are our

1. O'Connor, *The Habit of Being*, 90.
2. Guardini, "The Church and the Catholic," 55.

bodies incorporated into the body of Christ, though? By what processes do our unique bodies become participants in the risen and glorified body of Jesus? What does it mean for us to have this happen? For Christians in the more liturgically-oriented traditions, this occurs ritually in the sacraments, specifically those of baptism and Eucharist. These queer rites bring us into the queer body of Christ.

To discuss these queer sacraments, I will engage the work of three theologians who bring out their significance, but do so in very different ways: Elizabeth Stuart, Marcella Althaus-Reid, and Herbert McCabe. The sacraments are pivotal to Stuart's queer theology, but they are treated only occasionally by Althaus-Reid. They are also given very different valences and readings, with Stuart focusing on the traditional sacraments and Althaus-Reid minimizing those in favor of other rituals that are noticeably transgressive and practiced by the marginalized. Stuart's account is one that I find very rich and compelling, but is also troubling in its idealism. Althaus-Reid, then, serves to question some of Stuart's assumptions by taking the lived experiences of the queer and marginalized as her starting point, though her views are also not without difficulties. Taken together, however, I believe that a more compelling picture of the sacraments as queer can be constructed. Finally, McCabe—who is usually not identified with queer theology—will be discussed in order to interrogate Stuart's view of the church and hopefully provide a way of speaking of the church and sacraments that account both for their life-giving efficacy as well as their perceived failures.

Though Stuart discusses most of the traditional Catholic sacraments, I will focus only on the two that are initiatory, that is, bring us into and maintain us as parts of the body of Christ: baptism and Eucharist. The other sacraments are either later offshoots of these (confirmation),[3] intended to allow one to perform or participate in these (ordination and reconciliation), or else give further signs of the love into which we are initiated by these (anointing of the sick and marriage). All are important, but since my primary interest is about our queer incorporation into Christ's queer body,

---

3. Though numbered among the traditional Sacraments of Initiation, confirmation is a later separation of the anointing that was once an essential part of the baptism rite. The Eastern Catholic rites and Orthodox Churches generally maintain this more ancient practice. Stuart does not enter into any discussion of this sacrament. For more on the process of separation between baptism and confirmation in the Christian West, see Johnson, *The Rites of Christian Initiation*.

the aforementioned sacraments that emphasize this will be my primary focus.

Elizabeth Stuart and Parodic Repetitions

Elizabeth Stuart has exhibited a marked development over the course of her career, one that needs to be mentioned because of her current theological method. As she discusses in *Gay and Lesbian Theologies: Repetitions with Critical Difference*, her thinking has developed from what she terms feminist/lesbian and erotic theology to queer theology. In this text, Stuart discusses four kinds of gay and lesbian theologies—or theologies that can be loosely covered by that label. Though each of these has done very important work that must not be discounted, for queer theology itself builds upon them, Stuart ultimately finds all but queer theology lacking.

There are numerous reasons for this judgment on other types of gay and lesbian theology, but the key one for Stuart is that all these approaches treat sexuality or gender as stable markers of identity upon which theology can comfortably rest. In so doing, they have the tendency to set up a particular experience—gay, lesbian, female—as determinative of truth and value while viewing the Christian tradition with undue suspicion. The oppressive history of the tradition is emphasized, while its liberating potential is often ignored or downplayed. Christian tradition is ceded to reactionaries and conservatives, thus only further solidifying the view that they are the "real" Christians and conservatism is the same as orthodoxy. This is not to claim that Stuart finds experience to be useless as a category or analytical tool, but rather that she finds it more adept at deconstructive rather than constructive work: "But even among those of us who have constructed theologies on the basis of experience with some success, in that they have widened the horizons of others and rung true with at least a sizeable number of the people whose experiences were central, there is a growing conviction that experience may not be as effective a tool in construction as it is in deconstruction."[4] In other words, experience as a category helps to expose those points where tradition does exclude and thus requires transformation (deconstruction in Stuart's sense), but does not succeed as well at creating a unifying point for the work of re-creation. Work built largely on the so-

---

4. Stuart, "Sexuality: The View from the Font," 11. This essay was written during a period of transition from a more classically liberal theology to queer theology. The previous work Stuart refers to is her *Just Good Friends*.

called experiences of diverse groups tends to exclude many of those who are supposed to be liberated by it, an example of which is the development of womanist theology from feminist theology in response to the fact that white women's experience—who largely created the latter—was not the same as that of black women. It seems entirely reasonable to suggest that black, lesbian experience may also be different.

Queer theology, in Stuart's sense, does not share this innate suspicion of the Christian tradition, though it also refuses to be blind to the oppressive nature of many aspects of this past. Far from abandoning Christian history and thought to those who wish to use it as a weapon against the queer, it instead claims Christianity for itself. It tends "to argue that Christian theology was queer two thousand years before queer theory was invented."[5] It can also create a space for a broader range of experiences—such as the transgender and transsexual—by destabilizing any rigid notions of identity.[6] Gay, straight, male, and female are performatively undone as unbending markers of personhood. This is one reason why she sees queer theory as a form of "divine illumination": it allows us to approach our own tradition anew and see that which has long been hiding in plain sight.[7]

If gay and lesbian liberation theologies are about the freedom of these persons from hetero-patriarchy, queer theology is about the freedom of all people from the tyrannies of modern gender and sexuality construction. It regards the body as innately mysterious and, because the body is always about the exchange of signs, potentially sacramental—one definition of sacraments is that they are visible (bodily) signs that cause the very realities they signify. They are utterly mysterious, yet also intelligible. This approach to bodies applies not only to the body of Christ, as discussed in chapter 1, but to all bodies. Queer theory thus propels us towards an eschatological space, one in which the body is constantly being made and remade. In this, Stuart and Graham Ward elegantly cohere.

---

5. Stuart, *Gay and Lesbian Theologies*, 102.

6. Though queer theology has opened a space for these voices, the relationship of queer theory and trans-theory has often been fraught, precisely over the issue of stable gender or sexual identity. For an attempt by a queer theorist to engage with this issue, see Judith Butler, "Doing Justice to Someone" and "Undiagnosing Gender." For further discussion on this issue from a theological perspective, see Isherwood and Althaus-Reid, *Trans/formations*. On issues pertaining to theologies and intersex persons, see Cornwell, *Sex and Uncertainty in the Body of Christ*.

7. Stuart, *Gay and Lesbian Theologies*, 105.

The traditional Christian sacraments are dependent not solely on this mysteriousness of bodies in general, but specifically on that of Christ. Following the thought of Ward, Stuart affirms that, due to the queerness of Christ's body, which is the condition of possibility for the sacraments, they become spaces of Divine encounter as we undergo the process of becoming what we are, which is becoming what Christ is: "Not only is [Christ's] body available to Christians, they are caught up in it, constituted by it and incorporated into it, sharing in its sacramental flesh."[8]

Baptism

Though found in several of her works, the most developed treatment of sacraments given by Stuart is in the essay "Sacramental Flesh." She there argues that baptism is what incorporates us into the body of Christ, pure and simple. The ritual brings us into the very story and life of Jesus of Nazareth by participation in his death and resurrection. We enter into the waters, drown in them, and arise to a new life in Christ. Most significantly for Stuart, though, is what this does to our identities as persons and how it reshapes our desire.

Following Judith Butler, Stuart believes that life in this world—I use the term here in its Johannine sense—is a life marked by melancholia. Due to our constructions of gender and sexual identity, there are certain loves that are marked out of bounds. There are desires that cannot be legitimately fulfilled, at least not without risking the very subject that is created by their denial—the sexed, gendered subject: "Both heterosexuality and homosexuality are dependent upon each other for their existence but that dependence is based upon repudiating the desire each identity rests upon."[9] For Butler, there is no escape from this melancholia, this mourning over loves that cannot be. Stuart, however, sees a Christian alternative.[10]

For Stuart, baptism radically changes our identity. It transforms who we are in the most profound, primal sense. No longer are we bound into the creation of our own identities in a culturally-constructed give and take. No longer do we have to negotiate our selfhoods, always at the cost

8. Stuart, "Sacramental Flesh," 66.

9. Ibid., 65.

10. Importantly, Stuart believes that queer theory requires Christian eschatology if it is to become anything other than nihilistic and bound in cycles of impossible desire and loss: ibid.

of foreclosing love and desire. In baptism, we are given a new identity, one that is sheer gift, one over which we have no control. We do not have to "earn" our place in society by performing our genders or sexualities in a particular way; rather, in the rite, we receive "God's great 'Yes' to us, based not upon our own merits but upon divine love revealed in Christ."[11] It is precisely this recognition of ourselves as loved, as gifted into ourselves by God and part of the body of God in Christ, that exposes the place outside baptism as the site of melancholia that Butler describes. Because we now have an identity that is divinely given, we can have the courage to undo and expose those other identities that are non-ultimate: we can begin to live beyond melancholy.

Stuart is not trying to claim that sex and gender are meaningless categories or that baptism automatically sets us free of them. With queer theory, Stuart takes culture seriously and recognizes that we are bound up in these constructions and cannot simply "opt out" and live beyond them, or, at least, not yet. Baptism, then, shows us what we will be and what we are already in the process of becoming via the grace and love of God. It allows us to look with an eschatological horizon to the day when we will be finally freed from the constructions that cause us so much turmoil and loss here on earth. It does this by proclaiming our new existence in Christ, but also by reorienting our desire. Baptism shows us that our ultimate desire is to be the one whom God is gifting into being, that it is only here that we can truly become ourselves. The desires that create melancholy and close off love are part of an economy whereby we must shore up our own subjectivity by endlessly going after that which promises to fulfill, but cannot: "objects that fill gaps in our self-construction, so that what we desire is repletion, which is immobilization, a kind of death."[12] The categories that mark the modern subject—gender, sex, and sexuality—are exposed as non-ultimate and un-fulfilling in themselves; they cannot be what we are really about, for that is the gift of a new baptismal identity, and this in turn leads to our call as Christians to live beyond them.

What is this new baptismal identity, though? Granted that it exposes gender and sexuality as of non-ultimate value and shows us our true desire in God, what does this identity look like in history? In baptism, since we are united not only personally but also ecclesially to Christ, we are no longer the autonomous, atomized subjects that modernity trains us to be. Rather,

11. Ibid., 67.

12. Ibid.

we become, in Stuart's term, "ecclesial persons." We are still subjects and individuals, but that personhood is marked by a more fundamental reality, our existence in and with others as the body of Christ: "This personhood is characterized by a new subjectivity that is both communal and corporate, for it both shares in and constitutes the body of Christ, the new human."[13] Baptism brings us into the life of the new human, Christ, by perfecting that of the old.

Here, then, is a new kind of communal belonging. It is one that is not based on rank, on success in fitting in with social norms, but rather founded on our common participation in Christ's body and Christ's life. Baptism, for Stuart, requires that we do "not belong to the categories we thought we belonged in" in order that a new sociality can be formed. By receiving the unmerited grace of being included in Christ, we are now part of a solidarity that is unchosen and unnegotiated. We all arise from the font as part of the same new creation. No longer do we relate to one another as men and women, gay and straight, or via any other human identity: "There is no longer Jew or Greek, there is no longer slave or free, there is no longer male and female; for all of you are one in Christ Jesus" (Gal 3:28).

It should be evident that Stuart has great faith in the efficacy of the sacramental rites. In fact, perhaps she has too much trust in their efficacy. For her, baptism is obviously efficacious in its power; in classical terminology, it causes an ontological transformation in us that renders the baptized radically different from the non-baptized.[14] In her terms, there is a radical discontinuity that is a very real death: a death both to sin and to our former selves. But it is quite obvious that Christians are still bound up in the same cultural identities as anyone who is non-baptized. In fact, it is often the non-baptized who are more successful at exposing the non-ultimacy of these identities. One need only look at John Paul II's *Theology of the Body*, amongst numerous other works, to see that many Christians count our gender and sexual identities as enormously significant indeed.[15] The queer

---

13. Ibid., 68.

14. It should be immediately noted that this says nothing about the status of the non-baptized or their relationship to God, precisely because God is not bound by the sacraments: Stuart, "Sacramental Flesh," 68. It is important that she tends to think of baptism primarily in terms of the liturgical rite, which raises some questions about the broader implications of the term in the Christian tradition, such as baptism "by desire." I haven't the space to delve into these issues here though.

15. See John Paul II, *The Theology of the Body*. This work, which has become enormously popular in some Catholic circles, owes much to Hans Urs von Balthasar's theology

effects of baptism do not seem to be quite as evident as Stuart would like to aver.

As discussed above, Stuart tends to discount experience as a primary source of knowledge in her theology because of its tendency to exclude. Therefore, her account of the sacraments is not affective at all, that is, she does not discuss the sacraments in terms of how well they bring about or signify what they are intending. Baptism gives us a new identity, irrespective of our ability to perceive it. If I go into the waters and emerge again, I may very well notice no change whatsoever. For Stuart this is apparently not a problem, but for many contemporary persons, the inability to see or feel what is being asserted as happening is a difficulty. The opacity of the signs and the fact that often they seem to fail in achieving what they set out to accomplish is a serious issue that must be addressed if a sacramental account is to be credible. If they do not produce affective or behavioral change, then what is produced?

Stuart is not unaware of this problem, and thus emphasizes the eschatological nature of what is instituted in baptism. This seems to be how she wants to deal with the issue, by claiming that what most truly happens in the sacrament is something that is only fully understandable when it is consummated by our eternal union with the Trinity at the end of time. The death that we undergo in the rite is one that therefore places us in a liminal position in relation to the wider world, but does not remove us from it. We live in the body of Christ now, but also exist in the "not yet" of movement toward the eschaton. The gender and sexual identities that form us are not eradicated by the sacrament, but are shown to be under "eschatological erasure."[16] We are thus not called to remove ourselves from human culture—which is not possible anyway—but rather to transform it by living out these identities in ways that expose their non-ultimacy, dependent in faith on the identity we are given by God in baptism. This work is primarily God's, since it is she who will mysteriously bring about the consummation of all things in herself, but we also cooperate in it by enacting the lives we have even now as parts of Christ's body. Our efforts do not somehow bring about the fulfillment of creation separate from God, but since we are already part of the Divine Life by being part of Christ, our activity is also

---

of gender, found conveniently in *The Office of Peter*. For criticisms of von Balthasar on gender, and how his own basic insights should drive him in a more queer direction rather than the essentialist one he adopts, see Muers, "A Queer Theology" and Loughlin, *Alien Sex*, 152–61.

16. Stuart, "Sacramental Flesh," 68.

not incidental. We are part of Christ's body by grace, and called to manifest that life visibly in our historical existence.

Though this approach is important and avoids the dangers of utopianism, at times this eschatological trajectory is not emphasized sufficiently by Stuart. In turn, our new identities in Christ can seem to be as solid and present, perhaps even more so, than that of gender. We can undo gender and sexuality because we have a new, stable identity in baptism. Queer theory has to work hard to expose that gender is not, in fact, the stable, consistent identity we believe it to be, though, and it is far from evident that our ecclesial personhood is any different. It may be, as Stuart states, the only identity "stable enough to hope in," but that stability will not be fully revealed until the eschaton; if it were, then hope would not be the proper response. We are already part of Christ's body, but can only hope to live that fully hereafter.

The logic of Stuart's argument, especially in connection with Butler's views on melancholia, seems to be that Christians somehow can escape from this melancholy by simply embracing the identity that we are given in baptism as our true one, thus giving us the freedom to abandon our dependence on sex and gender categories to ground our subjectivities and identities. If Butler cannot completely undo her sex and gender identities for fear of ceasing to exist as a subject—all she can do is expose the seams and failures of their performances to point in that direction—Christians are not in this sorry situation for Stuart. Yet, if we attend more closely to Christian experience, we find that this simply isn't the case. The baptized are not granted some special privilege that allows them to avoid the same cultural constructions, negotiations, and maneuvers as anyone else. In fact, if we look at the controversies over sex and gender in the churches, we would be led to believe the exact opposite. If we have a new identity, it is one that is utterly mysterious and no more graspable than that of gender and sex.

This overstatement of identity, that it is somehow stable now rather than always being given anew, mysteriously, may be due to Stuart's use of Judith Butler as a conversation partner. After all, if the identity that we are given in baptism is not itself stable, it is far from clear how Christians can somehow escape the processes of becoming subjects that all other people undergo. Yet, if this identity is an eschatological reality that we are living into—as I believe it is—this does not seem to be sufficient answer to Butler, at least on Butler's terms. It could be all too easily dismissed as "fixing" everything in heaven. Thus, this new subjectivity presented as solid could be but a rhetorical technique to argue the superiority of Christian to secular theory on this point.

I think that Stuart is correct that we can risk our constructed subjectivities and the "death" that comes from them because we have already died and been raised with Christ. Yet this is a statement of faith, one that does not give us a more solid foundation for our subjectivity, but rather exposes all other identities as non-ultimate. It may give us the ability to risk ourselves, trusting that God will not allow us to be destroyed as Butler fears, but this is not the same as having a stable identity. I wonder if it is even helpful to discuss this baptismal, ecclesial personhood as an identity at all. It makes more sense to say that baptism gives us an "anti-identity," one which problematizes and exposes all other ones, but does not grant anything solid in their place.[17] After all, if baptism bestows an eschatological identity that we have now but do not know, then this is a very different kind of identity than what we mean when we discuss sex and gender. The very description of it as eschatological renders it quite different as an identity, since we are being identified and named by that which we do not understand. Stuart writes, "The nature of the elements of our Christian identity may be obscure to us and how we best act out our identity in our various contexts might be a legitimate subject of dispute but the identity itself is not negotiated, it is given."[18] Yet, if we do not even know what the elements of this identity consist of, or how to perform it, what makes it an identity at all? If identities serve the purpose of shoring up our subjectivities, this unknown identity seems unable to do that. As an anti-identity, however, baptismal faith gives us the courage to risk our subjectivities and identities in the trust that in so doing, we will become what we actually are. This anti-identity allows us to "lose our lives in order to save them" (Luke 9:24). It also has the advantage of avoiding the kind of dissonance that can come from reading Stuart between what she asserts is occurring and what we often see or experience.

Another way of grappling with this issue of already/not-yet might be the classical Catholic account of what occurs in baptism.[19] It is a commonplace that baptism frees us from the guilt of both original and actual sin, but that concupiscence—the tendency for our desires to be disordered—remains

---

17. I owe the term to Mark Jordan.
18. Stuart, "Sacramental Flesh," 67.
19. Stuart mentions this briefly, but does not develop it: see ibid., 68.

even after our dying and rising with Christ in the sacrament.[20] We are truly part of Christ's queer body, but we are also capable of living in ways that do not accord with that new life. We are at once free, and yet also bound; the outcome is assured eschatologically, but our lives in history remain in flux and mired in sin, both structural and personal. Simply because we are baptized into Christ's queer body, we may still opt to obscure this by grasping at identities made by our activity, attempting to create and shore up ourselves by excluding others who are themselves beloved of the Father. We may fear the loss of ourselves, and thus hold on dearly to the identities we know, choosing to "save our lives rather than lose them." And we may even do this in the name of the God into whom we have been baptized. In baptism and faith we have been justified in Christ, but we still have the task of sanctification; of working out—in cooperation with the grace of God, which is always prior—our salvation with "fear and trembling." In other words, it is quite possible, despite the very real effects of the sacraments as Stuart discusses them, to make idols, and it is precisely this that Stuart indicts the churches for.

For Stuart, the historical churches, and especially the Roman Catholic Church, have failed to recognize the non-ultimacy of all identities that do not come from baptism. Following the practices of modernity, they have made gender and sexuality matters of not only great concern, but even eternal concern. In this account, our sex differences are essential even to our relationships with God. They have a permanent ontological significance. Mired, as we all are, in post-baptismal concupiscence, the churches often seek to make the identities we have constructed eternal rather than welcoming those bestowed by the grace of God, or perhaps better, allowing our constructed identities to be undone as we are gifted with an identity we do not yet understand or fully inhabit. In so doing, they have failed to truly live out the baptism we have all received, and thus have been unable to recognize the queerness of the body of Christ and the gospel that undoes all these expectations:

> Heterosexuality and homosexuality and maleness and femaleness are not of ultimate importance, they are not determinative in God's eyes, and in so far as any of us have behaved as if they are, we are guilty of the grave sin of idolatry, and if we have further behaved as if they are grounds upon which to exclude people from the glorious liberty of the children of God, we are guilty of profanity and a

20. See *Catechism of the Catholic Church* (paras. 1263–64).

fundamental denial of our own baptismal identity which rests in being bound together with others not of our choosing by an act of sheer grace.[21]

These sins distort the reality into which we are initiated by the waters of baptism, which both drown and vivify.

Queer theory, especially the thought of Judith Butler, takes on particular importance in understanding Stuart's view on baptism. As discussed in the introduction, queer theory cannot promise that we can ever be free of sex and gender identities—they are too strongly part of our formation as subjects, even the very grounds on which we become subjects. Similarly, though she seems to overstate the clear efficacy of the sacraments in history, Stuart does not assert that baptism frees us from gender, sex, or any other fundamental aspects of culture. We die to any triumph of "the world," yet we remain in it, one where sex and gender are still dominating parts of who we are. The queer response to this situation is to expose the non-stability of gender and sexuality by performing them in ways that do not fit within the dominant narratives.

If this is how some queer theorists believe we should respond to the hegemony of sex and gender, it is precisely how Stuart thinks Christians should respond to the temptation of idolatry—of accepting this hegemonic narrative as truly eternal, natural, and given. Not only should they respond thusly, they *have* responded this way through much of their history already. Though we live in history distorted by sin, as members of Christ's queer, divine body we must strive to live the life granted us in grace by baptism: one that protests against every mechanism of exclusion and false worship. The Spirit acts both in and out of the church to subvert this sinful tendency to idolatry, of making ultimate what is merely contingent and unstable, even if valuable in itself:

> There is many a slip between the cities we build and the city of God and yet the Spirit is active within our creations, prompting and subverting. Sexual and gender identities have to be subverted because they are constructed in the context of power and are part of a matrix of dominance and exclusion. This has been the great insight of queer theory. Therefore these identities grate against the sign of baptism.[22]

21. Stuart, "Sacramental Flesh," 68.

22. Ibid.

Stuart does not think, however, that sex and gender categories are oppressive by their very natures. She recognizes how the categories of "lesbian," "gay," and "woman" have been used historically to advance justice, equality, and social space for otherness: "Feminism similarly took the category of 'woman,' exposed its patriarchal construction and then reinvested it with meaning."[23] Her queer approach is not meant to be a judgment on the genuinely important work these categories have done in the past. They are, though, ultimately inadequate and since they have become so essentialized in many quarters as to have become idols, they too must now be subverted. But how?

The answer Stuart gives is that parody is constitutive of our baptismal callings as Christians. Following theorist Linda Hutcheon, she defines parody as "repetition with critical difference."[24] Since we are not removed from culture by our baptism, but still dwell in the world of time with its own constructions and patterns, we cannot hope simply to escape them. We have no choice but to enact gender and sexuality, but the question is *how* to do it. Do we perform them in such a way that heteronormative and patriarchal assumptions are reinforced and reinscribed in our bodies? Or do our performances allow us and others to see the gaps and failures of gender and sexuality, gaps and failures that allow space for new life and freedom? Parody is not primarily about sending up or mocking normative discourses, but rather about performing our socially-scripted roles so as to expose their constructedness, their inadequacy. We are both called and given the freedom to play with these markers of modern subjectivity assured, in faith, that this play will not destroy us but rather allow us to become the creations of God that we truly are: "Parody is then the Christian way of operating, of taking what is given to us and playing it out in such a way as to expose the other world breaking through it."[25] Parody gives us the freedom to laugh with the *risus paschalis*, the laughter of Easter, delighting in the new world coming to be born.[26]

Stuart rightly believes that parody is the way in which Christians should live out their baptisms, but she also believes that we have become very bad at it. This is not only because of the aforementioned worship of heterosexuality and straight marriage that has become ubiquitous in much

23. Ibid., 69.

24. Ibid.

25. Ibid.

26. See Stuart, "Camping around the Canon," 25.

of Christianity, but as a correlate, the religious life that has begun to fall into abeyance. Stuart sees a strong connection between the life of vowed, celibate religious and the sign of incorporation into Christ's body that baptism marks. She does not in any way denigrate sex or marriage, but rather refuses to see sex as the ultimate way in which we are brought to God. Our erotic desire is not primarily for Christ's genitals, after all, but for his wounds; it is through these that God's gift of the Divine Life is made most manifest. If this is where all desire finds its end, vowed celibates attest to this reality. They live life as "single" persons in the general sense of the term, but they parody this because, in the church, no one is truly single or alone. The most solitary of figures—monks or cloistered nuns—are as fully enmeshed in the body of Christ as are the most social. Their singleness paradoxically attests to their rootedness in Christ and Christ's church.

Similarly, vowed religious attest strongly to the new kinship into which we enter at baptism. The church becomes a family, but it is one that parodies the biological family because it is based on grace, not nature. In the religious life, new forms of kinship are created where the community lives as mother/father and children who are brothers and sisters, but with nothing biological binding them together at all: "Celibates become 'mothers' and 'fathers' in their communities, presiding over groups in which a new type of kinship, no longer based upon blood relationships, united people as 'brothers' and 'sisters.'"[27] Similarly, in the classical way in which these communities were constructed and lived prior to the Second Vatican Council, non-members were also able to come to understand the constructedness and fluidity of gender and sexuality:

> Growing up surrounded by men wearing clothes that society labeled feminine, whom I had to relate to as "father," and taught by women who were my "sisters" or "mothers" with names such as Augustine and Bernard Joseph, taught me that societal categories were not fixed, that they could be played around with and that the church was a space in which gender shifted.[28]

This kind of gender queering was usually not perfect, as it tended to move in one direction only: women taking male names and characteristics rather than the opposite, with priestly cassocks and lace being an exception. Still Stuart's point stands that this kind of construction does seem to emphasize and expose the holes in our stable conceptions of sex and gender. This

27. Stuart, "Sacramental Flesh," 70.
28. Ibid.

parody is closely associated with baptism for Stuart, but it extends to other sacraments as well.

Eucharist

The Eucharist is itself a parodic act, a repetition with critical difference of the Jewish seder meal. For Stuart, however, it is not primarily an act of remembrance (at least in the sense that a seder is), but rather a dynamic participation in the eternal now of the Triune life. Thus, it too has a necessarily eschatological valence, for it is where the baptized "learn about and anticipate the eschatological life" where God will be all in all.[29]

It is cosmic, not simply for us here, but rather an activity of the whole church, living and dead. It is also, in its inclusion and transformation of the elements of bread and wine, a sacrament that discloses the ultimate consummation of all creation, not simply humanity. The whole company of heaven is present and our belonging is a function of the grace of God, not the ideas we hold or the identities we negotiate: "In the Eucharist the church stands on the edge of heaven in the company of cherubim and seraphim, angels and archangels and the whole company of heaven, and standing on the edge of heaven gender differences dissolve."[30] Or, similarly, one could say with Ward that our gendered differences are multiplied to a degree that they can no longer be a source of exclusivity, of "us" versus "them." Our community is not founded on our own transient desires or on the exclusion of others, but rather on the Divine, who calls us to be and to be present.

This point on exclusion is important, for the very essence of Eucharist is that it is radically inclusive. Stuart gives a further account of her Eucharistic theology and the importance of liturgy in her contribution to the memorial volume for the late Marcella Althaus-Reid.[31] Liturgical space, rather than solidifying and reinscribing hetero-patriarchy, is the place where this is smashed. The Eucharist must be inclusive because the Divine is inclusive or, to use Stuart's term, "radically catholic": "This is because catholicity is first and foremost an attribute of the divine in whom the pleroma, the fullness of being, exists, unity within its incredible diversity."[32] God is closer to every atom of creation than it is to itself: she refuses her presence and

29. Ibid., 71.

30. Ibid.

31. Stuart, "Making No Sense."

32. Ibid., 117.

companionship to nothing that is. The sin against this is contraction, exclusion, and every attempt to limit divine activity.

This divine catholicity, for Stuart, is focused in Christ. By entering into creation itself as a member who is also radically transcendent, God focuses the radical inclusion of all in the person who is fully human and fully Divine. It is important to note that this focusing is not, however, a contraction; the fullness of the Divine in Christ does not imply that it is somehow "lessened" anywhere else. Though she doesn't speak this way, other sacramental theologians describe this focusing as the "making visible" of the Divine Life and activity that is the primary purpose of the sacraments.[33] Christ focuses himself, in turn, in the church as his body, the body that can continue to make Christ visible once he has ascended from our sight, and the church, in turn, directs this focus to its ecclesial sacraments. This twin movement of radical inclusion in particular focus, is what the Eucharist is about: "This double rhythm of catholicity, the Divine Life of inclusivity and focus, is revealed and encountered in the Eucharist which stretches across time and throughout the cosmos." If baptism creates us as ecclesial persons, the Eucharist teaches us what that means and trains us for the life that is to come by allowing us to participate in it now.

The Eucharist undoes gender, because it also undoes our rigid, biologized notions of body. Following Ward, Stuart wants to emphasize that Christ's body in the Eucharist is no longer limited, and is certainly not bound to gender: "Embodiment can stretch across time and space and manifest itself in different forms."[34] Christ's body becomes bread and wine, which have no gender. The body is able to escape these constructs and no longer be demarcated by them. By becoming "re-incarnated" in the bread and wine, Christ discloses the manifold forms in which bodies can exist and yet be themselves. Correspondingly, Stuart believes that the Roman Catholic practice of ordaining only celibate men grates against this. After the ascension, Christ's body is made up of all genders and ways of life, and this must be reflected in those who minister at the altar to the church.[35]

It is the baptized self—the ecclesial person—who gathers with others not of her choosing around the altar, and according to Stuart, the liturgy is the place where we are given the strength and grace to resist the cultural

33. For more on this account of the sacraments, see Schillebeeckx, *Christ the Sacrament*.

34. Stuart, "Making No Sense," 122.

35. Stuart, "Turning Towards the Tomb," 39.

identities of sex and gender. We are placed in a different context, with a different vantage point, to have our desire re-oriented towards the Divine:

> It is this [baptized] self that is written over by hetero-patriarchy and cultural constructs but that remerges in the movement of the liturgy which provides a horizon and a context with which to engage and resist the cultural constructions of the self that act as entropic forces on our souls and bodies.[36]

If our baptisms are to be fulfilled and lived truly, we must participate in the Eucharist in order to have our subjectivities properly focused and formed.

I think that Stuart's reflections on what occurs in the sacraments are rich and compelling. As I have already indicated, however, I am troubled by the gap that exists between her very rich descriptions and what I can see of the sacramental results. There seems little room in Stuart's account for any ambiguity in the sacramental effects, and this makes it difficult to defend her account without significant revision. She is clear that her view is eschatological, but there is a danger in appeals to eschatology in that we may not attend enough to questions that need to be addressed in the here and now. Why does this description bear so little connection to what we see day-to-day? Does it serve to mask oppressive power structures and language, covered over by appeals to invisible, idealized realities? I do not wish to deny these realities, but I also think it is necessary to admit the incongruities.

For Elizabeth Stuart, baptism bestows a new character, a new identity that will persist eternally. In this, she is rehearsing an ancient Christian tradition. I concur that baptism effects this, and faith grants us the certainty of its fulfillment. But she also seems to want to make this identity into something so stable and secure—apparently in history—that we can rely on it to undo and subvert gender and sexuality. I think ultimately she is correct in this, though I believe that it needs to be emphasized that it is through faith and grace that this is possible, not by some automatic working-out of the sacramental ritual. The reason for this is quite obvious: many, perhaps most, Christians do not live out their baptisms in this way. Though we may be both assured of an identity gratuitously granted by God eschatologically and also affirm that we have this same identity now, it is also evident that we live in a confusing amalgam of other identities as well. We have been given a new name by God in Christ—our place in the queer body—but other

---

36. Stuart, "Making No Sense," 119.

than occasional, confused whispers, we do not yet know what this name is. The sacrament is indeed efficacious in faith, but it is often a complete failure to the eyes with which we are trained to view the world. When we arise from the font we are utterly new persons; we are also exactly the same.

A similar thing occurs with the Eucharist. Viewing the Eucharistic elements after the consecration as "a thing" (an inadequate view, granted), I have no difficulty believing that they have been re-created into the body and blood of Christ. The signs of bread and wine bring me into this communal sharing around the table of sacrifice; these visible signs bring me into the reality held in faith; they show it and do not contest it. The signs lead into the deeper reality of the Eucharist as true food and true drink, as what really gives life; they do not contradict it. Yet the Eucharist has as its primary end the enactment of another sign of God's life in the world: the church as the body of Christ, as the loving community of those called forth in baptism to be ecclesial persons. Like baptism, this sign is much more difficult, and thus raises questions about the efficacy of the Eucharist itself.

For queer persons, it is frankly a very difficult suggestion that the church is the effective sign—the sacrament—of God's love for humankind.[37] It is very difficult to see the church as the place where humanity is being brought together as a sign of our eschatological unity in the Triune God. Most often, we experience the church as a place that would like to expel us from the ranks of the human rather than calling us to embrace our humanity—which is to say to embrace love—all the more deeply. This has become only more evident as much of the church has accepted without question modern ideology on sex and gender; the community that once created the queer characters Stuart describes has found itself increasingly incapable of doing so.[38] Yet this is also the community that the Eucharist brings about, the community of Christ's body visible on earth. Faith tells us that baptism makes us into ecclesial persons, persons who are included in Christ's body now and forever; our day-to-day experience of that community seems not only to challenge this—as the bread and wine might challenge the real presence of Christ in the Eucharist—but to directly defy and contradict it. How can this be?

37. In this section, I confess that I am largely thinking of the Roman Catholic Church, but what is said can go for many other Christian groups or even for the body of Christians writ large. It has certainly been experienced that way by many.

38. For more on this point, see Jordan, *Recruiting Young Love*.

I do not think that Elizabeth Stuart is naïve. She understands these problems quite well. One way that she addresses them is through eschatology, but there are other possible explanations for why her work often seems to overstate sacramental effect. In the Catholic tradition in which Stuart is writing, sacraments are often discussed in two connected, but distinct ways: ontology and pedagogy. Ontologically, the sacraments are viewed in terms of what they do and effect in the person who partakes. They do create realities, they change us, though I have pointed out how calling these changes "identities" may obscure more than it enlightens. Presuming this first element, the sacraments are also used and discussed pedagogically, as ways in which God instructs humans in how to live. Someone like Thomas Aquinas wrote much about the sacraments pedagogically, presuming the beliefs about what they effect. Since the Reformation, however, this presumption cannot be as easily made. Perhaps Stuart, who has a penchant for Tridentine liturgy and thought, is presuming something on the part of her reader, and thus is not being clear about whether she is speaking ontologically or pedagogically. Her statements about the sacraments judging the churches on their adoration of modern sexual and gender categories make sense. They do so though, not as statements about the sacraments eliminating these identities—something the sacraments clearly do not do (at least in this life); rather, Stuart uses the sacramental rites to pedagogically call these identities into ultimate question. Unfortunately, Stuart does not clearly make these distinctions, so it can seem that pedagogical comments that are very useful and profound can have the ring of ontological statements that are difficult to justify.

When we look and see the church, queer persons often see a body built on exclusion, not the enfolding arms of the body of Christ that Stuart discusses. One might answer that this is simply the church failing to be the church; that when these exclusions occur it is not being a sacrament, but rather an altogether human institution. Others might claim that this is simply proof that the church is not, and cannot be, what it claims it is. For those who sincerely seek God, the only possibility is to leave and either join or, perhaps better, form new communities that are truly founded in the love of God for all. I understand and sympathize with each of these, but also find that I cannot accept them—at least not without reservation, or not right now. As much as it has been a place of exclusion, the church is also the place where I have come to know whatever of Christ and God that I do.[39] Even

39. "Knowledge" here being used in a very, very loose sense.

when I decided the church was wrong about something—for example, its current teachings on homosexuality—it was through means that I'd learned from the church itself (specifically the feeling of peace that is an essential part of Ignatian discernment). The church also taught me the value of truth, and that truth cannot contradict truth, so that the truths I was learning about myself had to annul some of the teachings of that self-same institution. Similarly, though I have been alienated from much of the church, I have also found many individual communities that truly embody their reality as body of Christ. I do not think I am alone in this kind of tensive relationship.[40] How then to account for this ambiguity, which Stuart elides, while also maintaining the faith claims about the ultimate significance of the sacraments and ecclesial community, which she powerfully defends? It seems to me that Marcella Althaus-Reid discusses sacramental realities in ways that highlight their ambivalences as signs without also negating their efficacy. In this, she can act as a useful counterweight to the sacramental idealism that Stuart sometimes seems to offer.

Marcella Althaus–Reid and Sacramental Ambiguity

Before bringing her in as an interlocutor with Stuart on the sacraments, there are a few preliminary comments that need to be made about Althaus-Reid. The first is that she has a very different writing style from Stuart, and this will affect how I engage her. Her thought, especially in *Indecent Theology* and *Queer God*, with which I am primarily concerned, does not flow in a linear pattern of logical progression or analysis. Rather, her writing style emphasizes the fragmentary nature of postmodern thought and tends to operate more as a collage of ideas and images that are anchored by a common, loose theme. Therefore, I cannot offer a systematic overview of her "sacramental theology," and I suspect she would decry the attempt. I will instead select a few salient passages and reflect on their significance in light of Stuart's contributions.

Theologically, she posits a distinction between what she calls "decent" or T-theology and her work of "indecent" theology. Decent theology is authorized by the churches and marked by its refusal to take gender and sex/uality seriously as theological topics. It may pay them lip service, but only so long as they remain within the comfortable zone of bourgeois values.

40. See Arsenault, "Worship in the Face of Rejection."

The queer, the gay, and those sites where economics and sexuality merge (especially prostitution) are systematically excluded from serious attention. In order to both expose and subvert this ideological and imperialist discourse, Althaus-Reid brings in indecent examples from the lives of the marginalized; by interrogating the permissible by the impermissible, she constructs her "indecent theology." She does this not simply to critique, but more importantly, to create new discourses that subvert the old, to allow new and alternative desires to flow theologically. The most discussed example of this is her analysis of female lemon vendors in Argentina who sell their fruit without wearing underwear, without separating their livelihood from their embodied existences, without separating their sexuality and economics: "The lemon vendor sitting in the street may be able to feel her sex; her musky smell may be confused with that of her basket of lemons, in a metaphor that brings together sexuality and economics."[41] Theology's primary role is to allow these marginalized voices to speak and show their relationship to the Divine, in order that the systems which oppress them may collapse. Theology must help change the world, and in this we see how Althaus-Reid is very much in the liberationist school, even as she applies devastating critiques to it.

This method also helps us to understand how she approaches the Divine. For her, God is primarily known through the intimate encounters and loves of the oppressed and marginalized, not in the dominant and hegemonic theological system of T-theology. The stories and lives of the poor, oppressed, and marginalized are therefore innately sacramental in that they carry and reveal the life of God. Sacraments are not primarily ecclesially-approved rites for Althaus-Reid, but any of those points where the Divine and human come together in the lives of the oppressed, creating new ways to understand and live both.

If, for Stuart, queer theology allows a recovery of the Christian tradition in its orthodox shape, Althaus-Reid approaches it rather as a way to allow the sexually marginalized to interrogate and, usually, critique the larger tradition(s). Stuart's approach is dogmatic, while Althaus-Reid's is materialist and Marxist. Much of the tradition that Stuart and I wish to

---

41. Althaus-Reid, *Indecent Theology*, 3. Some have found this example to be profoundly disturbing, and not in the sense that Althaus-Reid intends. Emilie M. Townes, for example, felt angry reading these pages because she "was being cast into the unwanted role of the voyeur—unintentionally, but deliberately." The lemon-vendors, to Townes, are always objects, never real people in the work: see Townes, "Marcella Althaus-Reid's *Indecent Theology*," 63–65.

recover would be seen as irredeemably patriarchal and colonialist in Al-thaus-Reid's account. Queer theory allows theology to become "indecent," for Althaus-Reid, by refusing to separate the economic from the sexual, gendered, political, and historical. In other words, classical Christian and creedal orthodoxy is not a rule or limit for Althaus-Reid the way it is for me and the other authors I discuss in this book. This does, to my mind, limit the value of her constructive work, but she nonetheless raises important questions and opens paths for understanding, even among those who remain ultimately unconvinced by her anti-dogmatic method.

This, of course, impacts how Althaus-Reid approaches the traditional sacraments. She is, at best, ambivalent about the claims that are made for them and refuses to separate them from the larger Roman Catholic system that she views as utterly complicit with the colonization of Latin America and the destruction of its native cultures. If Stuart's account of the sacraments gives little attention to their affectivity, the concrete results of the sacraments in history are what primarily concern Althaus-Reid. It should also be noted that she did not grow up within the Catholic tradition, but rather studied in a Protestant school. Yet living in Argentina made her at least a cultural Catholic with an interesting "insider/outsider" position vis-à-vis the Catholic sacramental system, and she largely critiques it in its ecclesially-authorized, decent form. Its effects, or lack thereof in terms of liberation, come in for harsh engagement.

In one of the few extended treatments that she makes of baptism, for instance, she offers a reading that interprets the sacrament as an attack on motherhood and the human in general. The newborn human is somehow seen as incomplete, thus the human itself is devalued: "However, it is also a devaluation of women, as if women are incapable of giving birth to children accepted by society as fully human."[42] The child must be redeemed—that is, completed—by the church. Similarly, the Eucharist comes to be seen in parts as a primarily cannibalistic act and, even though this reality is masked by decent theology, legitimates the devouring of Latin America by European colonialism.[43]

Because of Althaus-Reid's methodology of placing disparate texts, stories, and theories next to one another in order to produce new bodies of knowledge and ways of life, it is difficult to know how far to take these critiques. Do they render the sacraments of the church utterly illegitimate,

42. Althuas-Reid, *Queer God*, 136.

43. Althaus-Reid, *Indecent Theology*, 57.

places where only domination and destruction come into play? Can we make any ontological claims for them at all apart from these interpretations? Should we even try?[44] The reading is ambiguous. For instance, despite her reading in some places of the Eucharist as cannibalistic, she also hints that this might be due to the fact that she does not see the Eucharist creating what T-theology promises. In a later discussion of Klossowski's novel *Roberte ce soir?*, Althaus-Reid engages the idea of hospitality and how it operates. She critiques Eucharistic theology for its unanalyzed sexual claims and relations, but she also recognizes in it a site of potentially liberatory meaning. When she discusses how two characters from that book, in a truly hospitable act, invert the gender and social roles of host/ess and guest, she sees this as a fulfillment of what the Eucharist is supposed to offer: the "theological strategy has been to produce a radical exchange of identities: that the host will be the guest, and the guest the host in what we may see as a scene of truly Eucharistic exchange."[45] Despite this, however, it does seem true to say that Althaus-Reid is not concerned with redeeming the ecclesial sacraments for queer persons, but rather in showing how the Divine Life comes forth in the lives of the poor and marginalized: not primarily in the official churches themselves, but on their margins. What then, is the usefulness of reading her in light of Stuart's much stronger ontological and eschatological claims about the sacraments?

Even though Althaus-Reid is not dealing with the same rites and signs that Stuart and I are most concerned with, it is nonetheless true that she sees the symbolic and bodily as an indispensable way in which the Divine communicates itself and its liberatory power to humanity. Correspondingly, and again unlike Stuart, she attends to the ambiguity, the opacity, of these signs and symbols as well as their multivocity in both interpretation and action. Despite these ambivalences, however, the signs are still able to further the cause of true liberation, if not eschatologically as Stuart believes, at least in some sense (permanence is a theological category that

44. As Graham Ward points out, the issue of ontology's relation to epistemology is a question floating over Althaus-Reid's work. This makes it very difficult to discern both how absolute her critiques are meant to be, and also whether she is trying to talk about God at all or just "God," our images and representations of the Divine. I think it evident she is trying to say something important about the Divine itself, but it's very difficult to discern those passages from those that are just critiques of language. In fact, it is not even clear if there is a distinction that can be made between the two for her. This is an important point, but one that I cannot develop more fully in this chapter: See Ward, "The Limits of Libertinism."

45. Althaus-Reid, *Queer God*, 72.

Althaus-Reid believes deeply implicated in the imperialistic tendencies of T-theology). This ambiguity is precisely what I think Stuart needs to better address, and Althaus-Reid provides a way in which to begin that discussion, especially in relation to queer bodies, though I think that Althaus-Reid is too dismissive of the kinds of claims someone like Stuart makes.

Worship

I begin by considering how Althaus-Reid thinks about worship/celebration. It is important to note that she appropriately refuses to separate worship and politics; a march for the disappeared in Argentina under the banner of a saint or the cross-dresser carrying his rosary into a gay bar are both interpreted as acts of transgressive worship. In fact, worship inside an officially established church building is rarely analyzed by Althaus-Reid, precisely because she is interested in those marginalized from decent worship. In other words, she is interested in those spaces where church is made outside—or on the borders of—the "official" churches.

These rites seem to have three major functions: 1) enact a communal relationship to the Divine, 2) demonstrate radical inclusivity, and 3) offer resistance to hegemonic forces in church, state, and society. Althaus-Reid discusses several different festivities, and these themes seem to be held in common among all of them. Significantly, however, none of the events is simply reducible to any of these qualities, and the participating individuals may have very different interpretations of what is involved. It is also important to note that, in each of these respects at least, Althaus-Reid and Stuart are in complete accord as to what worship should do.

The first of these functions—relationship to the Divine—is both the most obvious aspect of worship and also, in Althaus-Reid, the most difficult to anchor. It cannot be interpreted as a one-way relationship in which worshipper offers oblation to the deity, or even in a binary two-way sense in which the deity returns some sort of favor in return for an offering or praise. Rather, worship brings communities into complicated relationships with the Divine that permeate the whole. Instead of thinking of worship in terms of actors (God/humans), it is better to think of it, for Althaus-Reid, as intricate inter-relationships and flows of desire. God, for Althaus-Reid, is desire; to be brought into this desire is to be involved in worship, and to therefore participate somehow in the Divine.[46]

46. Althaus-Reid, *Indecent Theology*, 147.

Sacraments: Queer In-corporation

Our models for God are intimately related to how we worship her, however. An example of this is Althaus-Reid's attempt to construct a bi-theology in *Queer God*. By looking at the festivities/worship of the Andean people who have an intermediary, bi-sexual divinity in their Christian imaginary, Althaus-Reid challenges Trinitarian theology in order to make it, to her mind, more authentically mutual and reciprocal. This divinity is called *Apu Yaya*, and is represented locally in the city of Moya by its division into three communities/neighborhoods (*ayllus*) that each represent a sexuality: male, female, and bisexual.[47] These sexualities, in turn, become significant in the annual rituals performed by the community.[48]

Importantly, the most bisexual of these rituals occurs at the time of Easter. Like many of the groups that Althaus-Reid discusses, these Andean peoples engage in an interesting combination of indigenous religion and Christianity, usually Roman Catholicism. For instance, each of the communities that are sexually marked are also represented by a Christian patron saint. The timing of these rituals, where gender and sexuality boundaries are crossed, is significant, since it occurs at the time when Christians memorialize the crossing of the border between life and death. For Althaus-Reid, all boundaries are porous and the Divine transgresses them all.

The border between sacred and profane is also crossed in these rituals. Though these rites occur at Easter and are deeply connected with the worship of *Apu Yaya*, they also serve to legitimate the authorities of the community, to whom power is handed over. In this, "bisexuality is represented in this power exchange by the symbolism of rituals which allow an interpretation of relocation and redistribution of gender roles in the communities."[49] The authorities are men, but their wives and children also occupy the town plaza. This masculine space is filled by women. Yet even here, there is not a complete reversal or subversion, because these women still fulfill a traditionally feminine role by handing out bread. Boundaries are transgressed, but they are not annihilated: "From the margins of the plaza, [the women] have come to the centre to distribute bread, but in the ritual of doing that, they incur a symbolic transgression."[50] Moreover, this

---

47. Because this is the language she uses, so will I. Her usage is a bit idiosyncratic, however, with "sexuality" being used for what is usually called "sex," and "bisexual" for "intersexed" or "transgended/transsexual."

48. Althaus-Reid, *Queer God*, 120.

49. Ibid., 121.

50. Ibid.

bread—tasked to the women—is wrapped in the poncho, which is a traditionally masculine garment. Men, though still the political authorities, are thus rendered ambivalent in this space, at least for the time of the ritual: "men become marginal to the political and religious space of the plaza by the temporal disorder symbolized by the presence of women and by the ritual cross-dressing for the distribution of bread."[51] The orders of male/ female are transgressed and the bisexual is given the place of honor.

The God that is indicated here is not only the intermediary divinity *Apu Yaya*, but, at least potentially, the traditional Christian Trinity. Though these rituals are strongly suggestive of new ways of relating the sexes, Althaus-Reid finds little to suggest that this has been particularly evident in the day-to-day lives of the community, especially the women, who still remain enmeshed in a structure of domination.[52] Althaus-Reid asks, in light of these rituals,

> whether the Christian Trinity is also a case of a theology based on a concept of mutuality and reciprocity which has been historically inefficacious. The deep attachment of Christianity to a non-reciprocal system such as heterosexual patriarchy shows clearly how a theology done from within a system of domination (as in the sense of an everyday doing of theology), ends as a theology of domination.[53]

The Divine must be rewritten in order to evade this trap, according to Althaus-Reid: simple reform of imagery or its re-deployment will not suffice. Worship, then, demonstrates a real connection to the sacred, but one in which both the divinity and the worshipper are opened for interrogation and transformation by the way they interact in the flow of desire in relation to each other.

The second aspect of Althaus-Reid's discussion of worship is that it needs to be radically inclusive. Worship that excludes based upon social patterns of decency cannot be worship where God—the Queer God—is truly manifested. Thus, she frequently mentions carnivals as paradigms of

---

51. Ibid. Althaus-Reid's text is ambiguous as to whether it is the women, or the bread, wrapped in the poncho. I believe she means the bread, but either way, the gender-blending is maintained.

52. This paradigm, by which sanctioned transgression solidifies the regnant status quo, is discussed by Foucault, "A Preface to Transgression."

53. Althaus-Reid, *Queer God*, 123.

worship/celebration, festivities that are the "revolt[s] of the Queers."[54] This is a rich site of theological reflection for Althaus-Reid, precisely because it is a place where poverty and sexuality, politics and religion come together in a tangle of transgression, desire, and freedom. She criticizes liberation theology for its refusal to take these seriously as theological sites, mired as it is in its own decency and desire for widespread acceptance as "legitimate" theology:

> What happens then is that if the shanty townspeople go in procession carrying a statue of the Virgin Mary and demanding jobs, they seem to become God's option for the poor. However, when the same shanty townspeople mount a carnival centered on a transvestite Christ accompanied by a Drag Queen Mary Magdalene kissing his wounds, singing songs of political criticism, they are not anymore God's option for the poor. Carnivals in Latin America are the Christmas of the indecent, and yet they are invisible in theological discourse.[55]

Note that it is the same townspeople in each example, the decent protesting for work and the indecent reveling in holy transgression. The boundaries between the two, as in so much of Althaus-Reid's work, are quite porous. Oddly enough, however, though mentioning the carnivals several times in her most important works, Althaus-Reid never gives them sustained analysis. Nevertheless, they are places where the most indecent and non-normative members of society (and those too frequently oppressed by their lives of normalcy) find themselves at home, able to both protest and to worship in freedom, as themselves . . . or at least the selves that they wish to be at that moment.

For another example of worship's capacity to bring about radical inclusion, Althaus-Reid discusses Batuque worship in Brazil.[56] This is a tradition that originated in West Africa and was brought to the Americas by slaves, where it was synthesized with Roman Catholicism, "but without giving up

---

54. Lancaster, "Guto's Performance," 19–20, quoted in Althaus-Reid, *Indecent Theology*, 25.

55. Althaus-Reid, *Indecent Theology*, 25.

56. Althaus-Reid bases her account and analysis not on first-hand experience, but rather the description offered by Fry, "Mediunidade e Sexualidade." I am utterly dependent on her account and have no experience with these communities. Though I certainly hope for accuracy, my primary purpose is simply to illustrate Althaus-Reid's view of worship as requiring fundamental inclusion of the marginalized and outcast.

[its] different cosmology or ways of affective relationships."[57] Its poor practitioners today manage to facilitate not only a relationship with the Divine,
but also a place for non-heterosexual identities. It is a religion of displacements and marginality, not only geographical (Africa to South America),
but also socially. It has maintained its indecency in poverty, while similar
traditions among the middle classes have become more and more "proper."
They have no true place in either the churches or the state, and this experience of marginalization caused them to seek out the marginalized as their
representatives and ministers, hence the preponderance of homosexuals
and queers among their ranks: "the point is what homosexuality can give
to the Batuque worship to enhance it, for instance in the splendor of the
liturgy which is so important and the transvestite aesthetics in spiritual incorporation (especially of goddesses)."[58] Queers are not only included, but
honored and given places of leadership.

This organizational pattern makes Batuque worship particularly hospitable to those who are outcast from the rest of society. Homosexuals and
transvestites find a place of welcome, not only by society, but also by the
Divine. This radical inclusion creates in the community the relationship
that we, as humans, require in order to thrive and flourish.

In addition, the Batuque provide a network of solidarity for other homosexuals who experience problems in their families or neighborhoods.
Their worship allows homosexuals to develop themselves as religious pro-
fessionals, if they so wish, in a context of respect and support and without
hiding their true sexual identity. At the same time they can provide a sense
of family to those who have been rejected by their own relatives.

Those who are either evicted or forced to hide themselves in decent
places of worship find here a place where they are not only valued and es-
teemed, but also are able to relate to God and act as conduits of divine
power and energy. For Stuart, this is precisely what the Eucharistic table
and community are supposed to do, and on this point—if not on matters
on the transformation of God by these rituals—her account of worship and
Althaus-Reid's once again align.

These same communities also address the third aspect of authentic
worship for Althaus-Reid: its capacity to critique the political, social, and
sexual hegemonies of society, state, and church. They are a community

57. Althaus-Reid, *Queer God*, 159.

58. Ibid., 160.

of the marginalized, for the marginalized.[59] This marginality, though, is viewed not as a liability, in which the community becomes some sort of support group, but rather as a source of profound power, a power that is not available through spiritual and social decency. Not only is there an obvious critique of social norms of imposed, decent heterosexuality in the community's elevation of queers to positions of power and authority, but also a deeper critique of where the source of authority and power originates. There are mystical powers, divine powers, which are available only to those who reside at the margins of decent society, of decent churches, for it is a Queer God that Batuque devotees worship.

This power enables the worshiper to live a life of profound holiness, but a holiness that has nothing to do with conformity to prevailing codes of propriety. It allows the worshiper to stand against the structures of oppression with those who are marginalized:

> Holiness then becomes a category of the marginalized, when we consider that the saint is meant to be an outsider to society, not in the sense of failing to participate actively in the political life of her community, but due to her dissenting role. It is participation in the transformation of the structures of society which marks the distance from the centres of order and power. That is Queer dissent, and divine dissent, as in prophetic or other models surrounding the idea of Holy women and men in popular spirituality.[60]

Those who worship in the Batuque communities recognize that their marginality—embodied in their worship—is precisely what allows them to stand against systems of oppression. The Divine empowers them to act in a prophetic capacity against the injustices of society by creating a community of inclusion and solidarity. They dissent from the codes and norms that ensnare and enslave the human (and, for Althaus-Reid, the Divine), and create spaces of true protest and resistance. This same defiance is found in the carnivals that Althaus-Reid so loves, and it is also found in the parodying of gender and sexuality that Stuart insists Christian liturgy must encourage and enable.

---

59. In this, the Batuque communities are quite similar to the church that Althaus-Reid eventually aligned herself with, the Metropolitan Christian Churches, which were created as specifically queer churches, places where those outcast from mainstream Christianity could find a place.

60. Althaus-Reid, *Queer God*, 160.

From the above discussion, I hope that it is evident why I believe Stuart and Althaus-Reid are excellent conversation partners on matters of worship and sacramentality. Their views of what worship should do align perfectly, even if the places they find that worship enacted differ radically. One of the additional things that I find valuable about Althaus-Reid is her ability to view the signs and actions associated with worship as empowering, while also attending to their ambiguity and opacity. This permits not only a rich account of what is going on in worship, but also a more realistic one from a phenomenological point of view. Althaus-Reid does not ignore categories of identity, but she also avoids the temptation to create ones of evident historical stability as Stuart seems to have done. It is here that I find her a valuable corrective to Stuart, and to that discussion of ambiguity I now turn.

Santa Librada

Saint Liberated: "The *Santerias* of Buenos Aires display statues and stamps of a young woman who looks like the Virgin Mary, yet she is crucified and her body hangs from the cross, reminding us of Jesus."[61] *Santa Librada* is a queer saint, a queer image, an amalgam of religious symbols that brings us an ambiguous cross-dresser, "the unstable image of a Christ dressed as a Mary."[62] According to Althaus-Reid, this image is particularly significant because of the ambiguous place that Christ holds in the Latin American, Christian narrative. It is Mary who is the primary source of identification for the poor, and Christ becomes difficult to approach without her: "*Librada's* worship fills that gap, because it is located at the intersection of Christ and Mary, with enough ambiguity for anybody to decide for herself her true identity."[63] S/he is a transvestite symbol that "emigrates from male/female locations."[64]

It is precisely due to this ambiguity that *Santa Librada* is an effective symbol in the lives of the poor, however. In her refusal to be bound to one side of a binary (male/female; Mary/Jesus), she also empowers the poor to refuse such binaries as well, particularly that of legal/illegal. In other words, *Librada* worship legitimates the experiences and lives of the poor as

61. Althaus-Reid, *Indecent Theology*, 79.
62. Ibid., 80.
63. Ibid.
64. Ibid., 81, discussing Garber, *Vested Interests*.

marginal, both socially and legally: the "Bandit Saints" who rob from those who steal land and deny jobs to those in desperate need of them; petty theft done in order to survive; prostitution as a career for those with no other economic options. These are all examples of how Althaus-Reid refuses to separate the economic from the religious, or any other aspect, of human life. *Santa Librada* is with the people:

> Lack of jobs, health problems are all perceived as enemies from which one needs protection and *Librada* protects those who cross legal boundaries in acting to fulfill these necessities. That is the starting point for her worship; acts of legal transgression where Christ or Mary cannot be invoked for protection.[65]

This is an important point for Marcella's critique of decent or T-theology. Jesus and Mary as symbols are given by the church to the people, yet they are presented in such a fashion as to render them unable to actually be with the people in their lives and struggles. Therefore, the people themselves have to negotiate the images to make them something liberating: "Curiously, as we do not seem to have presented dangerous memories of liberation in the Virgin Mary, indecent people just invent them."[66] This process goes against the temptation to close the meaning of a symbol or to deny its multivocity. It mitigates the Roman Catholic urge to limit the number of sacraments, to demarcate where and how the Divine can and does act. It serves the needs of those who gaze upon it, who invoke the saint depicted. Yet, for those like Stuart and myself, who want to hold more closely to Catholic-Christian orthodoxy, this approach can be troubling. After all, from that vantage point, Mary did not die for our sins or redemption ("completion") and it has been high on Catholic agenda for the past fifty years to restore the "proper" relationship between Mary and her Son.[67]

The very inability of the *Librada* to be pinned down mitigates against the need to read the symbol or its worship as simply against the wider tradition, however. Especially if read in light of Ward's account of Christ's displaced body, there is no reason why the salvific act of Jesus cannot be depicted in the person of a woman, since Christ has moved to a position

65. Althaus-Reid, *Indecent Theology*, 81.

66. Ibid., 79.

67. Stuart is ambivalent about this trajectory, especially how it has eliminated some rather rich imagery of Mary as priest, and how an older account of priesthood, suppressed by Pius XI, does a much better job of eliding the gender of the priest and the relation of Son/Mother than we do now: "Making No Sense," 120–21.

that encompasses all genders. Not only that, but simply because the figure is depicted on a cross, there is no need to read it as Christ at all; it can also be interpreted as any crucified or oppressed person. The name of the figure is *Santa*, Saint, and is taken in part from an earlier, marginal Christian holy person. Althaus-Reid herself points out that the image is clearly not the same as the *Christa*, (in)famously shown in New York's St. John the Divine Cathedral, precisely because that image was not ambiguous at all, but clearly a female Jesus. My point here is not to show how Althaus-Reid's account can be rendered orthodox (a move she would probably see as colonialist), but rather to emphasize the way in which the ambiguity of the symbol increases, rather than negates, its liberatory potential. Multiple transgressions are possible at once, all within the encompassing love of a queer divinity who has made transgression her key act: "This is the transvestite theology of the poor. The transgressive praxis accumulates one thing after another. One thing is to bless thieves; another, to be a Mary occupying a Christ space (the cross), or a Christ in his space, dressed as an elfin woman."[68] If legitimation of the outsider lives of the indecent poor is one way that the image is efficacious, so is its capacity to make clear the solidarity of the Divine with the people.

In light of its significance for those fleeing from either poverty or the police, *Santa Librada* is a dynamic symbol of motion and mobility: a symbol on the move. Althaus-Reid suggests that this is a theological response from people "to what does not fit into their lives, symbolized by what is considered indecent in Christian circles: to dress as the opposite sex (as condemned in Deuteronomy 22:5), to transgress sexual limits but also other limits as class barriers and the fixed locations of poor and rich in a Latin American country."[69] Yet Althaus-Reid is also clear that this image is one that has the potential to truly liberate people, to be with them on their path to freedom that the official images, she believes, often cannot do. The symbol is ambivalent, but also efficacious in its depiction of divine solidarity.

As is common in Althaus-Reid's work, the value of this worship cannot be restricted to the religious. *Librada* legitimates economic and legal transgression for survival and shows the Divine as accompanying the indecent in their plights and journeys. This dual efficacy extends as well to out-and-out political defiance as well. Althaus-Reid points out that, especially

68. Althaus-Reid, *Indecent Theology*, 81.

69. Ibid., 82.

in the days of the military *juntas*, but still today, gender deviance is carefully policed, both socially and politically:

> During the dictatorial regime, the politics of dressing was severely controlled. In Argentina, decency is closely associated with dress codes which are controlled by the media but also by politics at street level (a woman dressed "improperly" may be subjected to abuse by men in the streets, for instance). During the dictatorship, leaflets were distributed in public schools teaching adolescents how to dress properly. *Librada* ("Liberated") is the divine transvestite who opens the floodgates of political confinement.[70]

Librada worship allows the people to work for and exercise their freedom. It helps empower them to defy the oppressions of society, in full knowledge that God is on their side in the struggle. *Librada* responds to Pinochet's claim that he was saved from assassination due to his devotion and love of the Blessed Virgin. The official symbols of the church have been too easily co-opted by those who use them in hegemonic ways to enforce decency and violence. The ambiguity, the freedom, opened by *Santa Librada* legitimates resistance as well as evoking the solidarity of God.

What if we were to read baptism in this vein, not rejecting—as Althaus-Reid probably would—the eschatological faith claims that Stuart makes for the sacrament, but rather allowing a place for greater mobility and motion for those who have been initiated into Christ's body? Stuart wants to have baptism create a stable identity that makes us into ecclesial persons. In a sense, this baptismal identity is, in her account, a super-identity that allows Christians to engage the world in a queer way that seems impossible for the non-Christian. Yet the sign of baptism, the character that it truly imparts on those immersed in the waters, seems much less stable than that. It can be violated by sin and idolatry, as Stuart readily recognizes. The church that we are initiated into is as often as much an obstacle to God as a conduit to the Divine. But baptism is also a sacrament for those on the move, just as *Santa Librada* is. It is a sign that testifies to our new lives in Christ's body, but it is also a reminder of how far we are from that completion. Like those who worship *Librada*, we too are running to a promised freedom, and running from the police of gender and sexual enforcement. Yet we too are also always at risk of being captured, of capitulating, despite the assistance of the Divine guaranteed by the signs. This ambiguity does not negate the value or efficacy of the sign, but it does permit an account that allows the

70. Ibid., 83.

affective to be taken seriously, that allows us to be humble in the face of divine activity we seldom understand. Catholic theology has long been tempted by over-definition, by trying to state exactly what is accomplished by the sacraments, and yet the primary meaning of the term is that they are mysteries, signs of a profound reality we are a part of but can neither grasp nor fully understand.

This view of a sacrament for people on the move—a pilgrim people—with ambiguous but nonetheless real effects, is also significant if we are to take seriously the body into which we are brought by baptism. After all, if we accept the account discussed in the previous chapter, Christ's identity is nothing if not unstable, at least in terms of gender and sexuality. There is also the way in which Christ can be read as incomplete prior to the eschaton, when all will be consummated in him to the glory of the Father (see 1 Cor 15:20–28). In this account, Christ himself is still on the move, not in the same way we are (he is not mired by sin or ignorant as to the ultimate end), but nonetheless incomplete until all creation is brought to its proper place in and as his body. It is appropriate, then, that we attend to the ambiguity of the sacraments even as we celebrate the promise they offer, just as Christ is still not fully Christ—something is lacking—until all is brought to completion in fulfillment of that baptismal promise.

Herbert McCabe and Sacramental Failure

I have mentioned several times the issue of queer persons and their relationship to the Christian church. In the Roman Catholic imagination, as well as other traditions, the church is itself a sacrament, a sign of the loving community that God is calling humanity to become in Christ; it is a sign of God's kingdom. Throughout this book, I have made clear my belief in the church as the body of Christ in order to express this. Stuart clearly holds the same view. Yet, for her, the language of "church" can drift in the direction of the equivocal. The church *is* the body of Christ, our direct encounter with the Divine and our school for living truly just, parodic lives. It *is*, at the same time, an idolatrous institution that has capitulated to the sexual and gender mores of modernity. How can we account for, and be able to maintain, both of these disparate views?

One way to think through this difficult dilemma is offered by Herbert McCabe, who I would like to nominate as a queer theologian *avant la lettre.*[71] McCabe differs from Stuart because he pays great attention to the way in which we use words and how those words have meaning. He is a disciple both of Thomas Aquinas and Wittgenstein. Thus, he prefers to think of the sacraments in terms of language, but a language spoken by God in a human medium. Christ is the ultimate sign of God's love—the ultimate sacrament, with which Stuart would agree—precisely because he is God's Word, God's perfect language.

In our world, prior to the eschaton and consummation of all things in God, Christ is indeed present, but McCabe gives a slightly different argument than that of Stuart: "Christ is, indeed, to be found in the present but precisely as what is rejected by the present world, in the poor and despised and oppressed, he is to be found in those who *unmask* the present world, those in whom the meaninglessness and inhumanity and contradictions of our society are exposed."[72] Though he never uses the term, it seems evident to me that this language applies very well to the queer, as well as the proletariat he was referring to: of those who cannot fit in, exposing not an intrinsic problem in themselves, but rather in the society that will not accept them, not create or allow a place for them. In this world, to be rejected is part of what it means to be a disciple of Christ.

Sacraments are part of this world of rejection, and it is important for those who resonate with the name queer to be alert not only to their own exclusion, but also to where they exclude (for example, the very tense relationship between many gay men and transgendered persons). Sacraments are signs of a future breaking in, but not yet here, a future where love will be our language as human beings. Until this time, "the exchange of love, the Holy Spirit, between men [*sic*] is expressed in the language of the future: and this is what the sacraments are. Sacraments belong to our alienated world in which what we are really about cannot be expressed in our own language, we need a special sacred language, a magic." The very existence of the sacraments is a sign not only of what God is doing in our lives, but

---

71. Though I cannot go into my reasoning here, McCabe's work has a transgressive quality that emphasizes the ignorance of Christians in the face of the divine mystery. He also has sentences such as this that radically subvert gender, at least in God-talk: "How then can we all call upon God, beseech *Her*, gain *His* attention, when our very cry for attention is by God, more due to God than it is to ourselves for it must be God that brings it about that I pray as it is God that brings it about that I draw my next breath?" "The Trinity and Prayer," 59, emphases added.

72. McCabe, "Sacramental Language," 175.

also of our alienation from the Divine and one another.[73] The sacraments are both signs of our glorious, queer transformations, and marks of their own failures: they effect what they signify, and yet they haven't done so in a way that makes immediate sense. We are being taught a divine language through them that often remains so much gibberish.

Rather than seeing this as falsifying or negating the sacraments, McCabe states that we must approach them in an ironic fashion, quite similarly to how Stuart discusses parody:

> As Jesus before his death was Word of God (language of the future society) *in the flesh of this world*, so the sacraments of the Church are the language of the future in the language of our world and we have to be aware of the same ironic character in them, we have to treat them with the same irony. In the sacramental life we do indeed speak to each other in the language of the Kingdom, but only if we do not worship the sacraments themselves, only if we recognize concurrently that the flesh profits us nothing. Not that there is anything *else* to profit us.[74]

The sacraments, including the sacrament that is the church, must be looked on ironically, which is to say that we must be able to recognize their failures as language, as signs, precisely as we affirm what is being signified. Thus we should not be surprised that the church often fails to be the sign it claims to be: the sign of a humanity united in the love of God. It is a language of the future—an eschatological language—being spoken in a contemporary idiom. It cannot but fail, since it is made up of people who are themselves in the process of being divinized, and not yet there. But this does not, in itself, invalidate it as a genuine community on a common journey, a pilgrim people becoming what it already is: the body of Christ.

The last line in the above-quoted passage from McCabe is important: this language of the future cannot be adequately expressed to and in us yet, but neither can any other. "Lord, to whom can we go? You have the words of eternal life," said Peter when challenged by the difficult sayings on eating Jesus' body in the Bread of Life Discourse (John 6). The language that Jesus was using wasn't making any sense, but there was also no other place to go, no better language. So it is ultimately with the church. It is a failure; full of corrupt, hypocritical people constructing corrupt, hypocritical systems. It is also all there is, the place where Jesus becomes most fully present in the

73. Ibid., 175.
74. Ibid., 178.

sacraments and word. Nor is this incongruity a new reality, but one that has been a major problem from the beginning, as St. Paul makes clear in his exhortations to the Corinthians. McCabe, commenting on Paul's criticism of the Corinthian church for not attending to the most vulnerable among them at the Eucharist argues, "Like the historical death of Christ, the sacramental commemoration (and even celebration) of it takes place in a world of sin. A Church which is not a challenge to the values of such a world is one which, as Paul says, 'does not discern the body.' But the body is *there* to be 'discerned' and they are 'profaning the body and blood of the Lord' which is *there* to be profaned."[75] The church may fail as a sign of Christ's love, but it is nonetheless where Christ is to be found.[76]

Though it may seem counterintuitive, this failure is actually a key element of Christian belief. After all, Jesus dies a failure, the death of a broken, conquered man from a marginal backwater. In McCabe's telling of the story, Jesus' mission from the Father is a very simple one: to become human, fully human. This, of course, means to love, and Jesus fulfills his mission by utterly giving himself away, by loving without concern for the consequences: "To say that Jesus was without sin just means that he was wholly loving, that he did not put up barriers against people, that he was not afraid of being at the disposal of others, that he was warm and free and spontaneous."[77] Further, he tried to create around himself a community of persons that would be able to live this love as well, both with him and after him. In this, however, he failed. When he was arrested by the authorities because his love proved too threatening in a world that is terrified of it, this community scattered—except for the most marginalized, the women who remained with him throughout. If Jesus died because he was too human, most of the disciples lived because they were too afraid to embrace the humanity that Jesus would not shirk.[78]

75. McCabe, "The Eucharist as Language," 133, emphasis in original. McCabe is discussing 1 Corinthians 11.

76. It may be better to say that it is only through the church that Christ can be *explicitly* found. I am not here trying to get into wider discussions of Christ's presence and activity in the lives of those who do not know him, such as controversies about Karl Rahner's concept of the "anonymous Christian."

77. McCabe, "He was Crucified," 96.

78. The importance of the Spirit in the transformations of the early disciples cannot be overstated, for tradition has it that these same men who ran terrified into the night as Jesus was arrested would all—save one—themselves die as martyrs. They learned how to love without looking over their shoulders, and this process took time. This is particularly attested to in the remarkable passage in Scripture where Paul discusses rebuking Peter

This human failure, however, was not ultimately decisive: Jesus rose from the dead and the community that he had called around himself was re-formed in the Spirit as the church. The fact that the church still looks and acts in many ways contrary to how Jesus was should not surprise us, for it still exists within the muddle of history that has not yet been consummated. All we can see is the bloody corpse on the cross, we have not yet been granted the grace of resurrection. The church is the body of Christ, but it is that body crucified, aching for its fulfillment. All we can see, then, is failure. Yet within this failure, just as in the failure of the cross, the Divine is being revealed and made manifest.

I want to emphasize that this does *not* mean that we should adopt some sort of quietism towards the failures of the church. On the contrary, we must actively work for its transformation into a more loving, just community where gender and sexuality are not viewed as grounds of exclusion from either community or office. This is an act of love, however, an act of trying to get the church to be faithful to its own nature as Christ's inclusive, catholic body. The church is not an adversary, something foreign to us, for we are made as much a part of it by baptism as any bishop, minister, or pope.

Conclusions and Endings

If we take these caveats offered by Herbert McCabe and Marcella Althaus-Reid seriously, we can find something helpful and very profound in Elizabeth Stuart's discussion of the sacraments. If she sometimes overstates their immediate efficacy and makes the church and the "ecclesial persons" formed by baptism seem a bit too perfect, it is also true that she is writing with an eye to the eschatological horizon where what she says will be true, and reminds us that that transformation is already occurring. She gives us a very real account of what the sacraments do to us and our community, and how very queer it is, as well as challenges us and the church to live our queer baptisms more fully. Her work need not be abandoned because it is so very, very difficult to see the reality of what she's talking about, but rather it needs to be supplemented by greater attention to the failure and

---

"to his face" for failing to dine with Gentile Christians for fear of offending Jewish ones (Gal 2:11). If the "pope" who actually knew Jesus had such difficulty reaching out to the marginalized for fear of how it would look, we can scarcely be surprised if the one today does little better.

ambiguity of the sacraments due to their very nature as imperfect signs in an imperfect world. If she fails to attend properly to the ambiguity that Althaus-Reid and McCabe illustrate, this tendency does not invalidate her account of the sacraments but simply shows us what it is that we as Christians hope for and are becoming, rather than what we inhabit. This is a large oversight in her work, but not a fatal one.

But one aspect of Stuart's work remains to be discussed, and with it her account of the sacraments finds its *telos*. For Stuart, death is a kind of *ur*-sacrament, one that marks and creates the others, while they direct us toward it. Death marks both the ends of our lives, and their beginnings, and the Christian life can be thought itself as an *ars moriendi*. Finally, with this "sacrament," Stuart gets closer to holding onto the ambiguity of the sign while also affirming the reality of the signified. The transformation she rightly insists upon with the other sacraments is most evident, even as the final consummation is hidden from us on this side of the grave.

Death can be seen as a Christian sacrament because it connects us viscerally with the death and resurrection of Christ, a death that is already entered into sacramentally at baptism. As Stuart has said in other places, baptism writes these mysteries onto the very bodies of the believers, "their very characters are shaped by this drama (a fact symbolized in the wearing of a cross and in the act of making the sign of the cross) because they are part of the ongoing performance of it."[79] Not only is this connection evident, but it is death that allows the consummation of our lives, their entrance into the resurrection that Christ both reveals and causes. Death is no longer a place where God is not, because God has gone before us into it, transforming it into life: "We die, but are not consumed by death. We die to live and live more fully than we do now. Our dead are not lost to us but remain part of the Church. Their story continues."[80]

It is also through death that the transformations begun in the other sacraments reach their fulfillment, where the identity given in baptism— but inchoately—and nourished by the Eucharist becomes known and lived completely. Yet this resurrection into which we are brought is not something to be grasped, even after death. It is not something that we can now claim and understand, as if a riddle is finally answered. Rather, resurrection always remains a mysterious gift, because it is utterly bound up in the mystery of God and God's life, which is never a problem to solve. Death and

79. Stuart, "Queering Death," 63.
80. Ibid.

resurrection bring anything but closure, but rather a more profound open-ness to the mystery that is ever ancient and ever new: "The resurrection can only be laid hold of through re-enactment, and that includes performance of the space between the cherubim [that is, the space that is both empty and full of the Divine Presence in the Holy of Holies of the Jerusalem Temple]. It is a perpetually open sign, the last piece in the jigsaw that renders all meaningful. The meaning is not to be grasped but to be given."[81] The am-biguity of sign and signified, of presence and absence, that controls our sacramental language becomes most fully realized and fully transformed in our deaths and resurrection.

Yet these are queer sacraments that we are discussing, and, as Stuart has made clear, that means that we must camp and parody that which we are given culturally. Death, rather than being something hidden and elided, something repressed, is given a central role in the Christian imagination. For the secular world, death is a complete ending, an annihilation. It is oblivion, destruction, and final decay. But death, like gender performance, cannot be avoided. It is how we play it that matters. And for the Christian, death cannot be a space where God is absent, for God has gone there be-fore us, but is rather a space of encounter with the Divine. This encounter through our bodies—even the expiration and resurrection of them—makes death sacramental: "It was not just that God defeated death but that God did so in human flesh, and this has profound implications for flesh itself. It bursts from the tomb, the same but different: a flesh no longer meant for cleaving or for oblivion. Christians die, their bodies wear out or fall vulner-able to disease or violence, but a Christian death is a death with critical difference."[82]

This critical difference, this parody of secular death, is also important to contemplate if Christians are to live beyond the cultural constructions of sex and gender. The church is site of learning the resurrection, but it is also a site that too often forgets the significance of it. By ignoring death and the resurrection, the full inclusion of the human into the life of God, the church becomes beholden to notions of gender that are foreign to it:

> The absence of an afterlife deprives the Christian mind of a space beyond heterosexuality and homosexuality. It leads to, or at least allows, the identification of discipleship with heterosexual re-lationships and family life in dominant ecclesial discourse (and

81. Ibid., 59.
82. Ibid., 62.

homosexual relationships in the reverse resistant discourse) and with such identification comes the collapse of the religious life and the celibate vocation which challenges it. There is a great forgetting of the Church's "queer" tradition when death is evaded. Death is essential to the queer project.[83]

If we are to live our lives queerly, with space for those performances of gender and sexuality that evince their fleeting, non-ultimate natures, then we must attend to the sacrament of death that Elizabeth Stuart so ably describes. Thus, it seems now appropriate to turn our attention to another of theology's queer topics: Christian eschatology.

83. Stuart, "Return of the Living Dead," 218.

CHAPTER 3

Eschatology: Queer Consummations

On the third day the friends of Christ coming at daybreak to the place found the grave empty and the stone rolled away. In varying ways they realized the new wonder; but even they hardly realized that the world had died in the night. What they *were looking* at was the first day of a new creation, with a new heaven and a new earth; and in a semblance of the gardener God walked again in the garden, in the cool not of the evening but the dawn.

—G.K. CHESTERTON[1]

GARDENS ARE QUEER PLACES. They are sites of beauty and wonder, literary idylls and beguiling aromas. They are also places that remind us of death, of the summer that will soon turn to autumn, of flowers placed on graves. Scripture tells us that a garden is the place God creates for the first humans to live in, but it is also the place from which they are expelled. A garden is the delight of humanity, and also the reminder of our distance from happiness and from God. Christ suffers his anguish in a garden, and it is in a garden where the resurrection is first made manifest. Augustine hears the famous *Tolle, Lege* in a garden and is converted, and Hamlet's father, in a replay of the story of Cain and Abel, is murdered by his brother in one. Gardens are spaces of creation, exile, dereliction, burial, and new life,

---

1. Chesterton, *Everlasting Man*, 207, emphasis in original.

simultaneously. The whole of salvation history can be told as a story about gardens, of hopes that are lost, yet ultimately fulfilled. Queer places, indeed.

For this reason, it makes sense that one of the most important and powerful works of queer theology yet written, Gerard Loughlin's *Alien Sex*, should have its final, eschatological chapter deal with gardens, scriptural and cinematic. In the long Advent of our lives on earth, gardens remind us of our need for salvation and offer us testimony to the queer actions of God that secure it. This chapter will explore these eschatological themes in the works of two different gay, male theologians: Loughlin and James Alison. It will then offer a reflection on another cinematic depiction of eschatological, resurrected paradise by discussing the final orgy scene in John Cameron Mitchell's film *Shortbus* (ThinkFilm, 2006).

This chapter deals, by talking broadly of the creedal affirmation of the resurrection of the body, with hopes and desires that ache for fulfillment, but have not yet been brought to fruition. In other words, it is dealing with a subject that is extremely difficult to talk about, yet one that must be discussed if the queerness of the creedal Christian story and God's working through it is to be clarified. In the first chapter, I wrote about how queer it was that God should become a specific human being in the incarnation. This chapter will bring us full circle by discussing the other side of the classical dictum: God became human *that humans might become God*. Our deepest desire is to participate fully in the erotic life of God, to be immersed so totally in love that the Divine Life and our own become the same. In the terminology of the Christian East, we long to be divinized, to experience *theosis*, to become God by living God's life.

I do not intend to engage in speculative attempts to "predict" what resurrected bodies will be like or what we are going to be "doing" in heaven. All statements about the beyond are primarily statements about us today, full of our hopes, concerns, and fears; they involve projections and heuristics in order to think through them. The language that one uses for this must make this clear, genuinely speaking to our desires and offering visions of their fulfillment, but never allowing these to be mistaken for descriptions of that which neither I—nor anyone else—can know. Thus, this chapter will take a rather episodic form. For instance, I will not attempt to reconcile the very different approaches and methods of James Alison and Gerard Loughlin. Rather, my discussion should be seen as inquiring into variations on a central desire, variations that do not seek final harmony or reconciliation, but rather show the tensions in which we live and think about these matters as finite beings trying to understand hopes that can only be fulfilled infinitely. By making these tensions manifest, by using a multiplicity of images and approaches, I hope to avoid the idolatrous illusion that these matters can now be resolved; rather, I seek to propose ways of thinking about our desires and hopes that are useful while being honest about the vastly mysterious topic that is being engaged. These variations have less to do with disagreements about the fundamental longings that we have, but rather show a diversity that should be expected when dealing with a topic so necessarily elusive.

Gerard Loughlin and the Alien in the Garden

Loughlin's *Alien Sex* engages classical texts in Christian theology and cinema together. These forms cohere well with each other, in Loughlin's mind, because both are windows on desire, both sites—if done well—where our desires are enflamed and intensified. His entire project, echoing both Ward and Stuart, is a parodic and analogical one that looks at the distance between bodies as an incitement to desire and intimacy, which in turn echoes and manifests our desires for the Divine. In Loughlin's cinematic telling, his book is about the "cut that connects," distances that are both overcome and maintained in order that desire may grow ever stronger so that our intimacy may be as well. The gap between persons, the untouchable space that separates those to whom we are closest, produces desire which in turn bridges the very gap that creates it, while never eliminating it. As film editing splices two disparate images together in order to create a new understanding, a new way of viewing, so too does the utterly mysterious distance/difference between bodies allow for a connection that drives them ever onward into the depths of the completely Other: "The topic around and within which this book wanders—wonderingly—is the cut and connection of bodies, treated as analogy for the viewing of cinema and the seeing of God, with sight the analogy for desire, for the transversal of distance between."[2] Connections are created without ignoring differences; separation and distance—the vehicles of desire—are maintained within the most profound intimacy, for they are what permit it: there is a "necessity of disjunction for unity, of distance for proximity."[3]

---

2. Loughlin, *Alien Sex*, x.

3. Ibid.

This use of cinematic technique is not simply a metaphor loosely engaged, however. It marks the very method that Loughlin follows through the text. The idea of the "cut," of multiple images, separate yet brought together to create something new, is exhibited throughout the work. Each chapter, usually reflecting on a film or series of films, manifests this by its use of fragmentary discourse. We do not read a treatise from beginning to end, where ideas are clearly stated, laid out, and then concluded. Rather, we are brought into a reflection on multiple images and ideas that are often in tension with each other, but that cohere in a way that allows for new vision, new insight, new desire. We are able to see that which is new, and perhaps get glimpses of that which is not ordinarily there to be seen.

A classic example might here be useful. One of the most famous montage sequences is the shower scene in *Psycho*, where Marion Crane meets her untimely end.[4] The scene itself lasts only 45 seconds, but it took seven days to shoot and required over seventy camera setups. For its time, it was a scene containing almost shocking violence and nudity, but remarkably, taken individually, no shot actually shows anything tremendously violent or risqué. At no point do we see any more of Janet Leigh's body than is visible in the first scene of her dressing after an afternoon of love-making. At no point do we even see the knife touch her body. Yet, audiences to this day remain convinced that they saw the knife enter the flesh of Leigh or saw clear depictions of her breasts. The reason this is possible is the way the different images are assembled: each cut between shots becomes a cut of the knife in the mind of the viewer, and each glimpse of skin becomes a whole body that is never actually shown. In other words, montage allows us to see that which we cannot see, be it due to censorship, limits in technology, or limits in our sense and cognition. It allows us to see new visions, where the whole becomes more than the sum of its parts.

The chapters in *Alien Sex* operate in a similar way, as multiple angles on a common scene or film; angles that, taken in themselves, may seem disparate and unconnected, but when brought together, illuminate the whole. It hopes to allow us to "see" the mysteries he discusses, which cannot be glimpsed in themselves. Loughlin's text is not, in other words, a simple reflection on cinema and desire, but rather an attempt to create a textual version of the former in order to incite the latter. It enacts—largely successfully

---

4. At first blush, the use of *Psycho* may seem an inappropriate example, but Loughlin's book is full of readings of films that would not usually be taken as self-evidently theologically—or artistically—appropriate.

for this reader—what it describes. This approach is evident throughout the book, but it is perhaps clearest in the final chapter, "The Garden." Before we venture into that lush setting, however, we first need to attend briefly to the text's major themes.

As the title suggests, this book is about intimacy between foreign bodies, alien bodies. For this reason, most of the films that Loughlin discusses come from the science fiction, horror, or fantasy genres; genres where the alien is rendered most clearly. The image of the alien is also deployed on a number of other levels, however; not only between bodies, but also within them: "For the alien is just the other side of our skin; the inside of our outside. While it appears most distant, it is most close, our most inward but unacceptable being. It is thus all too often abjected, disavowed and destroyed."[5] This proximity, and also palpable disquiet and often even disgust, that exists in all bodies exists as well between bodies and, finally, between creaturely bodies and the analogically apprehended Divine. These diverse cuts are also connections, however, and desire flows across the boundaries, making the very differences between these bodies both absolutely necessary and necessarily complex and murky.

Difference is necessary for both relationship and desire, and eros transforms those differences, but does not annul them. In conversation with Levinas, Loughlin states,

> Eros is not so much the destruction of self or other [in a primordial unity that annihilates all difference and specificity], as their transformation, by making one present to the other, so that the other is not encompassed by the self, or the self submerged in the other, for that would be the destruction of their relationship.[6]

In other words, both self and other meet in relationship, in eros, and are both made "other" again, in a dance of transformation; the self goes beyond—transcends—itself to become what it is not and yet more fully what it is. Thus, for Loughlin, within erotic relationships among creatures, there is positive duality, but not that of subject/object or even that of subject/subject, but rather a "reciprocal asymmetry" where sheer otherness, that is mystery, is discovered.[7] In the closest, most intimate relationships there

5. Loughlin, *Alien Sex*, x.

6. Ibid., 4.

7. Though he shows less hesitancy with the notion of duality—as opposed to dualism—it seems to me that Loughlin's account is not far different from Wendy Farley's when she speaks of nonduality as transcending both subject/object divisions and unity

also remains an absence, the space of difference, the space where the other does not become an object for the self, but rather withdraws to be itself, even as both selves are transformed in the encounter. We become ourselves only in opening ourselves to the caress of mystery, of the other, of the unknown. Rather than trying to fulfill some fundamental lack, of absorbing the other into ourselves as objects to devour, we learn rather to delight in the mysterious intimacy that still allows the other to remain other. This constant interplay of intimacy and mystery, of presence and absence, is perhaps more clearly stated by Wendy Farley: "Lovers, besotted with their beloveds, are not less but infinitely more acutely attuned to the way their beloved remains mysterious, evanescent, sun glittering on waves. Lovers taste the sweetness of life in their beloved, a dance, a light to be desired but never possessed."[8]

This process of erotic love and becoming cannot be satisfied or understood simply as the slaking of need or thirst. These are important aspects of our desire, yet they do not end simply in the annihilation of desire—in sated appetite—but rather in new and deeper desiring. If we are really speaking of love, not simply lust or domination, then the other is never simply the vehicle for our satisfaction, but rather the way that we come to desire ever more deeply and profoundly, even when we do not know what it is we seek:

> But even if much sex is like this [grasping, possessive, lustful], Levinas points to the possibility of something more, to a transcendence of intensity of yearning that is other than want, a passing from need to a different, deeper desiring. When we caress the skin of the other we do not always know what it is that we seek to touch.[9]

In the caress and embrace of the other, in the delight found in her company and the potential ecstasy found in his flesh, we encounter the Other who animates all that is, an Other too present to be reified.

Loughlin's account of God is utterly incarnational and non-dualistic. God is Other, not even in a category of one, but beyond categories altogether; the Divine cannot be an object among others in creation. Accordingly, God cannot be in competition with creatures either, for to love and desire any creature is—at some level—to love and desire God. It is, in fact, the only way that we have to love and desire God, for all we can see and

---

or oneness: see Farley, *Gathering Those Driven Away*, 40.

8. Ibid., 64.

9. Loughlin, *Alien Sex*, 7.

experience is either that which God has made or else mediated through our own creaturely bodies and capacities (cf. 1 John 4:19–21). This is a classical Christian understanding, but one that also deeply informs his anthropology of human relating. God both approaches us in the erotic embrace and withdraws, pulling us ever onward into deeper desire of the Divine Otherness:

> That which withdraws in the erotic embrace is also that which approaches, and approaches by withdrawing. It is the approach of the Other, that, in a further venture, is also the approach of God—there being no other route by which God can come to us. God does not abandon the face of the beloved, but is so fully present, that there is nothing to be seen except the beloved's face.[10]

To love the one who shares our bed or our life—or even just passing namelessly in the street—can never be to take something from God, but is rather the very means by which we come to God. It is only through the created and finite that we may attain to the Uncreated Infinite.

Sexual desire, then, should not be seen as something dangerous that always risks drawing us away from God, but rather always as desire for something good. Pleasure is not something to fear, but a gift that we must learn to delight in, so that we might learn to go through, beyond, and with it to the source of our desiring: "Desire only becomes deathly when it mistakes a sign for that which is signified, an earthly for a heavenly good, turning us away from being itself, from the divine becoming that is excessive of all signs, the source of their coming to be and passing away."[11] Sexual desire can be a primer for our desire for the Divine, but only if we allow ourselves to be carried beyond, to find the Other who is always present and yet always withdrawing in the other. To insist on staying only in this place, to hold on to the pleasure and ecstasy we find, is to fail to become who we are by refusing to be carried onward.

Thus, a key thematic element of *Alien Sex* is the notion of "dispossessive desire." Eros marks us as creatures, for we are created both by and for the Erotic Divine, the eternal *perichoresis* of persons that we call the Trinity. That eros, that desire, cannot become something rapacious, however, if we are to be able to truly enter into the transformation we are called to in the Divine Life. Loughlin recognizes—following the thought of Gregory of Nyssa—that our desires always go beyond and behind what it is that we

10. Ibid., 8.

11. Ibid., 14.

think we desire, and since our ultimate desire is for the infinite, there is no way in which it can ever be quenched, but rather constantly deepened, reignited, and transformed.

Loughlin detects a pattern of withdrawal and return in that which we desire, particularly when that desire is for the Other, for God. We are given glimpses which delight, but we are pulled ever onward into ever greater intimacy. Discussing Gregory's *Life of Moses*, Loughlin states,

> Just as Moses, placed in the cleft of the rock, was permitted to see God pass by, from behind, so God's arrival and appearing is at the same time a withdrawal, since God is always going on ahead, infinitely. One can never get in front of God, and so never see his face. To see God is to follow God. To ascend the mountain and see God is to see God's unseeability, an ever further distance. It is to want to see God all the more.[12]

This Mosaic pattern is what we encounter in the Divine, and it does not cease at death, but continues eternally, as we are brought ever more deeply into the life of Eros.

Yet being brought into this Divine Life can be difficult, however, for it requires that we let go of our needs to hold on to others and our desires for obvious permanence and, often, exclusivity. This is not how God loves, for Divine Eros is promiscuous, enveloping and encompassing the entirety of creation, of the cosmos. Even when God has particular favorites—the people of Israel, for example—divine love is never limited to them alone, as it is only God's desirous and constantly creating will that keeps all the others in beloved existence. Thus, learning to love God and Christ, like learning to love a human being, requires us to be able to let them go, to be themselves:

> One cannot love Jesus possessively, since we are to be his, not he ours. Learning to love Jesus is learning to let him go. If we did not, we could not abide it that he loves others as much as he loves us, and loves them indiscriminately. The pain is not that Christ loves someone else, but anyone else, everyone else, even the person you most despise.[13]

This brings us then to Loughlin's concluding, eschatological chapter. As is often the case with this work, Loughlin begins this chapter with a topic

12. Ibid.
13. Ibid., 18.

that does not seem initially relevant to the larger eschatological issues that he will examine: the sexuality of Christ. Christ's sex life (or lack thereof) is discussed in very early Christian texts, especially those of the so-called gnostics. His sexuality, however, the "orientation" that he may have had, is a very modern topic, and one that has driven much recent, historical work. This is due, in part, to the fact that Christ is depicted throughout the Gospels as being enmeshed in human relationships that are often marked by passion and deep emotion. As Loughlin says, writing of Jesus' relationship with Lazarus and his sisters, Martha and Mary: "However fleetingly, Jesus is shown within a web of relationships, of endearments and affective bonds, of expectations and consolations. He is bound to others as they to him with ties of trust and affection, and some, no doubt, were ties of particular friendship."[14] Even if Christ was, as is most likely the case, unmarried, it is no doubt true that he loved deeply and passionately, and these are some of the facets of personality that we now discuss under the general rubric of sexuality. This long-attested tradition of thinking about Jesus and sex, and also the horror that we often feel from it, "reminds us that sexuality is at one and the same time most intimate to, and estranged from, Christ's body."[15]

At this point, Loughlin explicitly follows Graham Ward's lead on thinking through Christ's displaced body. For both, the resurrection and ascension make Christ's body not absent, but rather intimately present in *all* bodies and, ultimately, all creation:

> Jesus' body has a mercurial materiality that becomes less particular and more generalized as the [Gospel] story proceeds. Moreover, with each displacement the body becomes more desirable. . . . Jesus' body is gradually lost to sight with its crucifixion, resurrection and ascension. But it leaves only in order to return, infinitely transposed in the Eucharistic body that feeds the body of the church, which becomes Christ's body, not metaphorically, but actually, as its non-identical, analogical repetition.[16]

Christ's body withdraws only that it might come back in both greater intensity and greater mystery, pulling us along with it into ever deeper desire and beauty.

Loughlin, expressing some of the anxiety with Ward's language that I discuss in chapter 1, argues that what happens to Christ's body at

14. Ibid., 260.
15. Ibid., 263.
16. Ibid., 263–64.

the resurrection is less a displacement or disappearance, per se, than a deterritorialization. The risen body of Jesus cannot be bound to specific times and places, or even to a single corporeal form:

> Jesus is transfigured, but not just as Moses or Elijah. He has become the flesh of every foreign body, the touch of every stranger; the glory of an alien encounter. If Jesus' body is deterritorialized, and so no longer located in any one place, then every other body is set free, since Christ has become for us a common humanity, the difference in the same.[17]

Thus, to find Christ, we must attend to the bodily *more intensely*, and not attempt to skip over it to the spiritual. In order to love Jesus, we must learn to see him in the other, and to allow him to be himself in that other, by allowing them to become themselves, dispossessively. This learning to love dispossesively is an eschatological act, for it permits us to enact something of the Divine Life, the Divine Eros, in which we will finally be ourselves.

This way of learning to encounter Christ begins, for Loughlin, in a garden. The complexity of our relationship to bodies—that it is in the stranger that we discover the one most intimate to us—means that we must learn to see anew. This is what Mary Magdalene had to learn on that Easter day. She would, after that, no longer find her beloved teacher in the guise she had known; she would not be able to cling to him:

> Mary will learn this more bodily love of Christ through learning to love other bodies, that are the extended body of Jesus, and she will learn this love outside the garden. But the garden is where the learning begins, and to which the learning will lead, since love of the body-in-Christ—Christ's body—is the love of bodies in paradise, the garden of which we have hope of return. It will appear at the heart of the city, and be lit by the lamp of the Lamb.[18]

And in the heart of the city lies a house of flickering lights and illuminated shadows, which is why Loughlin at this point finds it appropriate to cut to Derek Jarman's *The Garden*.

This is a difficult film, as are many of those made by Jarman. The narrative—if it even is a straightforward narrative—is difficult to follow. Actors often play several characters and are edited into scenes at seemingly incongruous times. Loughlin is doubtlessly correct when he advises the viewer

17. Ibid., 264.

18. Ibid., 268.

not to seek after some code that will unlock the whole, but rather relax into "the 'ambient tapestry' of [the film's] 'random images.'"[19] Despite this, however, Loughlin is also correct—as Jarman often pointed out—that this is a Christian film, and motifs from the Gospels allow us to interpret it in part.[20] There is a gay couple who undergo a crucifixion and possible resurrection, while bringing a new Pentecost. A Madonna figure greets visitors bringing gifts, who then morph into paparazzi with murderous, Herodian gazes. A colloquy of officialdom—from the state and church—laugh as they wash their hands of the couple's fate, turning them over to the basin-bearer who becomes their eager tormenter. This is not scriptural allegory, however, for the story goes in its own direction and a Jesus figure from the classical Hollywood tradition (looking uncannily like Max von Sydow in George Stevens' *The Greatest Story Ever Told* [MGM, 1965]) enters frequently, looking plaintive and sad. Several figures are identified with Christ, but none in an absolute sense, for Jesus also stands apart, or in Loughlin's terms, withdraws as he approaches.

The film is shot almost entirely at Jarman's own home, a small cottage and garden on the Welsh coast. Like many others, Jarman sees the garden as a site of ambiguity, at once Eden and Gethsemane. For him, the garden is a space of "anguish and its comforting. In the garden time is touched by eternity and beatitude is momentarily embraced, promising infinite succor for life's inchoate yearning."[21] The film is set in paradise and shows its loss due to societal homophobia and the onslaught of AIDS (complications of which were killing Jarman even as he made the film). Christ becomes once again the innocent destroyed by hostile powers that are unable to abide his love—be it depicted in the "Hollywood" figure with his clear wounds, the gay couple in their tender embrace and closeness even in anguish, or in Jarman himself, who begins the story by showing himself dreaming it fitfully into being, imaging the creative Word.

This multiplicity of Christ's body has large import for Loughlin, for he sees Jarman attempting precisely what the church is/should be doing. For Jarman, Christ's life and passion are not historical events that are now complete. Rather, Christ lives—and suffers—today in the bodies of those who are persecuted for their loves: "Moreover, Jarman's telling of Christ's

19. Ibid., 272; quoting Jarman, *Dancing Ledge*, 129.

20. For Jarman's insistence on the Christian nature of *The Garden*, see Peake, *Derek Jarman*, 467.

21. Loughlin, *Alien Sex*, 272.

passion is not just about something that has happened, but is happening; in the same way that the church reads the scriptures as contemporary texts, needing present performances."[22] This dislocation of Christ's body allows the earlier question about Jesus' sexuality to be answered in a compellingly non-reductive (and non-anachronistic) way: The gay lovers' "story is transfigured into the mercurial space of Jarman's garden, and there into the story of Jesus, where they become analogical repetitions of his body, broken for loving. It is in this way that Jesus gains his homo/sexuality."[23] Jesus' body, risen and ascended, his eschatological body, longs for union with our own, and shows that our bodies have fulfillment only in his, the body of God. Our loves and sexual connections become Christ's, but he is not reducible to them, nor are we to remain locked into our own notions of our sexual identities. Rather, Christ's body gently guides us beyond ourselves into new ways of being, and new encounters with alien flesh, provided that we allow ourselves to let go, both of what we "know" about ourselves sexually and spiritually and what we "know" about him.

Loughlin's engagement with *The Garden* shows the necessity of entering into Christ's story so that this dissemination of his body might take place. But how is that possible, and is there anything unique in it? Is Jesus being treated as a simple archetypal figure in *The Garden*? For instance, Werner Herzog's film *My Son, My Son What Have Ye Done?* is a complicated (and loose) re-enactment of a true murder, in which a man kills his mother with an antique sword. Yet this action was, in itself, a self-conscious re-enactment of a scene from the myth of Orestes. Is there something in the story of Christ that makes the disseminations of his body different from those of Orestes, or Don Quixote, or any other figure that is frequently cited in cinema? It seems apparent that Jesus' historicity is key in *Alien Sex*, but more importantly, so are the realities of his resurrection and ascension, but why? Is there anything that makes entrance into Jesus' story—its non-identical repetition—different from that of any other literary or historical figure?

One possible response is that the historicity of Jesus' body, as opposed to that of Orestes, is what makes this possible. Historicity grants specificity, a real corporeality, that is simply not present in the case of myth. But is this always true? For instance, don't many literary figures—perhaps Ivan Karamazov—seem far more specific, far more "real," than many historical figures from the past? The many controversies and disputed questions

22. Ibid., 273.
23. Ibid., 274.

among those who engage in "Historical Jesus" work attest that it is quite difficult to get a solid, specific impression of Jesus, even from the Gospels. What then is the difference between Jesus and Orestes?

It seems to me that the only response that can be given is a theological one, not one that arises from some general theory of mimesis. On that account, there may be nothing more to Jesus' story than there is to Orestes, except perhaps that it is more deeply enmeshed in Western culture as an ur-text or archetype. This is precisely why Loughlin's attention to the resurrection and ascension of Christ is so important. Though the incarnation shows the entry of God into human history, it is also irreducible to human history. In other words, Jesus is a historical figure, but *not only* a historical figure. For Jesus is still alive, and still active in history in a way that is not true of others who have gone before us, or better, is true of them only because it is first true of him. The expansion, the dislocation, of this living Jesus is key to classical sacramental thinking. When I re-enact a scene from the *Oresteia*, I am doing only that: externally re-performing a motif. But due to the sacraments and Jesus' status as alive and risen, when something from his life is re-enacted, it is not simply extrinsic. The sacraments make my body and that of Jesus the same, even as they are also different. My baptism is not simply a re-enactment of a "scene" from Jesus' life, but rather an entry into that very life. My body and his body touch, merge, play. This is something which is simply not possible with a literary body, no matter how specific.

Jarman seems to depict this sort of connection in his film. There are clear scenes with baptismal and Eucharistic resonance, but like the ecclesial sacraments, these are not simply re-enactments of exactly what Jesus did. The gay lovers who together figure Christ play in a bath and have water poured over them by a child. A long table—re-enacting if anything the layout of Leonardo's *The Last Supper*—is shown throughout, most importantly at the conclusion in a Pentecost scene where the lovers emerge from their graves to be present to those gathered. This sacramental connection brings the couple into the story of Christ, allow his story to be told in their lives and his body to be shown in theirs. Indeed, it allows his body to be murdered and rise once again in theirs. This is something intrinsic and powerful that is more than simply "going through the motions." I suspect that Loughlin would concur in this reading, but I do wish he had given a bit more attention to the differences cinematically between extrinsic mimesis and sacramental participation.

Returning to the text of *Alien Sex*, Loughlin's reflection on Jarman's film leads to one more jump-cut, this time to a theological reflection engaging the thought of Gregory of Nyssa on marriage and sex in heaven. The angelic, young gay couple in *The Garden* is read as an instantiation of Gregory's ideas on heavenly life where all will be strangers to marriage (cf. Matt 22:29–30).[24] As we have seen so often, Christian eschatology is a non-identical return, a repetition with critical difference, a parody of Eden. There, according to Gregory, our first parents would not have needed sex in order to multiply.[25] Gregory, in accordance with the Christian Neoplatonism that formed him, sees the link between sex and procreation as accidental, as a remedy for the fall, and therefore in a pre-lapsarian state the former would not have been needed for the latter: our bodies would have reproduced as did the angels in heaven. Jarman—in a very different way and for very different reasons—agrees that sex and procreation are not necessarily linked in paradise, and Loughlin sees this state as celebrated by both.

It needs to be pointed out that Loughlin's reading of Gregory of Nyssa, though increasingly accepted and, to my mind, compelling, is not the one that is most self-evident. Recognizing that Gregory, like Plato before him, is a consummate ironist, Loughlin interprets the Cappadocian Father's *On Virginity* not as a polemic opposing chastity to sexual, married life—as has long been thought—but rather as a treatise on desire in all its embodied forms.[26] Gregory ultimately wants to see paradise as a future where reproduction occurs without sex; Jarman envisions it as a space where there is sex without reproduction. Loughlin argues, however, that these readings are not actually in opposition, for in Gregory, sexual desire "is not incompatible with heavenly yearning. For him, one form of desire leads to the other, and the second is a dispossessive form of the first."[27] As we encountered in Ward's discussion of Gregory in chapter 1, eros and agape are not in any way opposed, but rather eros is an intensification of agape and, Loughlin would add, agape is a dispossessive form of eros. Ultimately, therefore, marriage and virginity are not matters of sexual practice—much less attitudes towards reproduction—for Gregory, but rather signify states

24. Loughlin, *Alien Sex*, 274.

25. See Loughlin, *Alien Sex*, 274 and especially pp. 289–90, fn. 101.

26. Loughlin makes clear that his is a contested reading, and that the richness of Gregory's style allows for many different interpretations, including those of Mark D. Hart (which he follows), Viriginia Burrus, and Caroline Walker Bynum: see Loughlin, *Alien Sex*, 290, fn. 104.

27. Ibid., 275.

of attachment and detachment, possession and dispossession, respectively. Marriage is used as a metaphor for possessive relationships; virginity images dispossessive ones, where one looks not to have, but rather to partake in beauty in order to become beautiful.

In this reading, those who are married can be "virgins" and those who are celibate can be "married," attached in such a way to creatures and creaturely life that they are cut off from the source of all desire. Dispossessive desire of the creaturely is not meant to denigrate the earthly, married state or remove passion, but rather ensure that all desire is able to draw us to its source in the Divine Eros, not be exhausted by seeking it ultimately in creatures who cannot fulfill our longing: "Desire never ceases to flow, since it is the movement of an eternal source that knows no cessation. The only question is where it flows, and whether it is diverted into other channels that do not meet up again with the main course, but exhaust it in their diversions."[28] Thus, though Gregory makes clear that he envisions no sexual acts in heaven (mostly because, in his queer reading, gender and sex differences cease to exist altogether there), Loughlin argues that this need not be the case in order to maintain the larger point about desire. When Christ says that there is no marriage in heaven, this does not mean that there are no bodily desires or intimate, bodily encounters, but "the absence of attachments that detach us from desire, from the ecstatic dance of God's desiring."[29] This is the life that Loughlin sees depicted in Jarman's *The Garden*.

A salient point that Loughlin observes about the gay couple depicted in the film is that they look very, very similar.[30] This is not simply a matter of intriguing casting, however, because Loughlin reads this depiction as vitally important. Picking up on what Graham Ward has observed above, Loughlin argues there is no such thing as pure difference, but difference is always only observed in relation between two (or more) entities. Loughlin puts this a slightly different way by noting a preceding sameness in all differences, for if there is not some level of similarity, difference loses any significance at all: "Things that are not the same in some regard are beyond difference; which really only applies to the different 'difference' of God."[31]

28. Ibid., 277.

29. Ibid.

30. To this viewer, at least, the actor playing Judas could be added to this observation as well.

31. Loughlin, *Alien Sex*, 278.

The individuals in Jarman's gay couple are clearly two different persons, but there is also something the same about them. It is precisely this sameness that allows them to be different, and for each to reach out beyond themselves.

In many conversations about sexual difference, gay couples are perceived as necessarily narcissistic, because they do not recognize "true" sexual difference and instead seek out only themselves—oddly reducing human personhood to sexual organs.[32] The difference between male and female is thus made into such an ontological reality (a matter of ultimate concern, as Stuart would put it), that there seems to be difficulty accounting for any difference other than the genital. Ironically, however, this seems to imply either a thorough-going individualism where all people are already utterly themselves before entering into relationships—for how else could my difference from another be so absolute unless I already am exactly what I am meant to be in myself—or else an idea of "complementarity" whereby there is some fundamental lack in myself that can only be filled in by another of the other sex.[33] Both of these responses should be rejected, and Loughlin views each as fundamentally misunderstanding the nature of difference, sexual and otherwise.

As Loughlin is at pains to make clear throughout his text, the "alien" of the title is not simply about something "out there," be it other forms of life or the mysterious entity that may share our beds. It refers also to ourselves, about how we are alien to that which is closest to us, even internal to us. In order to build, citing Leo Bersani, a "non-antagonistic relation to difference," we have to recognize the sameness in difference, that the other is not something utterly monstrous. In order to do that, we must recognize that *"we are already out there."*[34] We are already the alien, and thus "we should find ourselves in the other, who is yet other; and the other in ourselves, who

32. Examples are numerous, but one of the most important is the *Catechism of the Catholic Church*'s statement that homosexual relationships "do not proceed from a genuine affective and sexual complementarity" (para. 2357). Complementary is how the current leadership of the Catholic Church discusses sexual difference.

33. As indicated in the previous note, this seems to be the way that the Catholic Church approaches the issue. The idea has been heavily critiqued, not least by Loughlin himself in *Alien Sex*, 152–62. For a detailed and, to my mind, rather devastating critique of how gender complementarity is read into Genesis and the later Christian tradition, see Moore, *Question of Truth*, 118–50, and *Body in Context*, 117–35.

34. Loughlin, *Alien Sex*, 278, emphasis in original, citing Bersani and Dutoit, *Caravaggio*, 48.

are yet ourselves, but other."[35] What this complicated word play is meant to emphasize is that sameness and difference are not in opposition to each other, much less in antagonistic opposition, but are rather mutually implicating. When it comes to persons—and perhaps much else—there is no such thing as simple sameness or difference, even in terms of the self.

To my mind, this has obvious echoes with the traditional language of Christian eschatology: the "already/not yet" paradigm. As was discussed in the last chapter in reference to the sacraments, Christian eschatology has often been about making sense of a particular tension—Christ has already come and saved us, but that salvation is not yet fully manifest. It has already occurred, but has not yet been consummated. These two elements are held in tensive relationship, but need not be antagonistic. Something similar is going on, it seems to me, with Loughlin (and Ward's) discussion of difference, sexual and otherwise. I am at once both myself and somehow other, somehow alien. Likewise, those I encounter are both themselves and also somehow images of me. Not only that, but I am also not yet fully myself, and come to be so only in and through the other, and the other in and through me (or those other than themselves). I am already myself; I am not yet myself. This final coming to be—self-realization in the other and, through them, the Other—is largely what Christian eschatology is about. We are ultimately only ourselves when we are consummated in the life of the truly Other, the Trinity.[36] In other words, we will only be who we are when we have been brought entirely into the life of the Triune God, and even then, our desiring and the infinite dance does not cease: God is infinite, and the depths of the Divine Life can never—even in paradise—be fully plumbed.

Loughlin's use of a same-sex, male couple to make this point about sameness in difference is potentially problematic, however. For years, many feminist writers have argued that attempts to simply "get beyond" gender function to simply reassert masculine privilege in a disguised light. Since maleness is considered in our culture (still!) to be both specific and also universal (man is both a sex and all humanity), trying to move beyond gender using all male examples can have the problematic effect of further

35. Loughlin, *Alien Sex*, 278.

36. The idea of sameness in difference that we have been discussing is ultimately rooted for Loughlin in this Triune life that we come to share: "For the rule of the triune God is that each divine 'person' is the same as the other two, but *differently*. The mutual gaze of gay lovers perfectly [!] repeats the Augustinian image of the loving Trinity: the lover and the beloved united through the love that passes between them." Loughlin, *Alien Sex*, 279.

occluding femaleness, if not the feminine. Loughlin understands this and responds by arguing that his example, drawn from *The Garden*, figures "not so much male bonding as same-sex union, and not so much same-sex union as the possibility of non-antagonistic relationships, in which the other is not irreducibly alien, but the same difference that we are from ourselves, and in which we encounter the different 'difference' by which we are given."[37] If anything, Loughlin's attempt is less about trying to move beyond gender and sex than it is to gesture toward a deeper, queer transgendering.

Loughlin points out that Gregory believed that not only is the resurrected body not differentiated sexually, but that the Edenic body was not either. Yet difference remained, even *before* sexual differentiation occurred: "For Eve was still helpmeet to Adam before their sexual differentiation, with each the other's non-identical double, so that though 'male' and 'female' it is impossible to say how they differed other than as one body from another. It is only with their fall into history, into social orders and cultural hierarchies, that it becomes possible to demarcate Adam and Eve as 'man' and 'woman.'"[38] Loughlin is most emphatically *not* trying to simply recover Gregory's view of sexed bodies, for it is indeed problematic, but rather trying to enact a paradisal hope where the body is instead sexed "in a way that is unspeakable and inconceivable." He wants to hold onto our embodied nature as sexed, but to allow that "sexing" to become something utterly mysterious and unknown. In fact, by positing this, he is also suggesting that our gender and sex roles are *already* that mysterious and inconceivable; this is not simply something that will happen after death. If maleness and femaleness do remain then, that difference is something that is fundamentally unstable and shifting, only understandable as the difference between bodies, rather than an ontologically irreducible reality. And as the differences are not reducible to sex, neither can the similarities be either. So it will be then, so it is also now. His point here is not simply to speculate about the mysteriousness of our sexed and gendered bodies in both pre-lapsarian and heavenly states, but more importantly to challenge, in light of the Christian tradition, the rigid ontology of gender assumed by many religious thinkers, especially in the Catholic Church: difference does indeed exist, and cannot be reduced to sexual difference, but how it exists and what this means is a far more complicated, queer, and fundamentally eschatological question. Whether this will address the anxieties of some

37. Ibid., 280.
38. Ibid.

over female occlusion, I cannot say, but it seems to me that if it cannot it is more a testament to a conflict between queer approaches and certain forms of feminism rather than a problem unique to Loughlin.

We have seen how Loughlin, using his cinematic methodology, has re-written/re-shot some of the key themes surrounding Christian eschatology: sameness/difference, already/not yet, and perennial questions on the ultimacy of our sexualities in light of the resurrection. We have discussed the eschatological entry into the Divine Life, and how that begins today via loving dispossesively and our ultimate coming to ourselves in and through others. Intimately bound-up in the whole conversation are Christian hopes for the hereafter and how they challenge us to live graced lives within history. I would now like to cut to another Christian theologian and his discussion of eschatology to cast a different light on many of these same topics.

James Alison and the Eschatological Imagination

Alison the Girardian

In order to understand Alison's theological project, especially in his *Raising Abel*, one must first know that Alison grounds his theology deeply in the work of René Girard. Girard is most famous for his "mimetic theory" of desire and violence, which, according to him and Alison, underlies all of human culture, identity, and action. For Alison, a cardinal tenet of Girard's thinking holds that all humans, by virtue of being human, create their identities and desires based on the imitation of another. From our earliest years as infants, all that we learn and know is done in imitation of others, for example, our parents. It is in this way that we first learn and understand language, which in turn underlies all of our attempts to form an "I" from then onward. Thus, all humans are by nature social, getting even their individual identities from other people: Alison's vision of the human is in no way atomistic. Thus, as Charles Hefling writes, "Desire is fundamental (though not 'foundational') to being human and to human being. Our consciousness is constituted by—in a sense it is—desire. The plural pronoun 'our' is deliberate, for the constituting is social."[39] This mimesis can either be pacific—usually when the imitator acknowledges and is comfortable with the fact—or violent—as often occurs when attempts are made to keep

39. Hefling, "A View from the Stern," 691.

the mimesis hidden. Take, for example, a case that Alison presents of two childhood friends and a girl.

One boy confesses to another that he likes a girl. Alison calls them Tom and Frank. Tom luxuriates in telling Frank about the girl that he's found he has discovered he's in love with. He does this for two reasons: to convey his desire and longing, but also to have it confirmed by Frank. After all, in Alison's thinking, Tom isn't capable of desiring something that Frank doesn't also find desirable. This desire, however, makes Frank start to desire the same girl as well. This, inevitably, leads to conflict among the friends, a common enough state of affairs among adolescents. Before this, Frank has been able to share the same things that Tom desires (Tom got an iPod and Frank could too; Tom got a new video game, and they could play it together). The girl, however, is indivisible. So Frank decides he's going to pursue the same girl, and Tom, in understandable anger, breaks off his relationship with Frank. Yet now Frank realizes that he's lost interest as well: "When Tom is distant, as friend and as rival, the girl loses her interest. Well, this story, where the male and female rôles can be changed around at pleasure, is so transparent that we all understand it at once: we all desire through the eyes of another."[40] Though this is where Alison ends this particular example, it can be taken further, so that our desire is not simply shaped this directly by one's friends, but is culturally shaped. The kind of men or women we desire is heavily shaped by what we learn is desirable from advertising, pornography, cinema, television, and myriad other sources. But our desire is always formed by our interactions with others.

Alison argues that this occurs not simply on the individual level, but also socially. Tensions and conflicts arise when what we desire through others' desiring is something we cannot achieve, or is somehow scarce. Profound rivalries and violence can result at these times. Thus, some third party group or person is labeled as a dangerous "other," one that is causing all our problems, and whose expulsion is required for our social stability. The treatment of Jews in times of war, famine, or plague in the Middle Ages

---

40. Alison, *Abel*, 20. It should be noted how well this example—particular the gender roles that Alison deploys but then universalizes—seems to perfectly model the way that women are often used in triangular relationships with men, so that they can relate to one another: see Sedgwick's *Between Men*, especially 1–20. This is Alison's main, "simple" example of the triangulation of desire and conflict that he takes from Girard. It has its value and truth, but it is also, I think, overstated, at least as a universal explanatory mechanism. My main interest in Alison is less about this methodology, but what he says as he deploys it, so I will not enter into more thorough critiques of the Girardian system here.

may be the classical example of this dynamic. Our capacity to live in society, desire, and yet also feel ourselves to be autonomous and "in control" cannot easily coexist. These tensions are then directed to a scapegoat who serves a vital social function, but whose guilt is invented.

For Alison, this mechanism of violent expulsion animates all of human culture, identity, and religion—with the one exception of Jesus Christ, to be discussed below. We are deeply imitative beings, yet feel threatened if and when our imitations are exposed as such, for then we can no longer see ourselves as utterly self-sufficient and autonomous. Because of this, we constantly try to find some weaker other on whom we can project our conflict. Though the above example may be relatively domestic, Alison sees this same mechanism of violent expulsion behind such things as wars, vast economic disparities, and other interpersonal and social realities. The cohesion of the group requires the sacrifice of an innocent, whose guilt cannot be questioned. If the victim is discovered to be actually innocent, the group cannot function as it once did, for its own violence would be made manifest. The entire process, then, would be subverted. For this reason, we often take our successful expulsion of a person or group from our midst as confirmation of their guilt by the gods, a mentality of punishment perhaps best demonstrated by the friends of Job.

Ultimately, in Alison's version of Girard, this pattern of behavior is bound up in a human obsession with death. We wish to assert our identities and wills over against another out of terror that we will somehow cease to be. This violence and fear, so endemic in us, seems only to be controllable by unanimous use of it against another: if we all decide to be violent against this person (who we have convinced ourselves really deserves it), then we will not be violent to each other. No particular group has a monopoly on this pattern, and no group is free of it—it is part of the human condition.[41] Since it is so deeply ingrained in all our activity, it is impossible for a human being to step outside and see clearly what it is we are in fact doing when we sacrifice others for our cohesion. It requires someone completely outside this system, one who lives entirely free of it, to show that to us, to reveal it. This, for Alison, is exactly what the incarnation of Jesus Christ accomplishes.

There is only one occurrence which, for Alison, could really expose our violent expulsions and sacrifices as the lies they are: the clear proof from the

41. Alison, in a later work, discusses this theory in connection with original sin: see Alison, *Joy of Being Wrong*.

gods that the victim is innocent. Jesus, then, in allowing himself to be killed as the cursed one "upon a tree," challenges this dominion of death and exposes it and the behavioral lie which it motivates. He is executed as a threat to social order, as a violator of the rules of society which are thought to be of God: his death is therefore justified and the order can go on. Then, however, a strange thing occurs, and this dead, cursed one is seen by his closest friends and disciples, raised by the power of God: "Naturally, then, if such a person rises from the dead and appears to his disciples, the whole system of thought which led to his execution is called into question."[42] This event, whereby the victim is shown to be innocent—and particularly *this* victim, one who associated himself so closely with all other societal outcasts—throws into complete disarray the entire mechanism that our societies are structured upon, and further shows that these violent structures have nothing at all to do with God. They are the products of a purely human violence.

The resurrection of Jesus, then, is the pivotal eschatological moment for Alison, the one that can truly give us hope. It is the breaking open of what we thought was immutable reality, empowering us to live as Jesus did, to imitate him above all. As he says, "The resurrection was the irruption into the midst of the normal human story, shot through with death, of a very different story, one which we do not know how to tell very well. This means that the study of eschatology is an attempt to study the fullness of the density of the resurrection."[43] Charles Helfing puts it this way: "The resurrection is among other things a disclosure of the human plight that it displaces."[44] The fear of death and ceasing to be, which motivated so much of our activity, is now shown to be without ultimate meaning: "O Death where is your victory?" (1 Cor 15:55).

When Jesus shows that God has nothing to do with death, that it has been stripped of its ultimate significance, he also reveals something else. By appearing to his disciples, still bearing the wounds of his bloody death, Jesus shows that our lives are not negated by God in being taken up to him, but are instead gloriously transformed as they are. As Alison writes, "[O]ne of the principal senses of the presence of the crucified and risen victim is to show that it is all of human history, *including its murderous vanity*, that has been taken up into the resurrection life."[45] Thus, all of our

42. Alison, *Abel*, 27.

43. Ibid., 28.

44. Hefling, *Stern*, 690.

45. Alison, *Abel*, 31.

history, and all that we are and have been, is taken up into the very life of God in the resurrection. Salvation, therefore, has a very clear individual component. Our actions and histories have meaning in that they will be transformed into the glorious life of God; they will not simply be abrogated and replaced by a heavenly story. To show a bit more clearly what he means, Alison discusses, quite appropriately for a thinker so rooted in the ways exclusion dominates life, a rather queer group:

> I try to make sense of it in terms of the transvestite prostitutes whom I knew in Brazil when they were in the final phase of their struggle with AIDS. I hope to know them again in heaven, not so transmogrified that their personal story has been, in each case, abolished, but rather so utterly alive that their fake beauty, arduously cultivated, their sad personal stories of envy, violence, frustration in love, and their illness have become trophies which are not sources of shame, but which adds to their beauty and their joy.[46]

Thus, risen life is one that is fully alive, having nothing to do with death, exactly how God is and how Jesus lived on earth. This is not, however, simply a hope for the hereafter. To understand better how Jesus allows us to live as risen beings now, in history, communally one with another, it is necessary to turn to the ascension.

For Alison, the ascension is one of the most important, and under-analyzed, Christian doctrines.[47] This doctrine, about Jesus' return to the Father and his opening of heaven to all, is understood by Alison as showing how Jesus makes it possible for us to also see God as our Father, and to live according to God's life, revealed in the resurrection as utter vivacity and forgiveness.[48] Thus, he states,

---

46. Ibid., 33. Though I haven't space enough to delve into the issue here, suffice it to say there would be many queer thinkers who would object to the idea that there is such a thing as "fake beauty." Camp, it could be argued, is precisely finding genuine beauty in that which is scorned as false or ugly.

47. *Raising Abel* was published before Ward's important essay on Christ's displaced body, which also gives sustained attention to the ascension, though in a very different way.

48. Some readers will find the sheer amount of references to the First Person of the Trinity as "Father" problematic in these pages. I recognize the concern about using solely male imagery, and try to avoid it myself, but as it is the language Alison uses, I will in this section as well. I suspect that Alison does not use it to subtly insist on God's inherent masculinity, but rather that it is both Scriptural and traditional and Alison wants to show himself as standing clearly in that tradition. Nonetheless, the steady repetition of "Father" as the sole image for the First Person is an issue that Alison should take more

> Jesus also tells us that it is *thanks to the fact* that he is going to the
> Father that we will be able to do the works which he does and,
> indeed, greater works still. This does not mean that it is in Jesus'
> absence that we believers will be able to do these things, but that
> *thanks to* Jesus' creative self-giving up to death we will be able to
> be possessed by the Father in the same way in which Jesus was. In
> this way, we can imitate him creatively, without rivalry, doing what
> he did and more.[49]

Alison sees the ascension, the return to the Father, as deeply linked with
Jesus' going to death, for by Jesus' return, he can empower us to live—and
risk all, even our lives—as he did.[50] By manifesting this self-giving love,
completely unconcerned with death and its effects,[51] Jesus shows us who
God really is and allows us to live fully as adopted children in imitation of
the firstborn Son.

It is very important for Alison that his readers understand that imitating Jesus is not something which binds and restricts us, but instead allows
us to enter fully into the creative activity of God that Jesus completes by
revealing who God really is in his utter non-violence and vivaciousness.
Living Christ's life is not about rigid adherence to rules or moralism. In
other words, imitating Jesus by rejecting the exclusionary mechanism that
dominates our lives and discourse is something that opens up infinite possibilities for creating new stories in the here and now. Christ opens up diverse
ways to live, to create genuinely human lives. In this way, the story of the
self that is being created anew for us by God in Christ, yet which we truly
participate in as well, is intimately linked to others and our treatment of
them. Really living Alison's eschatological imagination, completely focused
on the God who is utterly alive and who promises us an equally deathless
existence, requires us to abandon our own violence and exclusion of those
outcasts in our own lives—those outcasts to whom Jesus paid such attention. Though he does not use the term often, justice and the overcoming of

---

cognizance of, as it is not required for a vibrant Christian orthodoxy.

49. Alison, *Abel*, 62, emphases in original.

50. In this he seems to be following a more Johannine account, where Jesus' being
"lifted up" on the cross brings together the realities of death and glorification.

51. Alison, clearly, follows the Johannine narrative much more closely than the
Synoptics for his theology of the passion, though he is also clear that he sees the same
attitude shot through the other Gospels.

these violent systems is a constitutive part of really living the resurrected life manifested in Jesus.[52]

In order to do this, Jesus sends forth the Spirit and founds the church as the community of the Spirit. For Alison, the primary function the church serves, animated by God's Spirit, is to keep alive the memory of how Jesus lived and what Jesus showed God to be really like. This Spirit is, in a very literal sense, the counselor for the defense, the Paraclete of John's Gospel:

> The defense counsellor reads the same lynch [of accusation against the victim] but from the point of view of the victim: it knows that the victim is hated without cause, and constantly declares the victim's innocence. It does this by constantly bringing to memory the real story, which happened historically, of the teaching and the works of Jesus, the original defense counsellor, the original forgiveness of God. [. . .] This is the primordial function of the Holy Spirit, pleading for the defense, which corresponds exactly to the forgiveness of sins and the process of creatively producing children of God.[53]

It needs to be clarified here that Alison, in talking about innocence, is speaking very much about those who are hated without cause, or are hated for manifesting the same mechanisms of violence which we all share. They are hated so that the haters might deflect their own violence rather than perceive their own complicity. What the Spirit does in its defense is show that the victim, even if truly guilty of some crime, is not beyond redemption or forgiveness. The memory of Jesus, who died forgiving his attackers and approached his denier without recrimination after the resurrection, shows that forgiveness towards those who expel us is the way in which we truly show forth the unimportance of death and live as God's children.

This brings us to what can be perceived as either the greatest weakness, or the greatest challenge, of Alison's work. Forgiveness—the ability to offer it to those who are violent and exclusionary toward us, and the ability to accept it from those we are violent towards—is certainly seen as more important than justice, or rather, may be the only way that justice—truly right relationships—can be achieved. True humanity, true imitation of Jesus, is achieved not in demanding retributive justice for oneself, punishment for

---

52. Though he never addresses it, I suspect that Alison refrains from justice language because of the easy way in which it can be seen to simply invert the violent mechanism: justice as the oppressed becoming the new oppressors. Alison's insistence on forgiveness as primary probably also contributes to this decision.

53. Alison, *Abel*, 67.

the oppressor, but rather offering forgiveness and thus manifesting the ultimate impotence of the system of violence. This is an extremely challenging view, since it means that we have to dismantle every lust for violence and expulsion within ourselves. At the same time, however, it emphatically does not mean that we simply accept the status quo: we must stand against all violence, standing with all outcasts and victims, even if it means our own destruction. Alison realizes the difficulty here, however:

> Here is where there is produced what is perhaps the most difficult and substantial of the changes in the perception of God which we have been seeing. The god of victims becomes present not as rescuer, but as the One who gives hope to persons so that they may themselves run the risk of becoming victims. The tender and kindhearted Father, absolutely effervescent and vivacious, becomes present as the empowering of the subject to live the absolute twilight of being crushed when she casts light on dark places.[54]

The hope we possess is that we might be able to become truly free of the violent system, even at the expense of ourselves. Justice, insofar as it appears, cannot be seen as simple inversion of the system, with the former victims now able to victimize their oppressors or see them suffer, but is instead the complete dismantling of the system, so that victim and victor are words that lose all meaning. This is what Jesus effects and shows, since he is, in our language, victor and victim all at once, precisely by living among society's outcasts and exposing the lie of the system in his forgiving presence. Yet might this approach not effectively minimize the horrific violence that so many are subjected to? Does it ultimately dismiss it too quickly as too unimportant? Perhaps one way of thinking about it is to think in terms of standing with the victims and outcast. In such solidarity, we do not stand against other people, or the victimizers, but instead against the entire system which creates such categories. The distinction is a subtle, but important one, and it is how Alison is able to take real human suffering seriously while also asserting forgiveness as the only way forward, without it being but a blithe white-washing of historic evil. There is one area, though, that I think is pertinent to the question of salvation, and which Alison may not take seriously enough: responsibility.

A major issue I have with Alison's argument is that he seems to treat all humans, since we are all involved in the same mechanism of violence and expulsion somehow, as equally complicit or guilty. This makes him

54. Ibid., 165.

downplay the serious issue of responsibility and how it should be taken up by victimizers, no matter who they may be. It seems that he treats the acceptance of responsibility as synonymous with the acceptance of forgiveness. Thus, when he presents a parable of Abel coming quietly in the night, from beyond the grave, to forgive Cain, he says of the latter:

> This process of remembering his brother is not at all pleasant for the old man, since at every awakening to what had really happened, it shakes him to see what it was that had been driving him ever since then, what strange and fatal mechanisms of love and hatred interlaced; and his whole story of wandering, of searching for shelter, of killing and driving out to protect himself; all stand revealed as unnecessary.[55]

Cain understands, finally, by the forgiving encounter with his brother that much of his life as it was lived had been unnecessary. He is sorry for this. Yet at no point does he express contrition for his murder, but rather for the effects it had upon himself. This is a troublesome point, but at the same time, it is also one that challenges me. After all, Abel is clearly shown as one who, being able to forgive, does not need his brother's humiliation or contrition to be fully alive. It seems parallel to the father in the Parable of the Prodigal Son embracing his child, even though the son has shown little contrition (and, despite his words of apology, may not feel any, since he was mainly coming back because he was hungry). Does this, in fact, tell us something of the way of God—that human acceptance of responsibility is not as important as we think, since what is more important is that we stop living in the system of expulsion? Or is it instead, somehow, the "cheap grace" that Bonhoeffer warned against? To use an extreme example, is it enough for his salvation that Hitler simply realize that he need not have lived his life as he did, or is it rather necessary to take cognizance and responsibility for the massive damage that he inflicted? When our victims are not, like Abel, dead and beyond our capacity to harm, doesn't forgiveness and our acceptance of it have something to do with firm amendment of our ways? I will return to this point below.

It is clear that, for James Alison, salvation is ultimately rooted in what Jesus does in his cross and resurrection. By the innocent victim rising from the dead, we are able to see that God has nothing to do with the system of expulsion and violence that we live under. Through the power of the Holy Spirit and the memories that she keeps always before us, we are thus able to

55. Ibid., 133.

enter into this life and imagination, completely free from death, that Jesus possessed and live accordingly, imitating him by siding with all the expelled in the dismantling of the system. This process is not easy, or one that demands anything less than the complete overhaul of our ways of seeing reality, but this is what will ultimately allow salvation: the complete union of all humanity around God in loving solidarity, forgiving one another and yet denying nothing of who we are or have been, in a state where victor and vanquished cease to exist.

Subversion of Apocalyptic

Having discussed the general layout of Alison's thought, it would be useful to discuss the way he approaches the apocalyptic texts that appear in the New Testament, and how these both contrast with the eschatological imagination he describes—living without reference to death as Jesus did—and are subverted from within by Jesus. After all, many of the parables and language of Jesus seem to give evidence of a violent God, one who casts evil-doers into Gehenna.[56] This seems to contradict Alison's larger point about Jesus teaching us about the utter vivacity and non-violence of God.

In Alison's reading, the apocalyptic texts of the New Testament are best explained as examples of Jesus subverting the common imagination of his day. Apocalyptic as a genre precedes Christ and, as is shown by the preaching of John the Baptist and aspects of the Qumran texts, was a common vocabulary in his time. According to Alison, apocalyptic is built largely on two dualisms: social (good/evil, pure/impure) and cosmic (time and its violent ending in cosmic justice). This is the "imagination" that is created by this genre, but it fails to grasp the utter vivacity of God. Jesus uses this imagery and understanding, but he does so in order to challenge it from within, to show that instead of the violent God who comes from outside to rescue the pure and righteous, something else is going on. Apocalyptic thinking is subverted from within.

Alison discusses many examples of this, but I will focus on what may be the most famous case, that of Matthew 25 and the Parable of the Sheep and the Goats. On the common reading of this text, at the end of time Jesus will come as judge to separate the pure from the impure, the good from the wicked. Judgment is his and will be meted out, sending some to everlasting

---

56. See, among other examples, Matt 5:22, 29–30; 10:28; 18:9; Mark 9:43–47, and Luke 12:5.

fire. Alison, however, sees something radically different going on. In fact, Alison reads this not as some sort of prediction of heavenly retribution against the wicked, but entirely a statement about *now:*

> This is in no way a description of a future gathering beyond the grave. Rather, with all the splendor of apocalyptic language, the time in which we live is being qualified. The criterion for judgment is already present in the midst of the world; we do not have to wait until later. The criterion for judgment is the victim which is the principle of separation just as victim. [. . .] The final judgment adds *nothing* new to what has been lived out in the here and now. [57]

The end is subverted and becomes about what goes on now, with God's reign already breaking forth in the person of the innocent victim(s). There are no longer pure/impure people as there are in apocalyptic, and it is precisely how the outsiders are treated that becomes the criterion for access to the kingdom.

The concept of judgment is subverted as well. Rather than being an extrinsic process by which God separates those who are evil from those who are good, it now becomes an intrinsic proposition. Adhering to a way of life whereby some are to be excluded based upon worldly judgments is to place oneself outside of Jesus' way of life and example; it is to imitate the wrong source: "Those who, with all their spirituality and their adhesion to an established religion, have accepted the world's judgment on those [liminal] people, have been scandalized by them, Jesus knows not."[58] To make this clearer, Alison tells of when he first came to understand this way of "divine judgment," when he was working with AIDS victims in South America. He was accustomed, as I think we all are, to hearing some say that AIDS was a divine punishment—a judgment—against certain kinds of people and behavior, and this accordingly implied that nothing really needed to be done to alleviate their suffering: judgment from above had befallen them. Who are we to cast doubt on the dictates of God? Alison agrees that divine judgment was at work here, but in an inverse way:

> By separating ourselves from our sisters and brothers in need, alleging reasons of religion to boot, we run grave risk of eternal fire, because God's judgment arrives as the clamor of the neighbor in need. The judge is judge as victim. Whoever attends them confronts no judgment. Those who do not *have already separated*

57. Alison, *Abel*, 157, emphasis in original.

58. Ibid., 157–58.

themselves into goathood. I think that AIDS, for example, might be interpreted as a judgment of God, but it works as a question: a catastrophe has occurred; are you prepared to ignore the judgment of this world and stretch a hand toward those who are on their way out of existence? Or are you separating yourself into goathood, thinking yourself a sheep?[59]

Judgment, in other words, does not come at some end where we will be divided up from a mass; that judgment—that dividing—happens now, within history, based on our treatment of those the world judges as impure. Divine judgment, such as it is, is simply a passive permission that allows us to separate ourselves as we wish. The end result is the same—our exclusion from a salvation that is necessarily communal—but the agent is not a vengeful God, but ourselves, in the very acts by which we isolate ourselves from others. This is the eschatological, deathless imagination that Alison says Jesus uses to subvert the worldview of apocalyptic.

This subversion from within has many close parallels to the way that many queer thinkers talk about gender, not least Elizabeth Stuart. What Jesus is doing in these parables is what she would call parody, or repetitions with critical difference. Alison does not refer to this process of subversion as queer, but it is easy enough to see how it is. Though he is a gay man, and most of his work after this book specifically addresses that fact, the way that queer techniques saturate this text show Alison as, I think, a queer thinker. Eschatology, for him, is about subversion of the scripts in which we live daily—not pretending they don't exist, but rather playing with them from within in order to show forth their non-ultimacy, to demonstrate other ways of being. Paradoxically (or not), this internal subversion allows him to give a strong critique of a great deal of queer politics.

As we've seen, one of the main tenets that Alison gets from Girard is that most human activity is conflictual, since we learn our desires from another, yet that desired object then becomes a source of conflict between us. We each want the same thing, and some of these cannot be shared or purchased, they are singular and unique. This, in turn, can lend to a constant back and forth of recrimination, of both contesting and accepting the views that others have of us. Though the victim is the center of Alison's thinking, it is also possible to distort this, to create ourselves as victims in

59. Ibid., 158. When Alison refers to fire here, he is using it in a pedagogical, not prescriptive, way. As von Balthasar has discussed, there is nothing in Catholic teaching that indicates that any person is actually in hell: see Balthasar, *Dare We Hope*.

order to cast a disparaging eye on our victimizers. Our tendency to grasp hold of an identity—to assert who we are—rather than allowing that to be gifted to us by God, can cause us to define ourselves primarily against some oppressive other, rather than recognize ourselves as implicated with them. We canonize ourselves as victims in order to cast our oppressors as the ones who should *really* be expelled.[60] Alison makes this point explicitly in the context of much gay and queer politics since the sixties:

> [T]he emphasis of all that seems most bizarre and shocking in gay life was the consolidation of victim-status *by buying into a bad reputation*. The self-canonization of the self-victim. Thank God there has been no shortage of self-criticism of this tendency within gay culture itself, coming from people who only want to be thought of as just another human being: a pacific part of an "us," and not an "us" defined violently over against an oppressive and hypocritical "them."[61]

This tendency is delusional, because it masks our own hypocrisies and compromises, but more importantly, it simply reverses the same mechanisms of which we know the stings. It still allows our identity to be defined by a violent other. The only other who can grant us a life free of violence, for Alison, is the Other:

> The glory of heaven, the recognition which re-creates, is not given by the mere fact of having garnered for oneself a reputation as a rejectable transgressor in this world, but is given to those who, on account of their unconcern about their reputation according to the glory of this world have been able to stand loose from what is thought of them as they grow in solidarity with *things that are not*.[62]

Following the One who rejects no one, while giving no thought to whether one is earning a "good" or "bad" reputation from this, is what leads to transformation.

---

60. This is not simply an *ad hominem* against others for Alison, for he gives a lengthy discussion of his own move from this kind of thinking in "Confessions of a Former Marginaholic."

61. Alison, *Abel*, 184. It should be noted that this is not unique to gay or queer politics for Alison, as he goes on to say immediately following the cited portion: "The same process can be detected in almost all social groups demanding rights and probably in the relational history of all of us to a greater or lesser extent."

62. Alison, *Abel*, 185, emphasis in original.

Alison is not here advancing a moralistic critique of "gay culture" or "queer politics." He is not issuing this critique based upon some sort of hostility to "bad" behavior, but rather the motivation behind much of that behavior. As far as he is concerned, the reasons that much gay activism has focused on the supposedly scandalous and *outré* has less to do with genuine liberation as much as it does the human need for recognition, even if that recognition is for being "wicked." I once was at a talk by a queer activist (whose name I sadly cannot recall) who said that since we were often made to feel ashamed of ourselves, we needed to embrace this and thus act shamelessly. This is where we would find "liberation." But Alison is exactly right, for this is simply the flip side of shame, and still allows those who hate us to define who we are going to be: what is shameful will change over time, and its embrace simply because it is hated by others is the very definition of reactionary. Self-canonization as the "wicked oppressed" is not fundamentally different from self-canonization as "righteous." The same underlying mechanism creates both.

Struggles with Alison

Though I find the above critiques to be completely cogent and valid, I still find myself reacting against some of Alison's work. I find it both powerfully poignant and challenging in the best sense of the term; at the same time, I find some aspects troubling. Here, I would like to return to my point about responsibility and contrition. In his parable of Abel's return to Cain near the end of the latter's life, Cain seems mostly to be concerned with what has gone wrong in *his* life. At no point does he ever show any true realization of the evil he inflicted on his brother. Yet, can there be genuine transformation without some semblance of contrition? And if restitution is possible in a given case, is not amendment of ways key to reconciliation?

Or might it be that contrition is being shown in another way? Clearly there is no point at which Cain says to his brother, "I'm sorry for what I did," but the whole point of Alison's image is to show that Cain is nonetheless being transformed, and repenting in the truest way. Throughout his life, Cain has been roaming and wandering—terrified that someone will carry out the lynch on him that God has banned. After all, he was able to do to his brother what God had forbidden, why couldn't someone do it to him as well? This is clear evidence that Alison's Cain knew he was guilty of something, knew he had committed a terrible crime. He even knew it when he did it, since he tried to evade responsibility. Had he not known that he had done a terrible thing, he might have answered God precisely as to his brother's location, not the (in)famous, "Am I my brother's keeper?" (Gen 9:4). Alison makes it clear that this entire encounter with Abel is a terrible trial for Cain, waiting for the accusation that he feels *must* come, but never does. By truly receiving Abel's forgiveness, Cain can, for the first time in his life, approach his brother without envy and without fear: Cain "begins to glimpse that at the end of this trial he may have no physical strength left, but with all the strength of his heart which is unfolding into youth, he wants to kiss his brother before dying, the rest does not matter . . . ."[63] Whether or not Cain has spoken the words, relationship has been not only restored but transformed. Is that not the entire point of contrition?

Moreover, is this not the way that Jesus deals with those who should have been legitimately afraid of recrimination? What must Peter have felt when he heard of the resurrection? Not only bewildered confusion, the glimmerings of a hope he dared not entertain, but also, I'd think, some measure of fear. What would Jesus say to him? How could he face him after his denials in Christ's hour of need?[64] Yet how does Jesus, in fact, greet him when they are face to face? "Peace be with you." No recrimination, no expectation or need for self-flagellation on Peter's part. In John 21:15–19, Jesus asks Peter three times if he loves him—undoing the threefold denial—but this is not the same thing as Peter saying "I'm sorry." Isn't this what's going on with Abel and Cain? If one has a problem with this approach, doesn't she also have a problem with that of Christ? May not the point be that concerns about this are due to one being bound in this violent mimetic system that Alison describes?

One of the admirable things about Alison is that he doesn't claim that he is somehow "outside" this, but rather describes where he would like to find himself with respect to it. Like so much else in queer approaches, this violent system isn't something we can simply exit and stay out of. It's part of our formation as persons—according to Alison it *is* our formation as persons—and we can no more walk away from it than we can from gender or sexuality. But we can subvert it and begin the process of learning to live outside of it, with neither recrimination nor guilt. This is precisely what Alison means by the "time of Abel." As he says:

---

63. Ibid., 132, ellipses in original.

64. Alison raises similar issues about Peter in *Abel*, 92–94.

The task is to live in the midst of this, learning not to be scandalized either by oneself or by the process, nor by finding oneself living out simultaneous contradictions. [...] The only one who can cease fleeing from [the fear of the lynch and our oscillations from violence to violence] is the Cain who accepts forgiveness, accepts that he has no city, and that there is no need to seek to found it, because the Son of man has no place, like Cain, and his story is built wherever, and has no abiding city, because the new Jerusalem is coming down from heaven.[65]

As I have said, I find this quite compelling, especially in the long advent that is our lives on earth. But here is a different case.

A woman is being brutalized by her husband. She truly loves him, and believes that he, indeed, loves her. In fact, after every beating, unlike Cain, her husband actually apologizes and shows contrition, even swearing never to do it again. The woman consistently forgives him, in the hope that this forgiveness will effect some change in him. And then she is beaten again. Alison says that his reading means that, like Jesus, we will risk our lives by entering into this forgiving paradigm. But aren't there some lives that are already at risk? Doesn't the commandment to love our neighbor as ourselves require that we also have a degree of self-love, of not allowing ourselves to be brutalized needlessly? Now, I don't think that Alison intends his work to justify this kind of situation, but isn't there a way in which it nonetheless could, especially for some women who have been taught, with no shortage of Scriptural support, that their proper place is always to be nice and docile, submitting meekly to their husbands? Wouldn't forgiveness in this case be something much less free than Abel's? And isn't it important that Abel can give his forgiveness in part precisely because he's dead, just like Jesus grants his to Peter after the resurrection? Cain can no longer harm his brother, should the forgiveness be refused and transformation fail to occur. How can we simply retroject post-resurrection forgiveness and life into our own?

I think that Alison began to think about this question a little later than the text we've been discussing. In his essay, "Re-imagining Forgiveness," he discusses a bit more clearly what he means by the concept. Most importantly for him, he makes it clear that forgiveness is a creative act, something that changes a "you" and an "I" into a proper "we." It does not allow us to seal ourselves off from others, but rather to recognize how much we are like the person we have to forgive. It does not give us a claim to self-righteousness,

65. Ibid., 137.

but rather awareness that we are stuck in the same patterns as the other person and that we *have already been forgiven*. This is key. Forgiveness is not simply an act of will on our part to keep saying "Ok" to those who do evil to us, but is instead a recognition that we are both loved and forgiven already, and thus we are *given* the strength to forgive others, not simply call it up within ourselves: "I suspect that the first step in this task is to go through the effort of coming to see oneself as a recipient of forgiveness: in short, not someone who is primarily a victim and secondarily a forgiver, but someone who is primarily forgiven, and for that reason capable of being a forgiven victim for another, without grasping onto that, or being defined by it."[66] So passive taking of violence is certainly not what Alison means. Real forgiveness can only come about by recognizing yourself to be first loved, and loved deeply. Those who are in a cycle of passively taking abuse usually do not recognize their inherent worth and value. Were that not the case, the woman in question could both forgive from her heart, in a way that may indeed be transformative, and yet also decide that she can no longer live with this man.

In fact, Alison also states that,

> You forgive them by living with them with the twin attitudes of the wisdom of the serpent, knowing very exactly how to slither away to avoid being trampled on when danger is around, but the innocence of doves, who do not think ill of those whom they are seeking to forgive, nor are in any sort of rivalry with, but are able to give themselves "sacrificially" as it were to [those addicted to death], having the power to make of it the best show they can.[67]

But, in his view, this must be a free act of creative power, not the defensive or knee-jerk response of one being terrorized. It is *not* about moralizing or bending our will to that of someone else, but is instead "the straightforward objective way by which any of us can be created. It is only by a process of undergoing 'being undone' from various traps, dead ends and ensnarlments that any of us can be brought into being."[68]

This, however, raises a further problem: Alison tends to both treat all sins equally and he ignores the importance of power disparities. Mark D. Jordan asks, in reference to a different, but related, text of Alison's:

66. Alison, "Re-imagining Forgiveness," 38.

67. Ibid., 43.

68. Ibid., 44.

Pope and dissenter may be reversible in some acts of imagination, but they are not in institutional fact. [. . .] Alison knows this, of course. He has suffered himself. Still he insists that most forms of resistance simply continue the cycle of sacred violence, and so urges "brokenness" or even "death" as the way towards grace.[69]

Even if one finds this approach to be both compelling and, indeed, freeing with regard to oneself, what of our obligations to others? Isn't there a way in which Alison's approach makes it difficult to defend the weak and vulnerable, precisely because such action will often appear as violent? Can resentment and anger not be tools that further changes for the better? That which is beautiful as a homiletic reflection, as Jordan terms it, might become dangerous as a generalized recommendation. Does he move too quickly to the "in-breaking" of our eschatological hopes without attending enough to the very real disparities and violence that afflict too many in this world? It is this danger that I fear Alison does not attend closely enough to. The fact is, sometimes standing in solidarity with those who are oppressed—which Alison clearly defends—means standing *against* the oppressor. Not by seeking their destruction, but also not simply taking their violence passively; especially not in allowing *others* to take the violence passively. To stand with the battered woman I mentioned, we may have to stand against the husband. If forgiveness requires us to require her to take the abuse, it has become obscenity.

Wendy Farley also critiques the language of forgiveness, particularly if we fail to attend—as Alison does fail to do—to its history as a tool of gender control:

> The rhetoric of patience and endurance slides smoothly, seamlessly into a demand that the insulted and injured remain passive. Forgiveness is demanded of those who become angry or denounce injustice or talk about racism, economic injustice, or fiscal irresponsibility within the community. If some sharp stone of anger pricks someone's breast, the demons inside her head consort with the community's propaganda: "If you are only more patient, if you love a little longer, if you always forgive, if you quell your anger, you will save him. Love conquers all. By patient suffering, Christ saved all humanity, including your worthless hide. What if He asks of you a little forbearance? Besides, he cannot really hurt you; your soul is safe with Christ. And what about the children? Have you thought of them? Or are you so selfish you only consider your own

---

69. Jordan, Review of *Faith beyond Resentment*, 447.

happiness?" Many women know these voices only too well, but the demons are glad to afflict anyone motived by love with its evil twin, duty. Distortions of love crush those with a gift for love with a thousand reasons why they should never be angry, never live their own dreams, never leave an obligation unfulfilled.[70]

Alison offers a picture that I find quite compelling, but it will remain deeply problematic—perhaps even impossible—unless he is also able to incorporate a proper place for anger and resistance. If forgiveness only serves to blunt these, then it becomes a tool of power and the status quo, and loses the liberating energies that he lays out so beautifully.

Brian D. Robinette lays out a schema of analysis for resurrection language that may be useful in clarifying where Alison goes wrong. Robinette states that there are three overlapping "grammars" that must be present for any account of resurrection (and its corollary aspects, like forgiveness) to be complete and not distorted. The first of these is associated with apocalyptic language and the thirst for justice. He calls this grammatical mode "reversal": the unjust, deadly, destructive aspects cause grief and must be ended, must be reversed. The second mode is "double reversal," which correlates to reconciliation: this mode prevents the first from simply becoming an inversion of a deadly situation where the victims become new oppressors. Finally, the third mode is "fulfillment," which emphasizes continuity and speaks in the language of manifestation and participation of all of creation in God.[71] Alison is very good on modes two and three, but his fear of the dangerous possibilities of mode one taken in itself makes him neglect it and this, in turn, leads to the issues I've been discussing above. Alison is completely correct that there is a temptation to revenge in mode one, but it need not be the case, and to ignore it (or have it "subverted" too quickly and easily) neglects a vital and necessary aspect of the Christian tradition that, absent, leads to its own dangers.

The reaction I have to Alison is different in kind from that I have to Loughlin. With him, my critiques are more properly academic and intellectual; with Alison, something visceral happens. In part, this is precisely because of the strength of his arguments and the beauty of his presentation. I *want* to act as he describes, without resentment, without violence.

70. Farley, *Wounding and Healing of Desire*, 87, paragraph break elided. This critique is all the more powerful because Farley tends to see the power of the cross in the same terms of Alison: it exposes the innocence of the victim, placing a break between suffering and "just deserts," see Farley, *Gathering Those Driven Away*, 162–64.

71. Robinette, *Grammars of Resurrection*, 184–85.

But I also *need* that my non-violence does not end in other bodies being strewn upon the ground. Many of my general concerns about contrition and responsibility may be answerable through his interpretation of creative forgiveness, but I still fear something is lacking in his analysis of violence against the innocent other, or more specifically, lack of discussion on this point. As a generalized approach I think these are important questions that Alison has not yet sufficiently addressed.

The Eschatological Wedding Feast
. . . and Wedding Night

Still, there is much of value in his work, and much that allows us to think creatively about Christian eschatology. As is evident from the preceding discussion, Alison's entire approach to the subject makes it about the in-breaking of God's reign within our lives now, in history. His attention to the "hereafter" is thus much more muted, though he admits that it is only there that the fullness of our story will stand revealed and understandable. Nonetheless, Alison does not neglect the future entirely, for his final chapter in *Raising Abel* is precisely a reflection on heaven and the kingdom as the wedding banquet of the Lamb. Continuing his discussion on the eschatological parables of Jesus, and how they subvert our need to divide reality and people into good/bad, pure/impure, insider/outsider, Alison emphasizes how all are called to this feast, regardless of merit. All are invited into heaven, not despite their sinfulness, but simply because it is irrelevant. This is the meaning Alison finds in Jesus' parable of the Wedding Feast (Matt 22:1–14; see also Rev 19:6–9).

Alison is not afraid to look more closely at this very traditional imagery, however. After all, those who are invited to this wedding banquet are not simply guests, but also the bride, the church. The erotics of this situation are obvious, but very rarely discussed:

> The wedding which is celebrated includes the completely loving interpenetration of bride and groom, in a relationship which makes of them one thing, a relation of infinitely creative fecundity, freed, of course, from all the tensions, rivalries, and complications which surround and diminish our experience and living out of things erotic.[72]

---

72. Alison, *Abel*, 191.

We are desired by God, not despite who we are, but precisely in who we are. We are desired even as the sinners whose erotic lives are marred by rivalry and tension, yet in which we find glimmers of the Bridegroom who yearns to unite with us. This realization of our belovedness can serve to fire the imagination that Alison has been describing throughout his work, letting us begin to live this interpenetration of God and humanity—the cosmos, actually—in history.

Alison does not mention this point, but his use of the term "interpenetration" strikes me as both calculated and significant. The English term is one of the ways that the difficult Greek word *perichoresis* is often translated. In Christian theology, the word usually refers to the interaction among the persons of the Trinity, their distinction within unity. They are not the same, but they constantly interpenetrate one another; it is impossible to talk about one having a "beginning" or "ending" where another takes over because they are constantly and eternally implicated in one another. Distinct, but united; the same, but different. *Perichoresis* is often thought about in terms of a dance, especially a dance-in-the-round, where movement takes place but no one is going anywhere. It is an image of dynamism that also allows for a kind of changelessness. Alison's use of the term to discuss our relationship to God in paradise is a way of showing a deeper meaning to Christian eschatology. It is not only that we are saved, but that we are invited to enter into the very life of God, a life where interpenetration and desire define the persons of the Trinity. Salvation is being able to enter into the very erotic life of God, because of the prior entering into human life of God in Christ. We find ourselves back with the axiom we started out with in the Introduction: God became human that we might become God.

The wedding banquet has been one way to think about this heavenly life, but I do not think it is the only way. In fact, the neglected erotics of the language allows us to the think in more "earthy" directions as well. There are images of paradise that are not simply of the wedding banquet, but also of the wedding night.[73] But this is indeed a bizarre marriage, for it is not simply between me and God. Properly speaking, in Christian theology, the bride is not the individual believer baptized into Christ's life, but the corporate body of the church. My wedded bliss to God in paradise is also wedded bliss to all those who are united in the Divine Life, who are only the body

---

73. The two images also might not be as far apart as we'd like to think: remember that wedding banquets—in our time as much as in Jesus'—are not known for encouraging temperance and chastity. Their excess in celebration of eros is part of the appeal of the banquet image as an indication of the eschaton.

of Christ when they are many gathered into one. The erotics of heaven, in other words, is much closer to an orgy than it is to a sedate, proper wedding night of demure fumblings *à deux*. But this is not like any orgy that could exist on earth, either. It is one where the participants are united in the consummation of that covenant God made with all humanity through Israel, where all rivalries, fears, jealousies, and rancor are dissolved by the immediate presence of the Trinity.[74] After all, if we are to have resurrected bodies, doesn't it stand to reason that those bodies have a purpose in our heavenly lives and a role in our intimacy with all the others? Explorations of these implications using images of sexual intimacy get at some of the deeper insights of creedal belief in the resurrection of the body as both corporeal *and* corporate, and if they shock us into attending more to this difficult, but essential, doctrine, so much the better. I think one of these images can be found in the controversial, but powerful, film *Shortbus*.

Shortbus and the Orgy of the Lamb

John Cameron Mitchell's *Shortbus* is a rich examination of the intersecting lives of various broken people looking desperately for connection, intimacy, and love. It is (in)famous because the actors (and director) engage in

---

74. Thus, none of what follows should be read as an endorsement of unthinking and unloving promiscuity or utopian sexual projects in a world still mired in sin. Nonetheless, I find the image of orgy useful for thinking about resurrected bodies—and resurrected relationships—for a few reasons. First, as suggested above, the resurrection of the body is a core Christian belief that many Christians fail to adequately ponder. Many think of paradise as disembodied, a functional immortality of the soul only. The orgy image attempts to take seriously both our bodily natures in heaven and the reality that Christian hope teaches a paradise of us *together* in God's presence, not simply a collection of individuals relating to God alone. Secondly, it accounts for a desire that many do have to express intimacy sexually with many persons. Even if one would never do so because of the obvious risks and dangers, fantasy and imagination are not irrelevant to the spiritual life or theology. After all, that abjected desire may be pointing us towards something that we cannot achieve in history, but may enrich the holy paradise with God for which we yearn. Finally, many Christian images for heaven seem to make it a pretty dull place. The theological profundity of the reflections notwithstanding, there is a reason many more people have read Dante's *Inferno* than his *Paradiso*. Too often our images of life united with one another in God are lifeless, no doubt owing to the Platonic equation of perfection and stasis. This image is an attempt to suggest an alternative. Nonetheless, it is simply meant as an image among many others; some will find it useful, others not. The sex is a figure of complete intimacy—body, soul, and spirit—but as to whether there will actually be sex in heaven I claim no knowledge, any more than those more partial to images of "heavenly banquet" can say that eating will be part of heavenly life or not.

on-screen sex acts that are not simulated, but the film is not, to my mind, either pornographic or exploitative, even though it is often explicit and even raunchy. Indeed, the title was changed from *The Sex Film Project*.[75] It is about human relationships and the difficulties of achieving them. The film is lush with analytic possibilities, but due to space constraints, I will simply discuss two of the main characters—Sophia (Sook-Yin Lee) and James (Paul Dawson)—and how their lives come together in the club/commune/orgy that is Shortbus, a place for the "gifted and challenged"; a place for queers of all stripes.[76]

The audience first encounters Sophia in a mélange of sexual acrobatics with her husband of several years, Rob (Raphael Baker). Though impressive in their flexibility and creativity, there is something oddly manic about their couplings: a whiff of desperation is present. Rob and Sophia are not connecting as Sophia thinks they should and this is symbolized by Sophia's inability to have an orgasm, the running issue she faces throughout the film. When we next see her, she is acting in her professional capacity as a couples' counselor/sex therapist (the difference in nomenclature is a running joke, where she prefers the former but everyone else seems to see her as the latter) to the gay couple, Jamie and James. After hearing their problems, she breaks down and confesses the issue she is having and they invite her to meet them at Shortbus, a New York club where it seems anything goes.

Sophia meets them there one evening, and, with the audience, tours the facilities. Though there is a room where group sex goes on (the "Sex, Not Bombs" room), Sophia seems uncomfortable in it and instead engages in conversation with various people, including a group of lesbian women who share their orgasmic experiences with her.[77] She reveals her basic

75. Alfonso, "Permeability," 121.

76. The following will contain spoilers, so consider yourself warned, dear reader.

77. The lesbians have a separate room in the club, called the "pussy parlor." For a brief analysis of how this space encapsulates a host of tensions between the queer and women, see Alfonso, "Permeability," 123–24, fn. 10. Many have pointed out issues surrounding not only women, but other minorities in the film. As Nick Davis observes, "This 'spectrum' [of encounters], however, obeys evident limits. For instance, the lone avatar of the elderly [Tobias] [. . .] is summarily abandoned by the willowy male-model object of his desires [Ceth] in favor of a telepathically promised threesome with two shapely gym specimens [James and Jamie]. [. . .] One diegetically abrupt shot, ostentatiously inviting overweight bodies into the film's erotic party, cruelly frames its subject so that her head is cropped right out of the shot. The actors' palette of melanin tips heavily toward the lighter registers, especially in the centerpiece 'Sex Not Bombs' room of the Shortbus salon, and at least on surface evidence, no one manifests any of the forms of disability

straightness when asked if she's ever been with a woman, confessing she's "not wired that way." On her way out, she observes a couple (Leah and Nick, played by Shanti Carson and Jan Hilmer) that she had passed entering the club, engaging in passionate, but gentle love-making. Sophia makes eye-contact with this woman as she climaxes, and it is clear that a connection is formed, even if we—and she—don't understand exactly what kind.

After trying masturbation and sex toys in order to experience orgasm, and failing, Sophia invites Rob to come with her to the club to explore. Though they are going to go in their own directions, Sophia inserts a vi-brating "egg" into her vagina that Rob can control with a remote control, to "check in" whenever he wants. This attempt at playful intimacy goes terribly wrong, however, when Rob loses the control—he seems quite uninterested in the whole endeavor—and someone else picks it up to control the televi-sion. This causes Sophia to spasm and contort, injuring several people in a scene that borders on slapstick before turning quickly to sorrow. Sophia discovers that Rob had lost the control and she is infuriated. She takes the toy out of herself, hurls it to the ground outside the club, and destroys it in an explosion of rage, frustration, and despair. At just this moment a brief brownout occurs, symbolizing the emotional anguish of the characters, an energy so intense that it threatens to short the city's power capacity.

Sophia makes new friends at Shortbus who attempt to help her, but she can't escape the feeling that she is somehow lying to herself, especially when she is counseling others about their emotional and relational prob-lems. During one such session, she can no longer handle the tensions and rushes out into the wilds of Central Park towards the sea, where she tries once again to masturbate on a park bench. Despite the ferocity of her desire and hand work, she once again fails, and the city blacks out. In the dark-ness, she somehow finds her way to Shortbus . . . .

James is also striving for intimacy and love. He has been, for five years, in a committed, monogamous relationship with Jamie (PJ DeBoy), a for-mer child actor. We first encounter James filming himself in a bath, and then masturbating into his own face before breaking down in sobs. The next scene is also the second scene with Sophia, where Jamie and James are seeking her advice about whether they should "open up" their relation-ship to others. In the course of this session, and while he is again filming

---

that might secure passage on an actual shortbus:" Davis, "View," 626. I agree with many of these critiques, but do not think they negate the value of the film as an eschatological image. Rather, they indicate how much further our imaginations need to be changed to truly grasp the radical inclusivity of an eschatological imagination.

himself, the audience learns via flashback that James recently had to pull a dead body from the spa in the gym at which he works. The dead man "looks" directly into James' eyes after attempts at resuscitation, and the face that gazes from the corpse is both benevolent and serene. This triggers something deep in James, for he is seeking the same serenity and is unable to find it.

On the same night that Sophia first comes to Shortbus, James and Jamie meet Ceth (pronounced "Seth" and played by Jay Brannan), a young musician and sometime reluctant model. He comes home with them and, after some awkward conversation, the three have sex. In the course of this, we learn that James has never let Jamie penetrate him, despite their long relationship and obvious deep feelings for each other. Instead, James gently directs Jamie towards Ceth, handing his partner a condom.

While all this is going on, and unbeknownst to James and Jamie, they are being watched by a (surprisingly ethical) voyeur/stalker named Caleb (Peter Stickles), who lives in the apartment across the alley from theirs. The audience may have noticed that Caleb is always wherever James and Jamie are to be found, be it looking through the window of their therapy session or standing in the background at Shortbus.[78] The "Jamies," as they are collectively—and idealistically—known, have no idea, but Caleb is soon going to play a very important role in their lives.

On the same night that Sophia and Rob experiment with the vibrating egg at Shortbus, James and Jamie play a game of Truth or Dare with several other of the clubs' "guests, itinerants, and semi-strangers."[79] On a dare, James is sent into a closet with Severin (Lindsay Beamish), a professional dominatrix with a masochist's name.[80] Due in part to her openness about her sex work, James discusses his own past as a hustler and the brokenness left with him. Details are not given, but there is clear intimation of violence at the hands of some johns, and James reveals that he has never let Jamie fuck him. He needs to remain impermeable.

Finally, James' anguish leads to a not-unexpected suicide attempt in the pool where he works. He once again sets up the camera to video his

78. This is one of the reasons, among many others, that the film profits from multiple viewings

79. Davis, "View," 629.

80. Severin is a major character in the film and deserves more attention here, but due to space I cannot. Not only does her story enter importantly into that of James, but also of Sophia and Rob. She shares her name with the main character in the "original" masochist story, Leopold von Sacher-Masoch's *Venus in Furs*.

death, as he has all his intimate moments; he is only able to share them with another through the distancing of the camera's lens. He takes a handful of pills, ties a plastic bag around his head, and sinks below the surface. Fortunately, ever-present Caleb is there and pulls him out of the water and saves his life. Later, after leaving the intriguingly named Our Lady of Adequate Grace Hospital, James goes to Caleb's apartment so that he doesn't need to face Jamie, who is clearly shown panicking in the apartment across the alley. Here, James confesses that he was leaving the video as a suicide note to Jamie so that his lover would know that none of this was his fault. The suicide had been long-planned, and rather than simply "opening up" their relationship as Jamie thought, James wanted Ceth to become his replacement for his lover. When asked why he wanted to do this, James gives an excellent definition of hell:

> CALEB: Jamie loves you. You have so much . . .
>
> JAMES: I know, I see [love] all around me, but it stops at my skin. I can't let it inside. It's always been like that. It's always gonna be like that . . .

James is surrounded by exactly what he seeks and aches for, but cannot or will not allow it to enter in. It stops at his skin; his flesh—and the shame that it connotes—makes him literally unlovable.

The suicide attempt and encounter with Caleb function as a kind of purgatory for James. For reasons not made entirely clear—perhaps simply exhaustion at how he's been living—he asks Caleb to fuck him, and as he is being penetrated his mind goes to a host of images of himself and Jamie.[81] He tears up and, as he gently pushes Caleb out of himself, the room goes black . . . .

Before continuing on to a discussion of this pivotal blackout, where all the characters find themselves drawn to Shortbus, I want to discuss two things briefly. The first is the nature of the club itself. It cannot be reduced to a sex club, though sex certainly does go on there promiscuously and among strangers. The sex, however, is part of a larger matrix of creativity and shared self-expression. Under the benevolent (if sometimes bitchy) direction of Shortbus' mistress, Justin Bond, the club showcases music,

---

81. Among these is one of himself as a child with a person-shaped piñata, reaching into the ripped space between its legs for candy—perhaps hinting at a violent (and unwanted?) fisting that he once endured.

performance art, films of various genres, and simple conversation.[82] Desires are shared, screened, performed, enacted in this space where eros is free to flow and play. It is always an idealized space, where those of various body sizes, shapes, ethnicities, ages, and sexes appear to come together with limited rivalries and tensions.[83] This idealization—this unreality—is what makes the film useful for eschatological reflection. It would be very difficult to imagine such a place existing in historical New York, but less so in the transfigured City of God.

It is also a space that functions almost liturgically. There is a pivotal scene between Ceth and the elderly Tobias (Alan Mandell), a former mayor of New York who didn't do enough for those afflicted with AIDS in the 1980s because he was closeted, afraid, and impermeable.[84] In Shortbus, however, absolution and forgiveness come readily. As he reveals this to the much younger Ceth, the latter leans forward and kisses the old man gently. The betrayal the gay community felt from this mayor is absolved by a kiss, in a reversal of the encounter between Jesus and Judas.[85] Understanding, mercy, and compassion infuse Shortbus. Similarly, there is a Eucharistic promiscuity, of bodies giving themselves to bodies in delight and transformation, throughout. Indeed, though not in the club space itself, the film makes abundant use of water/baptismal imagery, especially at points of major transition, most obviously with James' attempted suicide. The waters, and his rising from them by the hand of another, bring him from death to a new life.

---

82. Justin Bond—most famous for his performance as "Kiki" in the "Kiki and Herb" drag shows and films—is playing "himself." I find that I cannot help being reminded of Dante and his "Pilgrim" as I think about this similarly fictitious self-performance.

83. Prior to the final scene, to be discussed below, there are fights and conflicts within Shortbus, but they are nonetheless open to the eschatological transformation I see depicted in the film. Kathy Rudy writes about the possibilities for Christian discipleship that clubs such as this (or, more specifically in her context, leather S/M clubs) exhibit in her problematic, but nonetheless important, essay "'Where Two or More are Gathered.'" She tends to idealize these clubs, neglecting the more eschatological dimension of her reflections, but the relationships and desires she describes are nonetheless useful.

84. Obviously based on Ed Koch, his name is never given in the film itself, but reads as "Tobias, the Mayor" in the end credits.

85. This depiction of forgiveness granted here is similar to Alison's reading of the Cain and Abel story, reproduced with a generational difference: the gay "father" who has betrayed his "child" is absolved and relationship restored. As the audio commentary on the Shortbus DVD makes clear, this scene was so important that it was one of the few performed exactly as written, not partially improvised.

Shortbus exists in a city that is, and is also somehow not, New York City. The film opens with an overhead shot (from the point-of-view of angels?) swirling around the metropolis, and the audience flies through the city from above. This is not a helicopter shot of NYC, such as opens *West Side Story*, however. Rather, the city is depicted in animation, with bright colors subsuming what is often—"realistically"—an urban gray, at least during the daytime. The city is made more beautiful than it is. The city is recognizable, with its bridges, Central Park, and the Statue of Liberty. But it is somehow different.[86] It is shown as the city might appear to those with different eyes, divine eyes. The entire space of the film is one that is both familiar and different, seen through the eyes of those who understand its final, consummated destiny in transfigured beauty.

The blackout that ends the film is, therefore, quite significant. It shakes the characters into new ways of living, symbolizing both their nadir and death, and also the new lives that are opening up. It is in the midst of this blackout, where the distractions of the modern world are laid to rest, that the club becomes most fully an image of paradise, one that goes through—and transforms—darkness. James and Jamie re-encounter one another. Jamie, desperately unsure of what to do about his lover's disappearance, looks out his window and sees James gazing at him across the alleyway from Caleb's apartment. James, however, is different. He has undergone his purgation and is now suffused with light, looking staggeringly beautiful. Though the audience knows that this light is ostensibly from the candles filling Caleb's apartment, it looks different. James is illuminated from within; he is transfigured. He has gone through a profound baptism and finds himself resurrected, through the ministrations of a strange Samaritan. The distance separating James and Jamie is decisive here. It was only in leaving Jamie, in withdrawing, that James could find the salvation he needed. He is now able to return and bring his lover along with him into a new kind of transfigured living. By allowing himself to withdraw into the mystery of his own existence, James can now allow the love Jamie (and, through Jamie, the Erotic God) offers to enter and penetrate. Jamie, in turn, seems to recognize this. We would expect that he would be furious: here he has been in anguish over James' absence and there he is calmly standing so close by. This is not,

---

86. Actually, this is not simply the case of the city, but the cosmos as well: when Sophia fails to achieve orgasm on the seashore and the city goes black, the camera pans upward and we see the moon, stars, and sky similarly transfigured by animation.

however, what we get. Instead we see a smile and a look of merciful delight come across his face. Jamie can let James be, and be with him, all at once.

The two go—together with Ceth and Caleb—back to Shortbus. It too is suffused with a new light, one that transfigures those caught in its glow.[87] As the characters come together in this space, Justin Bond begins a song:

> And as your last breath begins
> Contently take it in
> 'Cause we all get it in
> The End.

As this bizarre angel (are there other kinds?) sings this eschatological hymn, the persons in the club begin to join with one another, showing in their bodies the gratuitous gift that they have been given by Justin in this place. Sophia and Rob exchange looks of mercy and forgiveness. They let each other go and start to kiss and have sex with other people. They embody Loughlin's dispossesive desire: they love each other still, but that love can open to others, and rather than jealousy, they can delight in the delight of each other. Caleb and Ceth start to make out, and it looks like James finally allows Jamie to enter him. Around the club, others start to join into couples, trios, and otherwise. Some simply watch and smile, while others dance and sing along. Yet they are together, and acting in community to the rhythms of Justin's song.

The scene begins quietly and tenderly, and grows more and more passionate as a marching band—coming seemingly from nowhere—enters the club and joins in with Bond. The music becomes more percussive and loud, and the activity becomes more and more orgiastic. This is not, however, a violent orgy, but rather the Orgy of the Lamb. The bodies give themselves to one another Eucharistically, where the sex is a figuration of complete intimacy—body, soul, and spirit in the embrace of Light and Love. In the case of Sophia, no particular attention is given to the sex or gender of those she couples with: all that is significant in this new intimacy and connection is that they are in this place, a heavenly space of loving exchange. Nick and Leah, who we have seen earlier, invite Sophia into their love-making and, with them, she finally achieves the orgasm—the human connection, the erotic delight—that she has been seeking. Zooming in tightly on Sophia as she finally climaxes, the camera rapidly pulls out. She is the focal point of the club, which is focal point of the city. From her and it emanate a light

87. As Michael Bernard Kelly has pointed out to me, this imagery is also redolent of the liturgical rituals surrounding the Great Paschal Vigil of Easter.

that flows outward and we zoom up with our angelic camera to see light flow back into the city from Shortbus. Unlike its loss in the blackout, when it switches off in sheets according to the power grid, the light now comes in a way that is not explainable by electricity and its flow. It is an inner light, powered by desire and love, that illuminates the city, and then the country, and finally the world as the camera begins to spin and finally fades to black. The eschaton has come, and all is consummated in the light, and life, of Divine Eros.

As Alison has pointed out, this eschatological context changes the way the characters can view their past lives. Rather than simply understanding his years as a hustler as a dark time that must be moved beyond, those years are brought into the transfigured reality of the "new" James, who remains still the James he has always been. All of his history, his story, his past are brought into this new "resurrected" life, not annulled. The film makes this point through the lyrics of Bond's song, which includes the line that, in the end, "your demon is your best friend." Nothing, even that which we fear—our personal demons—is left out in salvation, the new communal life of resurrected bodies entering the Triune dance in promiscuous delight.

I find the images in Shortbus to be provocative and beautiful. They cannot, however, be adequate. One element that is lacking in my discussion is any clearly depicted presence of God. I certainly believe that Divinity is animating the love—emotional, physical, spiritual—among the persons, but God is still somehow not present, or at least not in the immediate way that we hope for in Paradise. If I simply accepted this as sufficient, I would be falling into the same analysis that I critiqued Ward for in chapter 1. If God is reducible to our loves and affections, what pulls us even deeper? Is God simply the candlelight that passively illumines the room? If so, isn't that too weak an image to fulfill our deepest longings for the Divine?

Yet is this a particular failure on the part of Shortbus, or is there something about eschatological imagery and language that militates against complete portrayals? If we were to depict God as a figure among the other characters—the Old Man with the Beard, the Ancient of Days, or even Alanis Morrisette[88]—aren't we reinforcing the view I have hoped to dispel throughout this work, that God is an object among other objects, or actor among other actors? But if God is not representable as a figure, what could

88. She plays God in Kevin Smith's interesting—if deeply flawed—Dogma (Miramax, 1999).

it be? Looking at the semi-eschatological end scene of *Angels in America*,[89] which projects hope, sadness, and the coming of a New Project, angels are present, but either as stone or watching silently from above. They are there, but they are not active; despite this, they still capture a hope for a future the characters long for. Yet angels are not God. In Norman Rene's *Longtime Companion* (Samuel Goldwyn, 1989), many characters who die of AIDS are reunited at the end upon the beach, in a deeply effecting scene of ached-for reunion. This is closer to the eschatological vision of *Shortbus*, but there is still no overt role or place for God, of whatever stripe. I cannot, in fact, think of any clear case of God being depicted in a film with eschatological thrust that does not reduce the Divine to the inter-connection of the characters or a figure separable from them. God as present in interpersonal connection is a vital element to a theological account of eschatology, but it is not sufficient, in itself, for a complete representation of eschatological hope, of seeing God "face to face." Thus, these gaps in cinematic representation are not, I would argue, artistic failures, but rather necessary absences for a presence that we yearn for, but cannot hope to depict. There are reminders and hints, however, that only something more can keep this desire flowing, that it might not end in stasis. May that help drive us, together, into the arms of the Beloved who awaits us all.

The zooming shot from New York in *Shortbus* is not the same garden with which we began this chapter and reflection. It is closer to the city imagery that Graham Ward utilizes in *City of God* than that of *The Garden*. Yet both are properly eschatological images, and both go well together—after all, the transformed New York has also a transformed Central Park. Cities, like gardens, are places that are full of both hope and despair, and Jesus goes forth from the place of resurrection to Jerusalem (cf. Luke 24:33–49). From there, however, he goes to the Father, expanding his body so that all bodies become implicated in it. The church—the body of Christ—will become like a Shortbus in paradise, when all the rivalries that Alison discusses are turned, via dispossessive desire, to delight in the bodies and lives of all others, united in the life—the body—of God.

89. Kushner, *Angels in America*.

Ways Forward for Christ's Queer Body?

I stay in the Church because the Church is more than its ignorance; the Church gives me more than it denies me. I stay in the Church because it is mine.

—RICHARD RODRIGUEZ[1]

SOMETHING BROKE ON NOVEMBER 30, 2005 between me and the Roman Catholic Church. I was twenty-four years old and had been discerning a vocation to the Catholic priesthood for years. I was also gay, and had spent years struggling with it, determined to be a Good Catholic Boy. I hadn't even been able to come out to myself, much less anyone else, until 2002 when I was twenty-one years old. And even when I did this, it was to a trusted spiritual advisor and my immediate family only. As far as I was concerned, it really didn't change much. The Church taught that one could be homosexual and not "practice," and that was fine. Naturally, this is what I was going to do: I was, after all, a Good Catholic Boy. I had been celibate to that point in my life; I couldn't imagine why that would need to change.

After completing my undergraduate education in 2002, I taught religion for two years in a Catholic high school. The first of these years went perfectly well, but with a slight nagging that wouldn't let up. The vast

---

1. Rodriguez, *Darling*, 117–18.

majority of what I was teaching—Christology, ecclesiology, social justice, church history—was not problematic for me at all. But when it came to teaching freshmen about "sex and chastity," there was something wrong. I presented the official teaching on homosexuality, and attempted to do it in a compassionate way by focusing on passages like this from the *Catechism*:

> The number of men and women who have deep-seated homo-sexual tendencies is not negligible. They do not choose their homosexual condition; for most of them it is a trial. They must be accepted with respect, compassion, and sensitivity. Every sign of unjust discrimination in their regard should be avoided. These persons are called to fulfill God's will in their lives and, if they are Christians, to unite to the sacrifice of the Lord's Cross the difficul-ties they may encounter from their condition (para. 2358).

This wasn't too harsh, after all. Compassion, respect, the counsel of the cross.[2] These are things one should expect from Christian teaching. But then the next paragraph says that those with "deep-seated homosexual tendencies" are called to chastity, which in this case, means celibacy. But isn't celibacy a special gift of God, one that not all persons can honestly live out? When Christ speaks of becoming "eunuchs for the kingdom" (assum-ing that this is in reference to renouncing marriage and sex, which is con-tested), doesn't he say that not all can do this (cf. Matt 19:10–12)?[3] Where does this leave those who have "deep-seated homosexual tendencies" and are not given the gift of celibacy?

Further, I knew something that I didn't share with these students. I knew that the Catholic Church had a much less capacious definition of "unjust" discrimination than I would; some kinds of discrimination, in fact, were explicitly just according to Church officials. As far as they were concerned, I really shouldn't have been in front of those students teaching in the first place. According to a 1992 Statement of the Congregation for the Doctrine of the Faith, "There are areas in which it is not unjust discrimi-nation to take sexual orientation into account, for example, in the place-ment of children for adoption or foster care, in employment of teachers or athletic coaches, and in military recruitment."[4] At exactly this same time,

---

2. For a critique of the damage this kind of cruciform counsel can do, see Crowley, *Unwanted Wisdom*, especially 104–26.

3. For discussion of various ways this text (among others) was interpreted in the early church, especially around the male body, see Kuefler, *The Manly Eunuch*.

4. Congregation for the Doctrine of the Faith, "Some Considerations," para. 11.

people with "deep-seated homosexual tendencies" were being scapegoated for the clerical abuse scandal that had erupted the previous year. The only way, under this regime, I was able to have my job at all was to keep my mouth shut, but that was becoming harder and harder. There were certain students in my classroom who were visibly wounded by these teachings on "intrinsic disorders" and as much as I could try to explain "authentic" Catholic teaching to them, it's very difficult not to get the message that, at best, one has some kind of disease and, at worst, one is God's regrettable mistake. All one's loves are somehow tainted and suspect, for any of them may somehow be infected with this evil desire. The sexual and affective urges that I was telling most of the class to direct into appropriate channels in marriage (pun intended), these students simply had to suppress. There was no "proper ordering" of them save by their elimination. Worse still, I, who was complicit in the laying of heavy burdens, could not—or at least would not—lift a finger to ease them, because of my own fears, insecurities, secrets, and lies.

This culminated in what I can only describe as a mental breakdown that began the summer before my second year teaching and ended in October. I would get sick whenever I ate, losing over thirty pounds by the time it was all over. I had panic attacks when I tried to teach. Eventually I was diagnosed with severe depression, generalized anxiety disorder, and obsessive-compulsive disorder; I was put on medication, and, after several weeks, was then able to return comfortably to the classroom. At this point, I had already been in counseling for years, and I was coming rapidly to the conclusion that I simply couldn't live this way. As non-ultimate as my gayness might very well be, I was forcing myself to deny a significant aspect of my own life, and for reasons that were, at best, unpersuasive. I am convinced that this whole experience was nothing less than the activity of the Spirit, showing me where my lies—even in the service of what I was authoritatively told was the truth—would lead. My attempt to be a Good Catholic Boy was psychically and spiritually ripping me apart. I knew I couldn't be teaching in a Catholic high school, so I decided to go to graduate school and try to explore some of these issues.

One would think that after all this I would have lost a great deal of faith in the Catholic hierarchy. It's true that I had basically concluded that the teachings on homosexuality (as well as birth control) were deeply flawed, but I also accepted that heterosexual marriage was somehow "normative" and that the Catholic bishops were basically trustworthy. They overstated their case and didn't give much pastoral help, but clearly these were just oversights. I had studied enough theology to know the acres of nuance that surrounded phrases like, "The bishops speak for God and the Tradition," but I essentially thought it true in a rather literal fashion. In hindsight, the Church had become, for me, an idol. It could not be wrong when it spoke in God's name, because in my mind, *de facto* if not *de jure*, it was God, and the diktats it issued were holy writ.

My experiences teaching began to undermine some of this easy equation between God and Church authority, but I still left them essentially unquestioned. When I went to Notre Dame to begin my Master's studies, ecclesiological questions were not at the forefront of my mind. The Roman Catholic Church was my church, and I was comfortable in it.

During 2005, rumors began circulating that a document was being prepared by the Congregation of Catholic Education in Rome about the admission of homosexual men to the seminaries. Much was written on whether it would simply reaffirm existing practice, by saying that these men would have to be celibate and accept the Church's teaching on homosexuality, or else go further and ban them outright as scapegoats for the sex abuse crisis. Even after what I had seen of the violence that Church teaching on this subject could inflict, I was absolutely sure that the document would not impose a total ban. Rome simply could not be that cruel and ignorant. The priesthood was full of gay men, and to claim that they should never have been ordained would be an act of extreme violence. For me personally, the priesthood was a "safe-place" for my own gayness, for it was a space where one could be unattached to a woman and still be praised rather than judged. The ideal of the priestly body was one with which I resonated, a body that was not simply male and not simply straight: it offered space to play with these identities.[5] It was inconceivable that Rome would rip that place away. Further, ample evidence of the devotion and holiness of gay priests had recently been dramatically demonstrated when Fr. Mychal Judge was killed while anointing wounded and dying rescue workers at the World Trade Center on 9/11. The Vatican could simply not be willfully blind to these considerations—or so I reasoned.

I was wrong. When I finally read the document on November 30, 2005—my name day as it happened, the Feast of St. Andrew—it announced

5. This was still true in my mind, but the "safety" of the priestly body had been severely—and properly—undermined by the revelation of widespread sexual abuse and cover-up. Though the priesthood gave this queer boy a place to imagine himself differently, it was based on an underlying clericalism that is dangerous and best discarded.

the ban that I was sure would not come.[6] I was flabbergasted. I felt as though I had been savagely attacked, not by strangers, but by those I still—somewhere, somehow—regarded more as parents. I went outside to a bench in the freezing South Bend air, called my mom, and wept. It was the first time that I really understood that the Church's teaching on this question was not, in fact, simply misguided; it was a lie. They claim that if you live a good, decent, celibate life, you live a life pleasing to God. But they didn't mean it, for if that were true, why was I not fit to be a priest? It seemed no more than window-dressing to mask the underlying cruelty of their view. This Letter, in fact, precipitated my final outing, when I wrote a rather intemperate letter to the Notre Dame *Observer* decrying the document. By banning me from the priesthood, the Vatican helped me to accept and live more fully the incongruity between being gay and Catholic, yet in a way that did not require me to sacrifice one part of myself to the other.

Thus, in hindsight, I am incomparably grateful that this Letter was issued. It shattered an idol I had been worshipping secretly, so secretly in fact, that I didn't even know it myself. The object of my real worship, my real awe, my real adoration was not God, but rather a particular kind of authority—an authority that allowed me to inhabit a world without contradictions or unanswered questions. Of course this, like all idols, was a lie, and it was precisely the awareness of the contradictions and tensions that sent it plummeting from its pedestal. For perhaps the first *real* time, I saw that the bishops and pope were men. They had authority because of their position, but they had no particular, special insight. What came from their

---

6. It was not interpreted as such by most bishops and religious superiors. Though I don't have the space to detail why I think these interpretations are wrong, I am convinced that the document meant to ban any priest with "deep-seated homosexual tendencies" and not simply those who would not be celibate or who "embraced the gay lifestyle" (whatever that means). It meant to ban anyone that I—and probably you—would describe as gay. The fact that it has not been implemented with this interpretation does not mitigate the force of its intent—later reaffirmed by the Cardinal Prefect of the Congregation—or the cruelty of its reasoning. If anything, the unwillingness of the world's bishops to challenge its logic and instead pretend that it says what it clearly does not say speaks volumes about the power of institutional silence on this issue, a silence which will only be exacerbated as more and more gay men enter the seminaries and are forced to lie about their orientations in order to maintain their place: Congregation for Catholic Education, "Concerning the Criteria." Benedict XVI also affirms a total ban, claiming "Homosexuality is incompatible with the priestly vocation" and that even *celibate* homosexual clergy manifest "one of the miseries of the Church": Benedict XVI, *Light of the World*, 153. For a view that agrees with my interpretation, but gives a reading so charitable that, it seems to me, certain facts must be ignored, see Alison, "Letter to Friends."

pens in this Letter was so evidently not the voice of God, not what I had been discerning in my own life and the lives of those around me, that I was actually set free from a particular kind of enslavement.

I am, as I said, grateful for this, but that doesn't make it particularly easy. Constitutionally, I am a person who likes clear authority, who finds it comforting and stabilizing. And even though this experience destroyed certain idols, it also allowed me to take more seriously the authority of the Christian community as a whole, not simply those who are appointed to lead it. Yet trying to discern the Spirit's actions within a messy amalgamation of humans, with all their own issues, fears, and insecurities, is a difficult—if exciting—project. In some respects, the shattering of my illusions about the hierarchy has allowed me to see more clearly the church as a whole as the body of Christ—bishops and pope included, but as members, not dictators. But as I've been discussing throughout, this is a queer body indeed, and life within it is anything but simple and stable.

At this point, many readers will wonder why I simply did not abandon Christianity or, at the very least, Roman Catholicism. Why did I not go to a more supportive and affirming church, such as the Episcopalians? The simplest explanation for the first concern is that this rejection by the hierarchy was never experienced by me as a rejection by Christ. As such, their violence at no point registered in my mind as a reason to abandon the loving Jesus I had been coming to know. I did not learn Jesus from the hierarchy, but from the much larger church, especially from grandparents, parents, teachers, and friends. Likewise, after coming out, I discovered that, unlike the bishops, these people—those I experienced most as church in my local communities and friendships—were not about to reject me due to my orientation. This is what I mean when I say above that this experience helped be to discern the Spirit more in the church universal, and not simply in its leaders. Catholicism is, for me, intimately bound up with family, friends, and warm, loving communities of worship. These were just as real, if not somehow more so, than the violence of the hierarchy. The latter did not in any way annul the former, but if anything broadened my own understanding of Catholicism. Something indeed broke the day I read that Letter, but something else was strengthened.

In addition to this, there is a way in which, despite my own various issues, the Catholic story, from its attention to the mysteries of the incarnation to its troubled, bloody missteps, is somehow *my* story. I resonate with what I read in histories of the medieval church in a way I simply do not with histories of eighteenth-century Anglicanism or Lutheranism. There is a way in which I feel connected to figures like Thomas Aquinas or even a vile pope like Alexander VI, which has no analogue in those other Christian traditions, even among figures I deeply respect and admire like John Donne or the other metaphysical poets. I do not understand precisely what this connection is, but it is nonetheless there.[7] There is also an ancient monastic view whereby stability—staying where God has placed you—is part of our discipleship. This has implications for contemporary ecumenism as well, as Robert McAffe Brown says in speaking of his own relationship to Protestantism:

> The critique must be an expression of loyalty. To criticize Protestantism is not to have entered a halfway house on the way to Roman Catholicism. Wherever a Christian finds himself [sic] within the family of Christendom, it is his job to stay there unless it becomes clear to him that it would be positively sinful for him to do so. [. . .] My task in terms of the coming great church is not to jump over into the Catholic Church or into another Protestant denomination, nor do I really want "progressive" Catholics to become Protestants. I want them to work for reform and renewal *within* the Catholic Church. Each of us must see that the stream of Christendom in which we have been placed becomes a more faithful transmitter of the Gospel.[8]

Despite these strong anchors in the Roman Catholic tradition, despite that it is the communion into which God has baptized me, I nonetheless find myself doing theology "amidst the stones and dust" of collapsed sanctuaries and ruined temples.[9] Much has changed in my own approach to my faith, and much has required re-negotiation. Idols once adored have fallen, but this has allowed the invisible presence of the True God to reveal herself more clearly—and queerly. The separation effected between hierarchy and God did not annul what I had learned from the Christian community, but rather strengthened it, and allowed me to explore it with eyes less afraid

---

7. As I hope is clear from this whole chapter, this is *not* intended as any kind of judgment on those who do not find the same connections or leave the Catholic Church for one they find more spiritually rewarding. It is evident, I trust, that these connections are always in tension with a profound dis-ease about much of contemporary Catholicism. I am here simply saying why I have chosen not to join a different community, not to judge anyone else for doing so.

8. Grandfield, *Theologians at Work*, 19.

9. The phrase is James Alison's: see Alison, "Theology Amidst the Stones and Dust."

to find God in spaces where the official Church refused to look or countenance. This is the great value of queer theology and the authors I have been discussing. This has been the gift that they have given me, even when it is difficult, imperfect, or I even disagree with it. With them, I can look at the creedal Catholic-Christian tradition in which I stand and explore its seams and lacunae. I can see God as far queerer than I had ever imagined, and yet have it be the same God that I had been worshipping all my life. I need not turn my back on the Catholic tradition that has so shaped and formed me, simply because I now see its leaders more clearly. It is still the body of Christ, but a much freer and capacious body than I had dared hope. By allowing me to explore these issues with them, with others who find the collapse of the modern ecclesial system (one based on the unquestioning assent of people to hierarchy or other authorities[10]) a sign of hope rather than despair, the authors I have discussed have helped me to live amidst these bare, ruined choirs with confidence and trust in the continued power of the Holy Spirit's activity within the Christian community. This side of heaven it is not always easy to inhabit the queer body of Christ, so it is good to be reminded that one is not alone.

I cannot help but notice that this collapse of ecclesial authority is correlated with the collapse of rigid gender and sexuality binaries.[11] In my particular case, they are certainly deeply connected. My movement from the heart of the Church as a Good Catholic Boy to its margins was correlated with my letting go of another identity that I had tried for years to shore up: that of heterosexual male. The multiple identities I now bear are not always simple to reconcile with one another, and at various times and in different places, some are more evident and important than others. This is precisely why queer theology is such a necessary project today, especially for those who take the tradition as embodied in the creeds seriously and as normative. The collapse of stable identities doesn't happen simply for gay, Catholic

10. There are many attempts by the hierarchy to reestablish this monolithic view of church which was the dominate one before Vatican II, but I interpret these as the last gasp of a dying system rather than the beginnings of genuine renewal. For the vast majority of Catholics, the bishops are simply irrelevant to their day-to-day lives of faith, though if more bishops chose to follow the lead of Pope Francis, this could change, with genuine authority flowing out of genuine encounter.

11. I wonder if the hierarchy did not notice this correlation as well, since they have become much more insistent on reaffirming and reifying the modern constructions of these categories in recent years. Why this may be—whether because their power depends on clear, stable identities and conceptions of gender, or some other reasons—is an intriguing question that I cannot address more adequately here.

men; the challenges some of our identities have on others is perhaps *the* key aspect of postmodernity. The growth of women toward equal places at the table in secular society has made it much harder to be a woman in a society like the Catholic Church, in which only men can exercise authoritative office; simplistic categorization of masculinity coupled with the rise of "metrosexuality" has made it more difficult to unbundle male, gay, and straight identities from one another; and there is increasing evidence that the younger generation is much less committed to any of these identity categories in the first place. This trend is not simply limited to sex and gender and their roles in our churches, either, but could be multiplied to include myriad others, such as our identities as consumers (for example, the rise of a "cult" of Apple), our nationalities (am I an American or a citizen of a globalized and shrinking world?), ethnicity, and even family.

Thus far, I have discussed these issues of identity as though they were self-contained, distinct units that clash disconcertingly together somewhere inside a person. This is both for purposes of clarity and because they are often experienced as such, but I think this approach is also misleading. The queering of identities is not only about the exposure of fluid boundaries *within* a given identity (for instance, sexual attraction to male or female and its relative fluidity in many people discussed under the rubric of "sexual orientation"), but also about the permeability *between* identities. I have already discussed the way that my gayness has impacted my Catholicism, which in turn impacted the performance of my maleness, especially when I was thinking about the priesthood. These identities form and shape one another, and cannot be considered simply as pre-formed puzzle pieces that need to simply be fit together: they act on one another as a constantly operative jigsaw, reforming and changing boundaries with constantly shifting edges. Queer approaches do not create this interaction; they simply expose it.

For some, this fracturing of homogenous identity or, perhaps better, of multiple identities that seamlessly fit together, is viewed primarily as a threat. I, like the authors discussed here, think that it provides wonderful opportunities to re-think and re-imagine our communities and relationships. This fluidity need not be viewed as simply the destruction of an idealized past, but rather an invitation to play and grow together. This kind of play does make it difficult, though, to demarcate clear boundaries, and even challenges their necessity.

This reality may help account for both the prevalence of the church as a subject in this book, as well as the "fuzziness" around its precise meaning. I come out of the Roman Catholic tradition, and remain committed to it, but when I speak of the church, I am well aware that I am using the term in a far broader sense than official Catholic ecclesiology permits. "Catholic"—open, universal both geographically (worldwide) and temporally (the communion of saints that have preceded and will follow us), liturgical, sacramental—is an identity of central importance to me, but increasingly the "Roman" part is becoming less decisive. I suspect that there are many other Christians in similar situations, not only with their own ecclesial communities, but also in their relationships to authorities like the Bible. How can one live and think through these various tensions? How can one do so while also remaining part of Christ's body?

This text has explored several key aspects of the Catholic-Christian tradition: the incarnation, the body of Christ, the sacraments, and our eschatological hopes. In each case, aspects of the tradition have been used to subvert rigid interpretations with more flexible ones. In other words, the tradition has been queered. Part of what queer theology provides are the tools and methods for remaining within certain traditions and places—ones that cannot be exited or may even be valued, despite hostile elements—while simultaneously undoing some of their more violent tendencies, or at least moving in that direction. These tools call for a greater openness and fluidity—not through the outright rejection of our identities, but also not allowing them to become "straight" jackets that close off avenues of love and connection. Queer theology as I have discussed it hopes to allow the Spirit room to transform us, to tell us who we are, rather than us trying to dictate the terms.

In many ways, therefore, this book has an apologetic function: it attempts to defend the Christian tradition in its best form, especially for the sake of those who are drawn to the gospel but repelled by many of the church's teachings that are, at best, incidentally related to the good news. It seeks also to be a counter-story to the moralism and modern hegemonies that have insinuated themselves as constitutive of the story of Jesus rather than being seen as the innovations they are.

Three aspects of the Catholic tradition have figured heavily throughout. The first of these is that the text takes a broadly analogical approach to the material discussed. Following Ward and Loughlin, this sense of analogy allows for an exploration not only of semantic similarities and differences, but also those that exist among persons, creation, and God. This is an *analogia entis*, but one that allows more maneuverability in terms than classically understood by that designation. For instance, the only strong ontological difference accounted for exists between God and creation, not within creation itself. This, in turn, permits greater fluidity in thinking about the relationship among differences within creation, especially among sexual and gender differences. Unlike current official Catholic teaching, gender differences are *not* ontological, but performative; they also do not exist as a simple dyad of male and female. Analogy in my usage has an apophatic purpose: by showing similarities in difference and, perhaps more importantly, differences within similarity, we are led to unlearn that which we think we know so well, allowing for new understandings and new relationships to emerge. The constant interplay of similarity and difference also emphasizes the essential mystery of the creedal topics discussed, which in turn permits a genuinely hopeful, but non-triumphalistic account of the Catholic-Christian tradition. Analogy in this sense allows us to gain real knowledge, but knowledge that is always marked by humility and openness to greater depths of understanding, and correction wherever it is necessary.

This apophatic analogy applies to the second area of Christian concern that this book dwells on: materiality and the mystery of our existences as embodied. Christ's resurrection as enfleshed emphasizes the importance of our bodies, as well as their essential unknowability and secrecy. It took me quite a long time to understand this. Years ago I read Henri de Lubac's *Corpus Mysticum* on the threefold body of Christ and the relationship between the various senses of body: historical and risen, sacramental in the Eucharist, and ecclesial in the church. Yet I could not understand how this was possible. I, like most of us, have held a very modern understanding of bodies in which they are autonomous, separate, and discrete entities that can be quantified and catalogued. If this account of the body is accurate, though, the traditional account of Christ's body makes no sense. How can it be both "in heaven" and on the altar? How can it be on multiple altars simultaneously? Even more of an issue, how can it possibly incorporate all the bodies of those who make up the church, without absorbing them into some kind of super-person? Absurdity added to absurdity. But what if, I wondered, our account of bodies is where the problem arises? What if, instead, we must first learn our bodies from Christ's, where it is enfleshed and specific, but in no way reducible to time and place? As the threefold body of Christ remains always Christ's body, but also more than simply Christ's body, how do ours exist and relate? My ultimate conclusion is that the best way to think of enfleshed bodies is that they are points and sites of intimacy offered and received. This is the point of the multiplicity of Christ's body: it opens up to greater and greater intimacy with all other bodies, finally the body of creation and the cosmos itself. This intimacy is not simply an extraneously shared closeness or proximity—though it can be mapped analogously in terms of distance and closeness—but rather a truly erotic love and desire: to unite in the most real, visceral, primal sense with all others. This union does not annul difference, however, but maintains it, that the intimacy between embodied selves is ever strengthened and deepened as fundamental mystery is explored and love exchanged.

Eros, then, is the third, and most contested, element of traditional Catholic thought that marks this book. Though conceptually important in much of the spiritual and mystical traditions, eros has often been viewed with suspicion, frequently even contrasted with agape. My approach follows that of Gregory of Nyssa, who thought of eros as agape brought to intensity. I also discuss it in terms of Loughlin's "dispossesive desire," where eros seeks to unite and overcome difference, but always as a genuine love that seeks the good, flourishing, and well-being of the other. This, it seems to me, is the most essential form of love, for it is the love that marks the persons of the Trinity and the deified life for which we hope. This emphasis on unity and intimacy obviously accounts for the way that eros is often viewed in terms of sexual love, but it is essential that it not be reduced to the purely sexual either. It includes the sexual, but is not at all exhausted by it. Our tendency to conflate the two has made it difficult for us to understand not only the past, where passionate friendship that did not imply sex was a straightforward commonplace, but also often our own feelings and bodily responses today.[12] Sex is a particular locus of eros, even a primary one, but we must not allow ourselves to reduce the erotic to the sexual. Therefore, these pages treat eros as the love with which God longs for us and that which will animate our deepest intimacies in the resurrection. It also allows us to visualize the church as the erotic community Ward discusses, but we must take our account of the church further if the desire for unity and intimacy that eros fires is to be made manifest.

12. For a critique of the way that modern scholars and activists tend to view erotic friendships in the past purely through the lens of sex and contemporary homosexuality, see Bray, *Friend*. For a contemporary attempt to recover a strong account of non-sexual eros, particularly that of mother and child, see Traina, *Erotic Attunement*.

Something seems to have cooled within the churches over the past several decades on the question of ecumenism. Many of the reasons for this can be traced to the hardening of various denominational identity markers, as my own story illustrates, and this makes me think that one of the next avenues ripe for exploration so that ecclesial eros might flow is the development of a queer ecclesiology. I can only speak from within my own church and tradition, but just as the identities "gay" and "straight," "male" and "female," "man" and "woman" need to be subverted to allow room for an ever-expanding multitude of characters and loves, so do our ecclesial identities. Denominational labels often serve to solidify "us" against some "them," in contrast to the genuine "we" that the Spirit works patiently—and erotically—to establish. For example, at least part of the motivation for the recent re-translation of the Roman Missal in English-speaking countries was not simply to bring it into closer alignment with some Latin original, but also to "Catholicize" it. The controversial document *Liturgiam authenticam*, guiding liturgical translations, states: "Great caution is to be taken to avoid a wording or style that the Catholic faithful would confuse with the manner of speech of non-Catholic ecclesial communities or other religions, so that such a factor will not cause them confusion or discomfort."[13] Ironically, as Maxwell E. Johnson points out, rather than the Catholic Church having been led into Protestant directions earlier, the Protestant churches had accepted much of the previous Catholic translations as their own. This great triumph for the ecumenical movement—one Rome claims to eagerly support—turned Catholic language into Christian language more generally. This success became a threat to a certain definition of "Catholic," however, and the new translations are partly in reaction to this.[14] In other words, a certain definition of catholicity seems to have become an idol for many in the Catholic Church, just as it once was for me: its preservation is seen as essential, even when this means undoing forty years of providential work towards Christian unity. A certain definition of "Catholic identity" has become more important than catholic inclusivity and openness.

This episode is a clear instance where denominational identities require queering.[15] One need not abandon those aspects of Catholicism or

13. Congregation for Divine Worship, "Fifth Instruction," para. 40.

14. Maxwell E. Johnson, "Ecumenism and the Study of Liturgy," 16–18.

15. Though my emphasis in on the Roman Catholic Church, I do not think that it is alone in this tendency to solidify certain ecclesial identities at the cost of greater movement against those "outside." Conflicts over homosexuality in the Anglican Communion, for instance, are as much about what it means to stand in that tradition and identify as

the other traditions that are genuinely life-giving and rich in order to allow greater play and fluidity in their structures, especially in relationship to our fellow Christians. In fact, there are aspects of the Roman Catholic tradition that already allow for this kind of subversion to begin. The Second Vatican Council both recognized the inter-connection of the church with the wider world and culture, and also recovered some aspects of early Christian thought on the communion of churches admitting of degrees. Some theologians, in fact, have already begun exploring these developments as ways to queer the current Catholic Church and allow it to move into a more flexible arrangement in relation to other Christians, and even the whole of humanity and creation.[16]

In *The Church Unfinished: Ecclesiology through the Centuries*, Bernard P. Prusak argues that Roman Catholic history already shows quite clearly that the structures of the church are variable and adaptable to given historical situations and locations. With the advent of a more historical consciousness among people over the past centuries, we have become more and more aware not only of what *has* happened in human history, but of what *could have* happened. In other words, we have become more sensitive to the manifold possibilities that exist within human life and culture. Vatican II's document *Gaudium et spes* took careful account of an eschatology in which there is a "future of history" that has a certain degree of autonomy and is open to human creation and construction.[17] This is not some Babelish rebellion against God, but is rather constitutive of how God creates: we are partners in the process and can make that which is genuinely new. Bearing this in mind, Prusak says, "Now the question to ask is, would God create through a process in which humans can choose among a surplus of possibilities for shaping a new future, but then completely predetermine the shape of the Church for all time? It seems unlikely." There is space for the church to become other than it is, while also remaining the same, both holding onto the gospel it proclaims, and boldly risking its own identity by allowing the Spirit to shape it. In addition to *Gaudium et spes* and its eschatological thrust—one that very much demands human effort and par-

---

Anglican—particularly its relationship to the Bible—as it is about sexual morality.

16. None of the authors below are particularly associated with queer theology, but they seem to me nonetheless to be engaging in its basic project of subversion of Catholic structures and ecclesiology in order to allow new forms of life to emerge. In other words, they use a similar approach to the one I discuss in the introduction when addressing queer as a strategy.

17. Prusak, *Church Unfinished*, 330.

ticipation—Prusak also reads Vatican II's *Lumen gentium* on the church as establishing a story of the church that covers much the same terrain that this book has: "*Lumen gentium* linked the origins of the Church to the trinitarian activities of creation, incarnation, and ongoing sanctification."[18] Within this framework, there is much work that can be productively done to queer the churches, that they might move closer to one another and, correspondingly, to God—whose innermost life and economic activity, I have argued, can only be described as "queer" within human categories.

Prusak's text is written primarily about the Roman Catholic Church, but it attempts to reach outside its boundaries to a wider ecclesiology. His method deals largely with "official ecclesiology" and is marked by the concerns that dominate it: structures of authority, who has final say in which circumstances, how various offices have developed, etc. There is a real question, however, whether these are in fact the issues that most Christians find particularly important. Raising this question is not meant to undercut the significance of these issues, but rather to set them in a more accurate framework. Do abstract questions of a bishop's theological authority, for instance, really energize many of the Christian and Catholic faithful? Are these issues, which have so long been the subject of ecclesiological debates, really the ones that most impact Christians on the ground level?

There is evidence to suggest that they are not. Forty years ago, shortly after Vatican II ended, Karl Rahner wrote an essay raising exactly these points. In this short piece, he coined the phrase "Third Church" to talk about the degree of practical, lived unity among the Christian faithful that exists across denominational lines. In the context he was addressing, it referred to the fact that more and more of Europe had moved out of state-sponsored religious enclaves, and thus many people who had previously been socialized into thinking that all other denominations were potentially hostile (both ecclesially and civilly), started coming into more and more contact with one another. When these people started to actually discuss and live their faiths together, they found that the differences they had been taught and which were still of primary importance to their leaders simply had little practical effect on their relationships with other Christians:

> [Confessional doctrinal differences] are, largely speaking, no longer realized at all, so that the modern Christian can hardly enter into the problems of controversial theology that used to exist, or feel in any way personally touched by them; and so he [*sic*] is

18. Ibid., 331.

bound to remain largely uninterested in the settlement of those questions, unless he clings out of pure loyalty to the denomination which has been passed down to him and to which he belongs as a simple matter of fact.[19]

Within my own tradition, this seems rather evident: most Catholics I know are not sure what makes them different from Lutherans (other than an obscure recognition that the pope is important), and those that most avidly defend "the tradition" and Catholic difference tend to be very superficially informed about it, often to the point that it is difficult to see their insistence upon their identities as anything other than tribalism, rather than informed theological positions. I do not want to overstate this, because the "pure loyalty" and "matter of factness" of one's ecclesial membership are not always expressed as facile fortress mentalities, and are often shaped by intense emotional and intellectual connections to family, friends, community, and history. There are ways of being committed, of being loyal, to traditions that do not use those traditions primarily as wedges against the rest of the world. That being readily acknowledged, however, it does seem to me that much recent discussion about Catholic identity does drift dangerously in the direction of constructing an "us" in opposition to some foreign or dangerous "them."

This "Third Church" is even more evident among queer Christians.[20] Coming from a multiplicity of different denominations, which have their own unique struggles and battles, many gay, lesbian, and transgender Christians have nonetheless found themselves being drawn closer to one another despite their confessional differences. The struggles that an Evangelical may have with the hegemony of certain scriptural interpretations, both intellectually and existentially, is analogical to the one that I have had with Church authority—and vice versa, if in less intense fashion for each. The strategies that we have learned to deploy, the lenses of interpretation that we have adopted, and most importantly, the conviction that Christ does not reject us but welcomes us as full members of his body bring us closer to one an-

---

19. Rahner, "Third Church?" 217.

20. And not simply for queers, either. Women, in particular, have often found the same solidarity across denominational lines in their mutual struggles for more voice and position within their churches. This paradigm is also manifested among non-progressive Christians, with Catholics and Evangelicals Together, and the journal *First Things*, being prime examples of Christians (and, to a lesser extent, non-Christians) from different denominations coming together in order to more effectively influence social policy in their preferred directions.

other than we are to many within our own denominations. Still, for a host of reasons, we may find ourselves either unwilling or unable to sever our ties with these same institutions that both cause so much pain and yet also form the matrix in which we have come to know and, however inchoately, love Christ and God through him.[21] It is precisely at this point that the need for a queer ecclesiology, one that subverts our denominational identities without utterly cutting us off from them, becomes important. What might this look like, though?

The Catholic theologian Roger Haight has attempted a project very similar to this in his three-volume work, *Christian Community in History*. Envisaged as an "ecclesiology from below," Haight sets out to show the wide range of ecclesial polities that have existed since apostolic times in order to establish the necessary grounds for communion among the churches, even if only partially. The work culminates in the third volume with an extended treatment of a "constructive transdenominational ecclesiology." Amid the staggering amount of divergences that Christians have enacted ecclesiologically over the centuries, Haight believes that we can nonetheless talk about an underlying level of common "ecclesial existence" that has remained surprisingly continuous since the days of the apostles. In fact, this existence is synonymous with a particular form of spirituality, defined as a dynamic way of life for those who embrace it: "Ecclesial existence refers to the apostolic faith in Jesus Christ as that is organized in the many churches that constitute the Christian movement. This ecclesial existence at its base is a way of life lived within the Christian community or by the community itself. But this is just the understanding of spirituality offered here: a form of life, lived in this case in community, with reference to the ultimate reality of God."[22] This common life of witness and commitment to Jesus Christ is lived within certain historical forms, is inseparable from them, and yet not reducible to them either. Moreover, these forms testify to a long process of development and change, where the greatest harms have been done not by too much transformation to new historical circumstances, but rather too little.

---

21. For purposes of brevity, I am simply discussing intra-Christian relationships, but it is important to note the multiple memberships that many queer Christians have with groups that do not consider themselves to be distinct denominations (the Metropolitan Community Churches, the Independent Catholic Movement) or non-Christian traditions (for example, the Radical Faeries or practitioners of various forms of Eastern spirituality). These issues would also have to be addressed in a more thorough queer ecclesiology.

22. Haight, *Ecclesial Existence*, 272.

In this work, Haight uses as his guideposts the documents of the World Council of Churches' Faith and Order Commission to guide his understanding of how a transdenominational ecclesiology can work, both by noting its possibilities and disadvantages. He challenges the hegemony and tribalism of certain ecclesial identities while also affirming their legitimate place. His project is not meant to replace denominational ecclesiology, but rather try to highlight where we already stand together. As such, this project is highly abstract, as abstract as the church is in the authors discussed in the chapters above. Haight doesn't view this as a liability, however, but rather as a means of allowing us to recognize one another in some partial communion that holds us in a fundamental, time-tested unity amid our many and strong differences. Questions can certainly be asked about whether this abstraction really allows us to move closer to one another, or simply covers over real differences by thinning out the definition of "church," but his emphasis throughout on plurality and unity-in-multiplicity, sameness-in-difference, makes his work resonate very much with queer theology.

It is also interesting to note, though he himself does not, that much in his final suggestions about the recognition of partial communion between the churches is itself an expression of ideas laid down in Vatican II's *Lumen gentium*. This statement on the church, as well as *Unitatis redintegratio* on the Catholic Church's relationships to non-Catholics, affirms that there is a real, if imperfect, communion that exists among all Christians via their reverence of Scripture and their common baptism in Christ, along with other elements that vary across groups. This partial communion *already exists*. As far as the Council was concerned, many necessary elements were lacking in many of these churches and communities, and the fullness of the ecclesial means of salvation "subsist in" the Catholic Church only. Yet many of these concerns are precisely the ones that have been existentially relativized for many Christians, as Rahner observed. Haight's use of the concept of partial communion seems a rich avenue for exploring how Christians can live together amid their numerous differences as true expressions of the single, united body of Christ. It takes what is already an accepted notion in many churches—though there are some which do not recognize any need for "communion" or find the language either unimportant or problematically sacramental, perhaps preferring "fellowship" or an equivalent—and recognizes that it can be taken much further than it has hitherto done.[23] An

---

23. Haight does not really push this concept very far, however, because his approach to "partial communion" is so explicitly tensive. Therefore, as far as the Roman Catholic

important concept already found in numerous groups may help unsettle many of their idolatrous attachments to their own solid identities. This seems a promising route for a future approach to queer ecclesiology, not only for discussing relations between denominations, but also the relationship of many *within* a given denomination.

As my own story shows, attachments to certain ecclesial forms have often drifted towards idolatry. Once one stands among their collapsed ruins, it is very difficult to know where to begin to rebuild. For this reason, the church must sometimes be treated in a very provisional, even abstract, way, because in this state of collapse what is essential and what is not—and how these relate to one another—are extremely difficult to discern. This is not, however, a necessary cause for despair in either the church or our fellow Christians. For as all the authors discussed in this book have been at pains to show, within these ashes are precious collections of liberating tradition and loving, Spirit-filled ecclesial practice. Christ is still present among us, even if we are in a situation where it can be difficult to know exactly where. The queer penchant for irony and parody gives us precisely the tools we need to form new ways of ecclesial life where all of those whom Christ has united in his body have both a place and a voice; we can enter into the constant process of reinterpretation and re-performance of traditions that have formed and shaped us, even in our queerness. The theologians I have discussed are signs of hope, and even when the road ahead seems dark and our enemies in the churches most violent, we might remember that the Spirit is praying and acting within us with inexpressible groaning (Rom 8:26) and that God will bring to good completion that which has been begun.

Church is concerned, it is unclear if his notion of partial communion really carries us any more forward than what that body already recognizes.

Bibliography

Ainsworth, Claire. "Sex Revisited." *Nature: International Weekly Journal of Science* 518.7539 (2015) 288–91. Also available from *Nature's* website: http://www.nature.com/polopoly_fs/1.16943!/menu/main/topColumns/topLeftColumn/pdf/518288a.pdf (Accessed February 26, 2015).

Alfonso, D. Rita. "Permeability and Impermeability in John Cameron Mitchell's *Shortbus*." *Radical Philosophy Review* 12.1–2 (2009) 121–36.

Alison, James. "Confessions of a Former Marginaholic." In *On Being Liked*, 65–77. New York: Crossroad, 2003.

———. *The Joy of Being Wrong: Original Sin through Easter Eyes*. New York: Crossroad, 1998.

———. "A Letter to Friends." In *Undergoing God: Dispatches from the Scene of a Break-In*, 220–30. New York: Continuum, 2006.

———. *On Being Liked*. New York: Crossroad, 2003.

———. *Raising Abel: The Recovery of the Eschatological Imagination*. New York: Crossroad, 1996.

———. "Re-imagining Forgiveness." In *On Being Liked*, 32–46. New York: Crossroad, 2003.

———. "Theology Amidst the Stones and Dust." In *Faith beyond Resentment: Fragments Catholic and Gay*, 27–55. New York: Crossroad, 2001.

Althaus-Reid, Marcella. *Indecent Theology: Theological Perversions in Sex, Gender and Politics*. London: Routledge, 2000.

———. *The Queer God*. London: Routledge, 2003.

Althaus-Reid, Marcella, and Lisa Isherwood, eds. *The Sexual Theologian: Essays on Sex, God and Politics*. London: T. & T. Clark, 2004.

Arsenault, Mark. "Worship in the Face of Rejection: Gay Catholics Find Community Despite Words from Rome." *Boston Globe*, June 27, 2011.

Athanasius of Alexandria. *On the Incarnation*. In *Christology of the Later Fathers*, edited by Edward R. Hardy, 43–110. Louisville: Westminster, 1954.

Augustine of Hippo. *Exposition on the Book of Psalms*. Edited by Philip Schaff. Grand Rapids: Eerdmans, 1984.

Balthasar, Hans Urs von. *Dare We Hope "That All Men Be Saved?" with a Short Discourse on Hell*. San Francisco: Ignatius, 1988.

———. *The Office of Peter and the Structure of the Church*. San Francisco: Ignatius, 1986.

Bibliography

Bauckham, Richard. *Jesus and the God of Israel: God Crucified and Other Studies on the New Testament's Christology of Divine Identity*. Grand Rapids: Eerdmans, 2008.

Benedict XVI. *Light of the World: The Pope, The Church and the Signs of the Times: A Conversation with Peter Seewald*. San Francisco: Ignatius, 2010.

Bersani, Leo, and Ulysse Dutoit. *Caravaggio*. London: British Film Institute, 1999.

Bray, Alan. *The Friend*. Chicago: University of Chicago Press, 2003.

Brown, Raymond E. *The Virginal Conception and Bodily Resurrection of Jesus*. New York: Paulist, 1973.

Burrus, Virginia. "Radical Orthodoxy and the Heresiological Habit: Engaging Graham Ward's Christology." In *Interpreting the Postmodern: Responses to Radical Orthodoxy*, edited by Rosemary Radford Ruether and Marion Grau, 36–53. London: T. & T. Clark, 2006.

Butler, Judith. "Beside Oneself: On the Limits of Sexual Autonomy." In *Undoing Gender*, 18–39. London: Routledge, 2004.

————. *Bodies That Matter: On the Discursive Limits of "Sex."* London: Routledge, 1993.

————. "Doing Justice to Someone: Sex Reassignment and Allegories of Transsexuality." In *Undoing Gender*, 57–74. London: Routledge, 2004.

————. *Gender Trouble: Feminism and the Subversion of Identity*. London: Routledge, 1990.

————. "Gender Regulations." In *Undoing Gender*, 40–56. London: Routledge, 2004.

————. "Introduction: Acting in Concert." In *Undoing Gender*, 1–16. London: Routledge, 2004.

————. "Undiagnosing Gender." In *Undoing Gender*, 75–101. London: Routledge, 2004.

————. *Undoing Gender*. London: Routledge, 2004.

Bynum, Caroline Walker. *Christian Materiality: An Essay on Religion in Late Medieval Europe*. Cambridge, MA: Zone, 2011.

de Certeu, Michel. *The Practice of Everyday Life*. Berkeley, CA: University of California Press, 1984.

Chrysostom, John. *The Catecheses*, 3. In *The Liturgy of the Hours: Volume IV—Lent and Easter*, 474–75. New York: Catholic Book Publishing, 1976.

Clement of Alexandria. *The Exhortation to the Greeks, The Rich Man's Salvation, and the Fragment of an Address Entitled "To the Newly Baptized."* London: Heinemann, 1919.

Congregation for Catholic Education. "Concerning the Criteria for the Discernment of Vocations with Regard to Persons with Homosexual Tendencies in View of Their Admission to the Seminary and to Holy Orders." November 29, 2005. Available from the Vatican: http://www.vatican.va/roman_curia/congregations/ccatheduc/documents/rc_con_ccatheduc_doc_20051104_istruzione_en.html. Accessed June 30, 2014.

Congregation for Divine Worship and the Discipline of the Sacraments. "Fifth Instruction 'For the Right Implementation of the Constitution on the Sacred Liturgy of the Second Vatican Council' (*Liturgiam authenticam*)." May 7, 2001. Available from the Vatican: http://www.vatican.va/roman_curia/congregations/ccatheduc/documents/rc_con_ccatheduc_doc_20051104_istruzione_en.html. Accessed June 30, 2014.

Congregation for the Doctrine of the Faith (CDF). "Some Considerations Concerning the Response to Legislative Proposals on the Non-Discrimination of Homosexual Persons." July 22, 1992. Available from EWTN: http://www.ewtn.com/library/CURIA/CDFHOMOL.HTM. Accessed June 30, 2014.

Bibliography

Copeland, M. Shawn. *Enfleshing Freedom: Body, Race, and Being*. Minneapolis: Fortress, 2010.

Cornwall, Susannah. *Controversies in Queer Theology*. London: SCM, 2011.

———. "Intersex and Ontology: A Response to 'The Church, Women Bishops, and Provision.'" Manchester: Lincoln Theological Institute, 2012. Available at the University of Manchester Religion and Civil Society Network: http://religionandcivilsociety.com/iid-resources/Intersex%20and%20Ontology.pdf. Accessed June 30, 2014.

———. *Sex and Uncertainty in the Body of Christ: Intersex Conditions and Christian Theology*. London: Equinox, 2010.

Crowley, Paul G. *Unwanted Wisdom: Suffering, the Cross and Hope*. New York: Continuum, 2005.

Davis, Nick. "The View from the Shortbus, or All Those Fucking Movies." *GLQ: A Journal of Lesbian and Gay Studies* 14.4 (2008) 623–37.

Doyle, Dennis M. *Communion Ecclesiology: Visions and Versions*. Maryknoll, NY: Orbis, 2000.

Dunn, James D. G. *Christology in the Making: A New Testament Inquiry into the Origins of the Doctrine of the Incarnation*. 2nd ed. Grand Rapids: Eerdmans, 1989.

Edelman, Lee. *No Future: Queer Theory and the Death Drive*. Durham, NC: Duke University Press, 2004.

Elizondo, Virgil. *Guadalupe: Mother of the New Creation*. Maryknoll, NY: Orbis, 1997.

Farley, Wendy. *Gathering Those Driven Away: A Theology of Incarnation*. Louisville, KY: Westminster John Knox, 2011.

———. *The Wounding and Healing of Desire: Weaving Heaven and Earth*. Louisville, KY: Westminster John Knox, 2005.

Foucault, Michel. "De l'amitié comme mode de vie," interview with René de Ceccaty, Jean Danet, and Jean Le Bitoux. *Gai Pied* 25 (April 1981) 38–39.

———. *The History of Sexuality, Volume I: An Introduction*. New York: Vintage, 1990.

———. "A Preface to Transgression." In *Michel Foucault: Religion and Culture*, edited by Jeremy R. Carrette, 57–71. New York: Routledge, 1999.

Fry, Peter. "Mediunidade e Sexualidade." *Religião e Sociedade*. (1977) 105–25.

Fuller, Reginald H. *The Foundations of New Testament Christology*. New York: Scribner's Sons, 1965.

Gaillardetz, Richard R. *Teaching with Authority: A Theology of the Magisterium of the Church*. Collegeville, MN: Liturgical, 1997.

Garber, Majorie. *Vested Interests: Cross-Dressing and Cultural Anxiety*. London: Routledge, 1992.

Granfield, Patrick, ed. *Theologians at Work*. New York: Macmillan, 1967.

Guardini, Romano. "The Church and the Catholic." In *The Church and the Catholic, and the Spirit of the Liturgy*, 11–116. London: Sheed and Ward, 1935.

Haight, Roger. *Christian Community in History*, Vol. III: *Ecclesial Existence*. New York: Continuum, 2008.

Halberstam, Judith. *Female Masculinity*. Durham, NC: Duke University Press, 1998.

Hall, Robert G. "Epispasm—Circumcision in Reverse." *Bible Review* 8.4 (1992) 52–57.

Halperin, David. *Saint Foucault: Towards a Gay Hagiography*. Oxford: Oxford University Press, 1995.

Hart, Kevin. "Response to Graham Ward." In *Sacramental Presence in a Postmodern Context*, edited by Lieven Boeve and Lambert Leijssen, 205–11. Leuven: Leuven University Press, 2001.

Hefling, Charles. "A View from the Stern: James Alison's Theology (So Far)." *Anglican Theological Review* 81 (1999) 689–710.

Hemming, Lawrence Paul. *Radical Orthodoxy? A Catholic Enquiry*. Farnham, UK: Ashgate, 2000.

Irenaeus of Lyons. *Against Heresies*. South Bend, IN: Ex Fontibus, 2010.

Irigaray, Luce. *Marine Lover of Friedrich Nietzsche*. New York: Columbia University Press, 1991.

Isherwood, Lisa, and Marcella Althaus-Reid, eds. *Trans/formations*. London: SCM, 2009.

Isherwood, Lisa, and Mark D. Jordan, eds. *Dancing Theology in Fetish Boots: Essays in Honour of Marcella Althaus-Reid*. London: SCM, 2010.

Jarman, Derek. *Dancing Ledge*. Edited by Shaun Allen. London: Quartet, 1984.

John Paul II. *The Theology of the Body: Human Love in the Divine Plan*. Chicago: Pauline Books and Media, 1997.

Johnson, Jay Emerson. *Peculiar Faith: Queer Theology for Christian Witness*. New York: Seabury, 2014.

Johnson, Maxwell E. "Ecumenism and the Study of Liturgy: What Shall We Do Now?" *Liturgical Ministry* 20 (2011) 13–21.

———. *The Rites of Christian Initiation: Their Evolution and Interpretation*. Revised and expanded edition. Collegeville, MN: Liturgical, 2007.

Johnson, SueAnn. "How is the Body of Christ a Meaningful Symbol for the Contemporary Christian Community?" *Feminist Theology* 17.2 (2009) 210–28.

Jordan, Mark D. Review of *Faith beyond Resentment: Fragments Catholic and Gay*, by James Alison. *Modern Theology* 19.3 (2003) 446–48.

———. "God's Body." In *Queer Theology*, edited by Gerard Loughlin, 281–92. Oxford: Blackwell, 2007.

———. *Recruiting Young Love: How Christians Talk about Homosexuality*. Chicago: University of Chicago Press, 2011.

Katz, Jonathan Ned. *The Invention of Heterosexuality*. New York: Dutton, 1995.

Kuefler, Matthew. *The Manly Eunuch: Masculinity, Gender Ambiguity, and Christian Ideology in Late Antiquity*. Chicago: University of Chicago Press, 2001.

Kushner, Tony. *Angels in America: A Gay Fantasia on National Themes, Part Two: Perestoika*. Revised Version. New York: Theatre Communications Group, 1996.

Lancaster, Roger N. "Guto's Performance: Notes on the Transvestism of Everyday Life." In *Sex and Sexuality in Latin America*, edited by Daniel Balderston and Donna J. Guy, 9–32. New York: New York University Press, 1997.

Laqueur, Thomas W. *Making Sex: Body and Gender from the Greeks to Freud*. Cambridge: Harvard University Press, 1990.

———. *Solitary Sex: A Cultural History of Masturbation*. New York: Zone, 2004.

Loughlin, Gerard. *Alien Sex: The Body and Desire in Cinema and Theology*. Oxford: Blackwell, 2004.

———, ed. *Queer Theology: Rethinking the Western Body*. Oxford: Blackwell, 2007.

de Lubac, Henri. *Corpus Mysticum: The Eucharist and the Church in the Middle Ages— Historical Survey*. Notre Dame, IN: University of Notre Dame Press, 2006.

McCabe, Herbert. "The Eucharist as Language." In *God Still Matters*, edited by Brian Davies, 123–35. New York: Continuum, 2002.

BIBLIOGRAPHY

————. *God Still Matters*. Edited by Brian Davies. New York: Continuum, 2002.

————. "He was Crucified, Suffered Death, and was Buried." In *God Still Matters*, edited by Brian Davies, 92–101. New York: Continuum, 2002.

————. "Sacramental Language." In *God Matters*, 54–63. New York: Continuum, 2002.

————. "The Trinity and Prayer." In *God Still Matters*, edited by Brian Davies, 54–63. New York: Continuum, 2002.

Martin, Dale B. *The Corinthian Body*. New Haven: Yale University Press, 1995.

Moore, Gareth. *The Body in Context: Sex and Catholicism*. New York: Continuum, 2001.

————. *A Question of Truth: Christianity and Homosexuality*. New York: Continuum, 2003.

Moore, Stephen D. "On the Face and Physique of the Historical Jesus." In *God's Beauty Parlor and Other Queer Spaces in and around the Bible*, 90–130. Stanford, CA: Stanford University Press, 2001.

Muers, Rachel. "A Queer Theology: Hans Urs von Balthasar." In *Queer Theology*, edited by Gerard Loughlin, 200–212. Oxford: Blackwell, 2007.

O'Connor, Flannery. *The Habit of Being: Letters of Flannery O'Connor*. Edited by Sally Fitzgerald. New York: Farrar, Straus & Giroux, 1979.

Peake, Tony. *Derek Jarman: A Biography*. Minneapolis: University of Minnesota Press, 2000.

Prusak, Bernard P. *The Church Unfinished: Ecclesiology through the Centuries*. New York: Paulist, 2004.

Rahner, Karl. "Third Church?" In *Theological Investigations*, Vol. XVII: *Jesus, Man, and the Church*, 215–27. New York: Crossroad, 1981.

Reck, Norbert. "Dangerous Desires: Catholic Approaches to Same-sex Sexuality." In *Homosexualities*, edited by Marcella Althaus-Reid, Regina Ammicht Quinn, Erick Borman, and Norbert Reck, 15–28. London: SCM, 2008.

Robinette, Brian D. *Grammars of Resurrection: A Christian Theology of Presence and Absence*. New York: Crossroad, 2009.

Robinson, John A. T. *The Body: A Study in Pauline Theology*. London: SCM, 1952.

Rocke, Michael. *Forbidden Friendships: Homosexuality and Male Culture in Renaissance Florence*. New York: Oxford University Press, 1996.

Rogers, Eugene F., Jr. *After the Spirit: A Constructive Pneumatology from Resources outside the Modern West*. Grand Rapids: Eerdmans, 2005.

Rodriguez, Richard. *Darling: A Spiritual Autobiography*. New York: Viking, 2013.

Rudy, Kathy. "'Where Two or More are Gathered:' Using Gay Communities as a Model for Christian Sexual Ethics." *Theology and Sexuality* 4 (1996) 81–99.

Ruggieri Giuseppe. "Beyond an Ecclesiology of Polemics: The Debate on the Church." In *History of Vatican II: Volume II: The Formation of the Council's Identity, First Period and Intersession, October 1962–September 1963*, edited by Giuseppe Alberigo and Joseph A. Komonchak, 281–357. Maryknoll, NY: Orbis, 1997.

Schillebeeckx, Edward. *Christ the Sacrament of the Encounter with God*. New York: Sheed and Ward, 1987.

Sedgwick, Eve Kosofsky. *Between Men: English Literature and Male Homosocial Desire*. New York: Columbia University Press, 1985.

Smith, James K. A. *Introduction to Radical Orthodoxy: Mapping a Post-Secular Theology*. Grand Rapids: Baker Academic, 2004.

Somerville, Siobahn B. *Queering the Color Line: Race and the Invention of Homosexuality in American Culture*. Durham, NC: Duke University Press, 2000.

BIBLIOGRAPHY

Steinberg, Leo. *The Sexuality of Christ in Renaissance Art and Modern Oblivion.* 2nd ed. Chicago and London: University of Chicago Press, 1996.

Stuart, Elizabeth. "Camping around the Canon: Humor as a Hermeneutical Tool in Queer Readings of Biblical Texts." In *Take Back the Word: A Queer Reading of the Bible,* edited by Robert E. Goss and Mona West, 23–34. Cleveland, OH: Pilgrim, 2000.

———. *Gay and Lesbian Theologies: Repetitions with Critical Difference.* Aldershot, UK: Ashgate, 2003.

———. *Just Good Friends: Towards a Theology of Lesbian and Gay Relationships.* London: Mowbray, 1995.

———. "Making No Sense: Liturgy as Queer Space." In *Dancing Theology in Fetish Boots,* edited by Lisa Isherwood and Mark D. Jordan, 113–23. London: SCM, 2010.

———. "Queering Death." In *The Sexual Theologian,* edited by Marcella Althaus-Reid and Lisa Isherwood, 58–70. London: T. & T. Clark, 2004.

———. "The Return of the Living Dead." In *Post-Christian Feminisms: A Critical Approach,* edited by Lisa Isherwood and Kathleen McPhilips, 211–22. Burlington, VT: Ashgate, 2008.

———. "Sacramental Flesh." In *Queer Theology,* edited by Gerard Loughlin, 65–75. Oxford: Blackwell, 2007.

———. "Sexuality: The View from the Font (the Body and the Ecclesial Self)." *Theology and Sexuality* 11 (1999) 9–20.

———. "Turning Toward the Tomb: Priesthood and Gender." *Theology and Sexuality* 10 (2003) 30–39.

Sullivan, Francis A. *From Apostles to Bishops: The Development of the Episcopacy in the Early Church.* New York: Newman, 2001.

Tillard, Jean-Marie Roger. *Church of Churches: The Ecclesiology of Communion.* Collegeville, MN: Liturgical, 1987.

———. *Flesh of the Church, Flesh of Christ: At the Source of the Ecclesiology of Communion.* Collegeville, MN: Liturgical, 2001.

Townes, Emile M. "Marcella Althaus-Reid's *Indecent Theology*: A Response." In *Dancing Theology in Fetish Boots,* edited by Lisa Isherwood and Mark D. Jordan, 61–67. London: SCM, 2010.

Traina, Cristina L. H. *Erotic Attunement: Parenthood and the Ethics of Sensuality between Unequals.* Chicago: University of Chicago Press, 2011.

Ward, Graham. "Bodies: The Displaced Body of Jesus Christ." In *Radical Orthodoxy: A New Theology,* edited by John Milbank, Catherine Pickstock, and Graham Ward, 163–81. London: Routledge, 1999.

———. *Christ and Culture.* Oxford: Blackwell, 2005.

———. *Cities of God.* London: Routledge, 2000.

———. "Divinity and Sexual Difference." In *Christ and Culture,* 129–58. Oxford: Blackwell, 2005.

———. "The Limits of Libertinism." In *Dancing Theology in Fetish Boots,* edited by Lisa Isherwood and Mark D. Jordan, 173–80. London: SCM, 2010.

———. "The Politics of Circumcision (and the Mystery of All Flesh)." In *Christ and Culture,* 159–80. Oxford: Blackwell, 2005.

———. *The Politics of Discipleship: Becoming a Postmaterial Citizen.* Grand Rapids: Baker Academic, 2009.

BIBLIOGRAPHY

———. "On the Politics of Embodiment and the Mystery of All Flesh." In *The Sexual Theologian*, edited by Marcella Althaus-Reid and Lisa Isherwood, 71–85. London: T. & T. Clark, 2004.

———. "Redemption: Between Reception and Response." In *Christ and Culture*, 113–28. Oxford: Blackwell, 2005.

———. "There is No Sexual Difference." In *Queer Theology*, edited by Gerard Loughlin, 76–85. Oxford: Blackwell, 2007.

Zizioulas, John D. *Being as Communion: Studies in Personhood and the Church*. Crestwood, NY: St. Vladimir's Seminary Press, 1985.